PROFESSIONAL IDIOT.

A MEMOIR

STEPHEN STEVE-O
GLOVER

WITH DAVID PEISNER

HYPERION
NEW YORK

Library of Congress Cataloging-in-Publication Data

Steve-O, 1974–
  Professional idiot : a memoir / Stephen "Steve-O" Glover, with David Peisner.
—1st ed.
      p.   cm.
  ISBN 978-1-4013-2433-9
  1. Steve-O, 1974–   2. Entertainers—United States—Biography.   I. Peisner, David.
  II. Title.
  PN2287.S67845A3 2011
  791.092—dc22
  [B]

                                                              2011007236

Design by Renato Stanisic

FIRST EDITION

10 9 8 7 6 5 4 3 2

THIS LABEL APPLIES TO TEXT STOCK

We try to produce the most beautiful books possible, and we are also extremely concerned about the impact of our manufacturing process on the forests of the world and the environment as a whole. Accordingly, we've made sure that all of the paper we use has been certified as coming from forests that are managed, to ensure the protection of the people and wildlife dependent upon them.

DEDICATION

This book is dedicated to everyone I shit all over for telling me exactly what I needed to hear, when I didn't want to hear it.

ACKNOWLEDGMENTS

Writing this book was more than a little bit scary for me, and I couldn't have done it without plenty of help, love, and support from numerous people. First and foremost, I'd like to thank David Peisner, whose calm and soothing approach to talking me into including controversial information that I wasn't comfortable with won out about 99 percent of the time. David is an incredible writer, and working with him has been both an honor and a pleasure.

I also want to thank Dad, Cindy, Sophie, Jeff Bernstein, Laura Nolan, Beth W., Nick L., Jeff H., Ian Rosenberg, and Cynthia Colonna; Jill Schwartzman, Colin Fox, and everyone at Hyperion; PJ Clapp, Jeff Tremaine, and everyone at Dickhouse; and everyone else who offered their recollections, opinions, and support.

I SWEAR, I WAS
BORN LIKE THIS

It was March 1996, and I was in jail. The Orange County Correctional Facility in Orlando, to be exact. A couple months earlier, I'd gotten my second DUI in less than a year. I was pulled over for swerving badly while making an illegal U-turn through a red light. I tried to tell the officer I wasn't drunk, just tired. The arrest report actually reads: "Defendant declined roadside sobriety tests stating he'd prefer to take a nap." Upon my arraignment, I pled guilty and asked the judge if I could just start my ten-day sentence immediately, since I couldn't really afford round-trip bus fare home to South Florida and back.

Actually, "home" is a generous way of describing my living situation at that point. Mom had kicked me out of the house, and not without good cause: I was an irresponsible slob who seemed completely incapable of keeping any sort of job. I was mostly crashing on friends' couches in those days or, when things got really desperate, sleeping in my car, which I'd been driving around with a suspended license and expired tags. I liked to tell people that I was a stuntman, but except for some free T-shirts from a very fledgling Florida-based clothing company called Bizo, I had nothing really to show for six years of videotaping myself skateboarding, jumping from rooftops into shallow pools, and doing whatever else I thought might get people's attention. Also, my front teeth were all busted up from a drunken face-plant I took off a second-story balcony trying to impress some girl at a party more than a year earlier. I hadn't quite gotten around to getting them fixed.

Anyone with any sense would've looked at my life at that point and seen nothing but a grand fucking disaster. But sitting there on my bottom bunk in jail—an unemployed, homeless college dropout with some gnarly-looking front teeth—I was absolutely stoked. I was so sure that it was just a matter of time before the world found out how totally rad I was that I decided what I really needed to do was get a jump start on my memoir.

"They call me Steve-O," I wrote. "I'm thinking about switching back to Steve Glover because now I've kind of begun a career and I don't know if I want a nickname when I'm famous."

When I'm famous. I love that. As I was writing those opening lines, there was no question in my mind *if* I was going to be famous; it was just a matter of *when*. My life at that point may have been an unholy mess that was destined to get much, much messier, but a part of me is envious of that twenty-one-year-old daydreamer. That kid may have had very little going for him, but he knew what he wanted and was absolutely certain he was going to get it. It's still baffling to me how I was capable of such unbelievable enthusiasm and optimism when I had seemingly so little to be enthusiastic or optimistic about, yet years later, once my dreams had basically come true, I could be such a miserable prick.

As I wrote my "prison memoir," I'd pass each one of the pages around to some of the other inmates, who—apparently overcome by the stifling boredom in that place—actually read them. It wasn't enough for me to be completely jazzed on how great I thought my life was going to be—I needed other people to know too. Everyone always says that if you have to go to jail, you should just keep your head down and not draw attention to yourself, but I was totally incapable of following that advice. I needed an audience.

IT'S KIND of been that way since the beginning.

I was born in London, England, on June 13, 1974. At the time, my dad was the marketing director for Pepsi Europe, and I'm told he was in the delivery room dressed in a business suit as my mom was pushing me out. He took some pretty gruesome photos of the delivery and its immediate aftermath, then, right after I was born and the doctors determined that all was well with Mom and me, he rushed off to a meeting. A few days later, when it was time for us to come home from the hospital, Mom's friend had to drive us because Dad was tied up in more meetings. That kind of set the pattern for my younger years: Dad running around as a rising corporate executive, while Mom, my sister, Cindy, who is three years older than me, and I stayed at home.

My parents were an odd couple. Dad comes from a family of strivers and achievers. His father, Richard, was born and raised in England, graduated from Oxford, and then went on to get a Ph.D. in history from Harvard. He served in the Canadian army during World War II and then spent many years as a university professor in Winnipeg. He died when I was eleven, and I remember him mostly as a hard-ass who seemed to disapprove of my antics. When he was around, he made it clear that whatever I was doing, saying, or wearing was unacceptable. In his defense, it probably was, and all the things that rubbed me the wrong way about him back then are things I'm sure would make me respect him now.

Dad's mom, Constance, graduated from Vassar and then got a master's degree in English from Mount Holyoke College—this at a time when very few women even went to college. Her family had some money—they were in the paper business—but she and my grandfather lived very frugally.

I got to know Grandma Constance pretty well as I grew up. She was an incredibly sweet woman whose kindness—and failing memory—I totally took advantage of. I don't think she had Alzheimer's, but after my grandfather died, her mind definitely started to go, so it was pretty easy for me to coerce her into doing what I wanted. When I would visit her in British Columbia, I was constantly taking her to go buy me shit. Among other things, I convinced her to get me a stereo with a dual tape deck and my first decent skateboard, a Powell-Peralta. She was as good a person as I've ever known, and in retrospect, I feel crappy that when she was suffering from dementia, my main priority was what I could get out of it.

Dad's brother and sister both got advanced degrees as well. His sister became the director of two leading art galleries in Canada; his brother was a career naval officer and later a historian. Dad's extended family is also full of academics, and going into the business world made him kind of the black sheep.

My mom's family is a whole other story. She came from a long line of alcoholics, addicts, and depressives. Her parents were both born in Canada and Mom grew up in Ontario. I never knew Mom's father, Ed, because he blew his brains out when I was a year old, but what I've heard about him doesn't paint a pretty picture. He was a tall, charismatic guy who liked to walk around with a big wad of cash and show off a lot. He had inherited quite a bit of money and owned some car dealerships, but he spent a lot of time hanging out at the horse track, gambling, and getting drunk. It's my understanding that he pissed away whatever money he had.

Ed was an alcoholic and apparently a particularly volatile and unpleasant one at that. Mom had been a straight-A student in school and won a scholarship to help with her university expenses, but my grandfather refused to give her any money for tuition, telling her repeatedly that it was a waste of money to send a girl to college.

Another story I heard about him is even more disturbing: When my sister, Cindy, was a baby, Mom took her to visit our grandparents, and my grandfather got into a drunken argument with my mom, during which he apparently pulled out a gun and pointed it at Cindy. It's possible this story has been exaggerated over time, but the police were definitely called, and my grandfather spent a night in jail before the charges were eventually dropped. Not surprisingly, he and Mom had been estranged for a while by the time he killed himself.

Mom's mom, Thelma, was also a gnarly alcoholic. I didn't see her that much, but it seemed whenever I did she was drunk. As she got older, her hands were always beet-red from cirrhosis and she couldn't even sleep through the night without getting up for a sip of something to fend off the withdrawal tremors. At some point I heard a story about how she got drunk, passed out, and left a cigarette burning, which set fire to the living room of her apartment. I don't remember anyone thinking this was terribly shocking. After my granddad committed suicide, she married a guy named Wayne Howell, who had had a long career as a TV announcer with NBC. He was also an alcoholic, so he fit right in with the rest of the dysfunctional family.

Not all my memories of Mom's family are negative. Mom and her sister Janice were pretty close, and I remember them hanging out together and joking around pretty frequently. Around the time I got accepted to Ringling Bros. and Barnum & Bailey Clown College in my twenties, my cousin Neil, Janice's son, was in school to become a mortician. I can remember Mom and Aunt Janice sitting at the kitchen table in Mom's house, laughing about whose son was a bigger loser: the one who was going to be wearing floppy shoes and a big red nose, or the one who'd be embalming dead bodies. They spent hours cracking up about it and I can't say it really hurt my feelings because, frankly, they were hysterical.

I think Mom's family stressed her out though. There would

occasionally be late-night drunken phone calls during which her mom would lash out at her. I don't want to make it sound like Mom's family were just awful people—I know that's not fair—but alcoholism and depression are very real illnesses that many people in her family have struggled with, and they tended to overwhelm just about everything else about them. As Cindy once put it, "That family tree, every single branch, is dripping with booze, drugs, gambling, and suicide, going back as far as anyone can remember."

My parents both seemed pretty intent on keeping Mom's entire family at arm's length from us while we were growing up. I'm sure the idea was to insulate Cindy and me from their negative influence, but I think my life is pretty strong evidence that that's impossible: you can't escape your genes.

Over the last two decades, as I became a reckless and borderline suicidal alcoholic drug addict, it wasn't hard to see that I was the natural product of my mom's family. But I'm equally convinced that my ambition and drive to turn all my misbehavior into a successful career is the legacy passed on to me from Dad.

MY PARENTS met at an office party in Toronto in 1966. Dad was working at Procter & Gamble's Canadian office at the time, and Mom came to the party as someone else's date. They hit it off and were married in Toronto two years later. It was a tiny wedding—just them, the minister, and four other people. Mom decided at the last minute that she didn't want her parents there, so Dad's parents weren't allowed to come either.

Mom had gotten a graduate degree in nursing—although her dad wouldn't pay for university, nursing school was free in Canada—but she gave up working after she married Dad. I think she probably came to regret not having a career of her own, but that's just the way it was done back then. Besides, with all the moving around that resulted from

Dad's work, it would've been nearly impossible for Mom to keep a career going herself. After Toronto, they moved to Connecticut for a few years and then to London in 1972. Our first relocation after I was born was from London to Rio de Janeiro, Brazil, when I was six months old. I have no memories of living there, but apparently, I spent most of my time with our live-in maids and actually spoke my first words in Portuguese.

I was a hyperactive toddler. At eighteen months old, I knocked out one of my top front teeth running full-speed into a piece of furniture in our apartment and thus spent my early years with a big gap in the front of my mouth. My parents' friends started calling me Rocky.

When I was two and a half, my dad got a promotion at Pepsi and we moved to Caracas, Venezuela. On my first day of nursery school there, my mom picked me up and was told by the teacher that I was *"tremendo."* Mom assumed that meant "tremendous." She reported this piece of good news to Dad, but as they consulted their Venezuelan friends it became clear that there was a little nuance lost in translation. What that teacher actually meant was that I was like a whirlwind—horribly behaved, too much to handle, basically a pain in the ass. This would be the first of many teachers, coaches, friends, bosses, colleagues, and strangers who would make this observation. Even at that age, moderation was not my thing.

We left Caracas after a year—at the time I was fluent in English, Spanish, and Portuguese, though I quickly forgot the latter two—when Dad got transferred to Connecticut. My earliest childhood memories are from our time there. We lived in the upscale suburb of Darien, and I remember running through the woods near our house with the girl who lived next door to us, showing each other our butts. I think I thought it was sexy.

When I went to kindergarten, there were problems pretty much from the beginning. My enduring memory is how much I hated naptime. I just had so much energy that the thought of having to lie down for a while in the middle of the day was nothing short of torturous. This was a pattern that would repeat itself for years. When we were working on *Jackass* and I'd be traveling in the same bus, car, or van with Johnny Knoxville on road trips, he'd sometimes stick sedative pills in my food in the hope that they'd shut me up so he could enjoy some peace and quiet. Never once did it work. Each time, I think he was truly amazed at the doses of downers that failed to quiet me down.

After two years in Connecticut, we moved to Miami. My first day of first grade, I got off to the kind of start that was already becoming the standard for me. As the school day wound down, I remember sitting at my desk, staring out a big window that spanned one whole wall of the classroom. I could see my mother outside, waiting to pick me up, so I jumped up, waved my arms around, and generally acted like an idiot. My goal, I suppose, was just to get attention—from my mom, my classmates, my teacher—but no one was impressed, only annoyed, and Mom was furious. Again, it was just too much. A few years later, I got a report card that kind of spelled out the basic problem for me.

"Socially, Steve's attempt to impress his peers frequently has had the opposite effect," my teacher Mrs. Iacuessa wrote. "Perhaps if he had more empathy and were more self-effacing he would have greater social success."

Mrs. Iacuessa really nailed it on the head in a way that's still a little painful for me to acknowledge. Years later, most of the *Jackass* guys would have nearly the exact same initial reaction to me. When we filmed the very first season of the show, my parts were done in one five-day stretch in Florida. After a few days of drinking, doing crazy stunts, and just clowning around together, those guys had already had enough.

CHRIS PONTIUS (cast member on *Jackass*, *Wildboyz*): The first few days I spent with him, I couldn't wait for him to go home. Every chance he got to show off, he would. The first day

I met him, me and him ate at IHOP together really late at night and he was doing back flips for the manager. It's neat at first, but when you're around him all the time, after like two days, you see that he does the same thing to everybody and you get really sick of it. Right when he left, the whole crew was like, "Ahhhhh."

JOHNNY KNOXVILLE (co-creator/star of *Jackass*): When I first met Steve, he was very sweet even though he was kind of a pain in the ass. He had this insane desire to perform at every second. I'm an attention whore myself but he's an attention whorehouse. He loved attention and would do any-thing to get it. On a scale from 1 to 10, he was about an 11½ of being "on."

That's pretty much how it had always been. I was the kid who drank salt straight from the saltshaker in the school lunchroom in third grade in an effort to win other kids' approval. It'd be easy to blame this stuff on the fact that our family moved around so much—after three and a half years in Miami, we headed back to London—but there was more to it than that. I felt uncomfortable in my own skin, like I wasn't good enough, and somehow all my antics, all my efforts at impressing people, were a way of trying to make it right. When I was about ten, I remember sitting in class next to a pretty girl and telling her, "I'll bet you I'm getting out of class today." She sort of looked at me like, "How are you going to do that?" at which point I took hold of a tooth that was a little loose in my mouth and violently yanked it out. I then calmly raised my hand and, with blood dripping from my mouth, asked the teacher if I could please be excused to go to the infirmary. Mission accomplished.

Ever since I was little, one of my favorite ways to get attention was to dress up in costume. As a toddler, I used to turn my bib around to look like a cape and ride my Big Wheel around our driveway, pretending to be a superhero. Even better than actual costumes, my favorite thing to wear for attention—probably even to this day—has always been my own blood. For as long as I can remember, there was little I loved more than the sympathy, shock value, and unadulterated gawking I got from bleeding—accidentally or on purpose. It always made me feel special.

In fifth grade I had a homeroom teacher named Mrs. Cornish. It was already my general policy to blame all my troubles on my teachers, but Mrs. Cornish had it in for me. Playing on the playground one day, a kid named Kenneth Harbaugh pulled my arms behind my back and tripped me. The ground was a mixture of pebbles, tar, and asphalt and the first thing to hit it was my head. On contact, a jagged pebble punctured my forehead and blood began spurting out. I had already done a lot of bleeding in my life, but this was by far the most blood I'd ever seen. There was no question I needed to go to the hospital. Instead, I went blazing into school, running to my homeroom so I could go terrorize Mrs. Cornish. I showed up in her classroom, my shirt soaked with blood, open head wound gushing, just to make her scream. Later I did go to the hospital, started puking, and was diagnosed with a concussion, but I think it's telling that my first thought on impact with the ground was, *How can I get more attention out of this?*

As a kid, a lot of my relationship with my dad revolved around sports. He signed me up for baseball, football, soccer, whatever, and those were things we could always talk about or do together. I was a decent athlete but had all sorts of anxieties about actually playing sports: *Oh no. If the ball comes to me I'm going to blow it.* What I really liked most about sports were the uniforms. Somehow, to be decked out like that made me feel important.

I loved the ritual of laying out my baseball uniform the morning before a game, so when I came home from school it would be there ready for me. Hell, I even used to wear my uniforms when we didn't have games—to school, to the movies, wherever. The photo on my Canadian citizenship ID card from when I was nine actually shows me in my full football uniform, shoulder pads and all. Anyone who has ever played football knows how impractical that stuff is to wear around, but I insisted on going to that photo office dressed for kickoff. There is something sort of fitting about the fact that it was for an *identity* card: here I was, nine years old, completely uncomfortable in my own skin, dressing in a football uniform to try to find an identity I could live with.

SCHOOL WAS never really my thing growing up. Nearly all my report cards said some version of the same thing: "Steve isn't stupid but he just doesn't apply himself." I actually did okay—mostly B's and C's—but my sister was a straight-A student from birth, which probably gave me a bit of a complex. I knew I wasn't going to outshine her in that area, so why try?

Because we moved so much, Cindy and I spent lots of time together when we were younger. We'd often stomp through the woods, and in Miami, we spent a ton of time swimming, diving, and just making up all kinds of crazy games in the pool in our backyard. I don't recall feeling like I had any special athletic or acrobatic prowess as a child, but I was maybe a little more willing to try things other kids wouldn't. I remember diving headfirst off the three-meter high dive at our country club pool in Miami despite the fact that it scared the hell out of me. In fact, the fear was a little rush.

CINDY GLOVER (sister): Steve was always a bit of a daredevil, always had delusions of grandeur and superhero obsessions. If he had been born twenty years later, he most likely would've been diagnosed with ADD or ADHD and medicated, but I'm not sure he actually had that. He had a really good imagination, but he did lack some of the "look before you leap" instincts that you want in a fairly athletic child.

Dad traveled for work all through my childhood. When he was around, he could be—and hell, still can be—an intimidating figure, but I really looked up to him and badly wanted his approval. When he was home, he'd sometimes sit around with friends drinking beers, and I'd often hang around just to be a part of it. As such, I kind of became his little party trick. He'd say things like, "Hey, for a dollar, my kid will do a hundred push-ups." I probably couldn't do a hundred push-ups, but I'd always hit the floor and give it a try. There was a lot of physicality to my interactions with Dad that I'm sure must have had an effect on my becoming the kind of guy who'd always be willing to toss his body around for the attention and appreciation of others. With Dad, if I came home with a shitty report card he'd be disappointed, but then we'd go play catch in the backyard and he'd say something like, "I'll give you ten bucks if you can throw the ball so hard that you break my finger."

Dad had a mischievous side. I remember a family wedding we all went to when I was in third grade: He wanted to show me how he could light a whole book of matches on fire, but what he didn't realize is that he was standing under a smoke alarm. The entire reception had to be evacuated. Mom was embarrassed, but I thought it was cool.

I don't know whether he'd admit it, but I think Dad really liked playing with fire. Whenever he'd light the charcoal grill, he'd purposely overdo it with the lighter fluid, then when Mom would freak out and tell him to stop, he'd squirt some more on there. I was a budding pyromaniac as well: A favorite childhood hobby was pouring out gasoline from a gas can then igniting it by hitting rolls of cap gun caps with a hammer. It scared the crap out of me, and I loved it.

As I got older, I remained pretty obsessed with fire. I'd spit it from my mouth, set various body parts ablaze—in fact, it was an utterly ridiculous fire stunt that went wrong that first earned me a place in the crew of guys who'd go on to make *Jackass*. While I would never blame anyone else for my own stupidity, at the very least I was getting some mixed messages as a kid: if "Don't play with fire" is one of the basic rules of Parenting 101, it didn't exactly come through loud and clear.

2

IN WHICH I DISCOVER THE JOYS OF ALCOHOL, SHOPLIFTING, MÖTLEY CRÜE, AND THROWING EGGS AT THINGS

My parents drank together a lot when I was young, and they seemed to have a pretty good time. They'd have "company" over, and Cindy and I would either be banished to the basement or we'd just float around the edges of this adult world, listening to stories and jokes we often didn't fully understand. Pretty early on though—certainly, by the time I was eight or nine—I began to get it that Mom was an alcoholic. I'm not sure if I knew the term back then, and I certainly didn't understand what it really meant, but I noticed that she acted differently when she was drinking— which was often. When she was drunk, she was out of commission. She'd hardly ever leave her bedroom. I'd need to go to a Little League game, Dad would be out of town, and Mom would refuse to get out of bed to drive me there, so I'd have to beg a ride off a neighbor. When she was on a bender while Dad was away there were no rules. Dinner was a fend-for-yourself affair and school was optional.

Mom wasn't the type of drunk who'd get wasted at night and then be hungover the next day. She'd just camp out on the couch or stay in bed, watching TV for days or even weeks on end, drinking, passing out, waking up, and then drinking some more. All the while, her appearance would deteriorate and the house would just get gnarly. Cindy was unbelievably responsible for her age and picked up a lot of the slack, but we both were left to take care of ourselves a lot growing up.

Mom had allergies, so her nose was often running, and she'd frequently claim to be sick when she was actually drunk. She'd come into the kitchen, clutching a tissue, and say, "I'm not feeling well so I'm going to be in bed today." Eventually, she made this claim so often that she invented shorthand for it: "It's just drip, drip, drip." It was her way of saying she was sick and her nose was running again, but Cindy and I quickly understood what it really meant.

When I was about nine, Mom gathered the family around the kitchen table and told us she had some very serious news: she'd been diagnosed with a form of cancer called non-Hodgkin's lymphoma. Dad had recently bought the family an encyclopedia set, and the first thing I did after that family meeting was look up "lymph node cancer" to find out what was going to kill my mother.

The news of Mom's condition made our house feel silent, dark, and lonely to me. I can look back now and see that the house was actually none of those things, but I think that was just how depression felt to a nine-year-old. For nearly a year, Mom's "cancer" hovered around the house until somehow the truth came out: Mom didn't actually have lymphoma at all. It was all an elaborate lie. She was just drunk. We'd all been fooled, even Dad. Strangely, I was never mad at Mom for lying—I just felt relieved she was going to be okay.

CINDY: Mom was so depressed, I'm sure she *felt* like she was dying of non-Hodgkin's lymphoma, but it wasn't true. She was incredibly intelligent but not very articulate about her feelings. I'm sure that was a story that would help communicate how she was feeling. She needed sympathy, she needed attention, she needed concern, but didn't know how to say that.

It probably didn't help that Dad was largely in denial about Mom's alcoholism. Mom would routinely claim to have the flu—"drip, drip, drip"—and Cindy and I would understand she was drunk, but Dad would insist, "No, she's really sick." We'd have these periodic family-in-crisis meetings to discuss some issue that needed addressing—a new potential move, problems in my parents' marriage, my shitty grades and bad behavior, whatever—but the elephant in the room was always Mom's drinking. Dad just didn't see the elephant. In his defense, Mom used to try to plan her benders around when Dad would be out of town, then clean up by the time he got home. Really, though, she wasn't that good at planning it, so he shouldn't have been in the dark as long as he was.

TED GLOVER (father): On more than one occasion, she blamed her hangover symptoms on chemotherapy treatments for the lymphoma, but never allowed me to meet or talk with the doctor who supposedly performed these treatments. The excuse she gave was that her self-esteem demanded that she handle this herself.

Despite all this—or maybe because of it—I always felt extremely close to Mom. Cindy often says that she was Dad's kid and I was Mom's, and I understand what she means. Cindy and Dad were highly motivated, articulate, serious, and logical. They loved arguing and debating, and seemed to relish confrontation. Mom and I, on the other hand, saw the world differently from them. We had similar personalities and senses of humor. Cindy and Dad were often the target of our jokes.

Appearances definitely mattered to Mom, and by that, I don't mean she was particularly superficial but just that grace and class were important to her. She wanted to show her best side to the world, and her heaviest drinking almost always went on behind closed doors.

Mom wanted us to be successful, too. When I got older and became a college dropout who couldn't keep a job, I think it bothered Mom because she felt it reflected poorly on her. Once I started doing all sorts of insane stunts, I'd show her videos and she never seemed worried about my getting hurt. She was more ashamed of the fact that I wasn't doing more with my life. To her credit though, she had a way of voicing her disapproval with humor: She'd make fun of me but in a way that never made me feel like crap. Instead, it always felt like she was on my side, rooting for me. She wanted me to make her proud.

Mom was also a lot of fun. She was charismatic and sociable, and seemed to make friends pretty easily. She had a wicked sense of humor and was not above telling the odd dirty joke. She was also extremely intelligent. When I got a little older, we'd sit and watch *Jeopardy!* together a lot, competing to shout out the right responses when we knew them, and she whipped my ass every time. She would murder everyone at Scrabble.

Ultimately, there were two Moms: Drunk Mom and Sober Mom. Unfortunately, as time went on, Drunk Mom got worse and worse. Every time she sobered up she'd claim she was done with drinking. But it was never too long before I'd come home and see her with a glass of wine. I'd say, "Mom, I thought you'd quit." She'd promise, "I'm just having a couple. I'm going to keep it under control." But I knew she couldn't control it. The wine invariably turned into vodka, and soon enough she'd be in bed for days on end.

GROWING UP, we had always had enough money to be comfortable, but beginning with our move back to London when I was in fourth grade, our fortunes improved considerably. Dad had been a player in a major corporate merger—between R. J. Reynolds and Nabisco— and our standard of living began changing pretty dramatically after that. Our houses got considerably larger. A few years later, in Toronto, our house wasn't far from a public housing project where a few friends of mine lived. The thought of any of them coming over and seeing where I lived made me very uncomfortable. I also felt like my parents themselves were subtly affected by the money, and not for the better. As a kid who was already pretty uncomfortable in his own skin, having money just gave me one more thing to feel uneasy about. Recently, I've come to understand that a lot of the amenities we enjoyed—company cars, chauffeurs, country club memberships, private school—were actually paid for by Dad's employers in return for his willingness to work overseas.

When I was in fifth and sixth grade, we were still living in London and Dad was the president of Del Monte Europe (which was then owned by Nabisco). One of his responsibilities was to oversee a pineapple plantation and canning factory in Kenya, so he traveled there five or six times a year. Each year, he coordinated one of those trips to coincide with our spring break from school and took the whole family along on vacation. We stayed in upscale lodges, went on safaris, took a hot air balloon ride, and chartered a small plane to travel within the country. It was all pretty extraordinary, though one of the distinct emotions I came away with from these trips was an overwhelming guilt for my own good fortune.

When we arrived in Nairobi that first year, we were ushered out of the airport into a limousine. As we sat in the car, partially clothed children swarmed around us, clawing at the windows and begging for money. This was my first experience as a witness to real poverty, and I remember thinking, *What have I ever done to deserve to be inside this limo as opposed to clawing at its windows from the outside?*

When we stayed at these lodges and resorts, I often hung around the staff and visited them in their own quarters. I even became pen pals for a short while with a guy who worked at one of the places we stayed. It's not that I was some budding humanitarian who felt this deep connection to the world's impoverished masses—I just wasn't very comfortable living the life of a rich kid. To some extent, I never have been.

On one visit to Kenya, we accompanied my dad to the pineapple factory. I was absolutely horrified by the conditions people were working in. Flies swarmed around their faces, it was unbearably hot, and the place just stunk. I asked Dad, "How can you let people work like this?" His answer: "The list of people who have jobs here isn't nearly as long as the list of people waiting for jobs here, so if anyone doesn't like it, they can leave and be replaced by someone who will work harder than they did for less money." After I heard that, my first thought was, *What a dick!* But it was really just a lesson in how the world works.

I remember, years later, we were shooting an episode of *Jackass* for MTV and one of our cameramen, Rick Kosick, was complaining to the director, Jeff Tremaine. "I just worked fourteen hours shooting a national television show," Rick said, "and I made less money than I would've if I'd shot a photo for a skateboard magazine ad." Tremaine's response: "Then go shoot a skate ad." It was really the same Economics 101 lesson that Dad had given me in that pineapple factory, and one that would stick with me: If you want to get paid, you've got to prove your value by doing something nobody else can (or will) do. If you can be replaced, you will be.

That was hardly the only thing from my early travels that stuck with me into adulthood. When I was in eighth grade, I went on a school-sponsored trip to Egypt. At the time, the trip seemed notable for the trouble two buddies and I got in while we were there. We got put on some sort of probation at school because we were pouring bottles of

Kool-Aid and piss out our hotel room window onto passersby below. But something else from that trip proved more consequential.

We'd been warned repeatedly not to drink the tap water in Egypt, not to even drink a soda with ice cubes in it. The water was unsafe, we were told. One day, we were sitting at a restaurant along the banks of the Nile River and I watched an old Egyptian dude dunk a toothbrush into the river and brush his teeth. I thought to myself, *If tap water around here is so bad, what the hell is the Nile?* It occurred to me that our bodies build up immunity to whatever they're regularly exposed to. As such, it seemed the healthiest thing I could do for myself would be to travel the world, drinking tap water everywhere I went. Years later, when I was filming the *Jackass* spin-off *Wildboyz*, I got the chance to put this theory to the test. Without fail, the first time I brushed my teeth in each new country we visited, I'd think of that Egyptian dude and gulp down a bunch of tap water. Not only did I never get really sick, I'm convinced it gave a major boost to my immune system.

I GOT my first skateboard for Christmas when I was in sixth grade. Just about every kid I knew had recently seen *Back to the Future* and it seemed like there was a skateboard under every Christmas tree that year. I took to skating immediately, and got pretty good at "tick-tacking"—generating momentum by pivoting your front foot back and forth—which was about all I thought you could do on a skateboard at the time. But that summer, my family moved from London to Toronto and none of the kids I met there were into skating, so I quit.

You might think that being forced to uproot every few years would be traumatic for a kid, but to be honest, I was never sad to move. My personality was so over the top, generally by the time we packed up to leave, I had more than worn out my welcome wherever we were living. Each move felt like a chance for a fresh start, to wipe the slate clean and leave behind all the problems I'd created wherever we were.

With skateboarding out of the picture, I quickly found other things to occupy my time in Toronto. A big one was heavy metal. My initial discovery of it was purely by chance: I was ten, in a London department store, browsing through the music section when the cover of Iron Maiden's *The Number of the Beast* caught my eye. I didn't know anything about the band or about heavy metal at all, but to a ten-year-old who wanted to be a badass, that cover image—the band's iconic ghoul, Eddie, playing puppet master to a horned, pitchfork-toting red devil— just looked like the coolest thing I'd ever seen. I bought the cassette and listened to it over and over for a few days. Then I'd run around the house singing the lyrics of "Run to the Hills" ("Raping the women and wasting the men!") for the benefit of my mother. Once Mom heard that, she ripped all the ribbon out of the tape, but it wasn't long before I dubbed a new copy from a kid across the street.

Something about Iron Maiden and metal, in general, just appealed to me. I felt like I didn't fit in anywhere and here was this music that seemed to celebrate this social discomfort and provide a tribe of similar misfits to commune with. I've always liked to say that when I was ten, my first Iron Maiden album taught me I was a metalhead, when I was eleven, my first Mötley Crüe album showed me why I was a metalhead, and when I was twelve, my first Slayer album proved how bad the situation really was. Although that's an oversimplification, it's basically true.

In Toronto, heavy metal became who I was. I wore black concert T-shirts, kept my hair in a short-on-top-longish-in-back style that was positively mulletesque, and just generally got unreasonably obsessive about it. Kids at school teased me and called me a devil-worshipper, which made me upset, but really I had it coming. Like everything else I did, my interest in heavy metal was over the top. I wanted to be rebellious and shocking, so I forced this metalhead version of myself on everyone.

Ozzy Osbourne and Mötley Crüe were not necessarily the healthiest role models for a hyperactive kid with a family history of addiction problems. Mötley Crüe, in particular, became a passionate and unhealthy fixation. As a twelve-year-old, I wanted to be just like those guys, and

even though I didn't have the inclination to learn to play music, I figured I could just model the rest of my life on their example. Many years
later, I actually became friendly with Tommy Lee and when he wrote his
book, *Tommyland*, he asked me to write a testimonial for it. I wrote: "You
were my hero because you behaved horribly badly, not because you were
a great drummer." That pretty much sums it up.

I didn't waste much time, either. On January 17, 1987, the sixth an-
niversary of Mötley Crüe's formation, I decided I needed to do something special to commemorate it. So I snuck a bottle of red wine from
my parents' wine cellar and slugged a little down on the way to school
that morning. Then I stashed it in the snowy yard of a nearby house
that was under construction.

I was twelve and this wasn't my first taste of alcohol. A few years
earlier, my parents had begun letting Cindy and me have one drink on
New Year's Eve. I'm sure they thought this was a way of demystifying
alcohol to us, eliminating the "forbidden fruit" appeal of it, but needless to say, this little experiment in European permissiveness was a total
failure. I still thought of booze as forbidden—in fact, that was initially
its major appeal—but this just encouraged me to think of it as special
and fun too. Besides New Year's, my sister and I had occasionally snuck
alcohol out of my parents' liquor cabinet as well, but Mötley Crüe's an-
niversary marked the first time I'd taken the initiative to get drunk all
by myself.

I had a little buzz when I went to class that day, but I saved most of
the wine for my way home from school. I picked the bottle up out of
the snow and pounded it. When I arrived at my house, I was the only
one there, but I was dying for someone to know I was drunk. I called a
friend from school, Patrick Lundy, and told him all about it. He told
me, with as much seriousness as a twelve-year-old could muster, "You're
an alcoholic." The accusation made me feel like I was treading into the
same dark, dangerous territory where my mom spent so much of her
time, which actually gave me a happy little jolt. I then stormed into the
kitchen to play with a novelty Breathalyzer that someone had given my

parents as a gag gift. I blew into it and was thrilled as I watched the needle climb, confirming my drunkenness. I left the Breathalyzer sitting on the kitchen island, went upstairs, puked into the toilet, and then passed out on my bed.

When my dad came home a couple hours later he found the phone still off the hook, the Breathalyzer on the counter with its needle still jacked up, vomit still in the toilet, a bottle of wine missing, and his son passed out on his bed in his green private-school blazer. It did not take a whole lot of detective work to figure out what had happened. He woke me up, walked me down to the basement, and gave me the whole, "I'm very disappointed in you" talk. For some reason though, he decided to give me this speech while we shot a game of pool. I distinctly remember kicking his ass at pool, which, to me, seriously undermined his point. In fact, it gave me a sense of accomplishment.

Mötley Crüe's influence was not all bad. In October 1987, the band was scheduled to play a concert at Maple Leaf Gardens in Toronto on the "Girls, Girls, Girls" tour. Dad had taken me to my first concert, Twisted Sister, in London a year and a half earlier, and I'd only grown more rabid about metal since then.

> **TED:** At the time, I was president of Nabisco Brands in Canada. I came home and proudly announced that I was going take Steve to the Mötley Crüe concert, and that I'd reserved the company's skybox at the Gardens for the two of us. I even arranged for our driver to smuggle Steve's tape recorder into the box so he could make his own illegal recording. Steve's reaction was, "Dad, that's really lame! No way I'm going to sit in a corporate skybox at a Mötley Crüe concert." So I told him, "Okay, then, you get tickets that you like better and we'll sit in your seats." He rose to the challenge.

The day before the show, I saw on the local news that the band was already in town, and it occurred to me that they must be staying at a local hotel. I figured they wouldn't check in under their own names, but guessed they might be registered under their manager's name. I checked every Mötley Crüe album sleeve and worked out that their manager was a guy named Doc McGhee. I grabbed the Yellow Pages and began calling every hotel in Toronto and asking for Doc McGhee's room. I spent literally hours going down the list one by one. After a while, Mom began to get annoyed that I was tying up the phone line, but Dad convinced her to back off. He'd never seen me so motivated to accomplish anything, and he loved it. Finally, after calling one of the numbers toward the bottom of the list, a hotel operator patched me through to a room.

"Hello, Doc McGhee?" I asked.

"This is Doc's brother, Scott," the voice answered.

"As in Mötley Crüe?!?"

I'm sure my prepubescent voice made me sound like a little girl, and Scott initially seemed slightly annoyed.

"How did you get this number?" he asked.

When I told him what I had gone through to find the band, his attitude completely changed.

"That's awesome! How would you like it if I put your name on the list for a couple of backstage passes and tickets for tomorrow night?" he asked. "I can get you in the fifth row."

I was fucking stoked. Dad took me to the show, and the passes were there as promised. It was amazing. Afterward, the arena emptied out, and we were allowed backstage. I met and hung out for a little while with Tommy Lee and Nikki Sixx, got autographs and photos, and generally fulfilled the biggest dream my thirteen-year-old brain could've possibly imagined. Those guys didn't really impart to me any lasting nuggets of wisdom and I didn't really have anything to tell them either, but that night was the first time I ever really saw myself as someone capable of accomplishing anything he set his mind to.

Unfortunately, I didn't really set my mind to much else that was productive while we lived in Toronto. I remember saving my lunch money so I could use it to buy eggs to throw at stuff after school. I'd get up on a highway overpass and wave at people in their cars while they were stuck in traffic. When they saw this cute kid waving, they'd inevitably smile and wave back, at which point, I'd pelt their cars with eggs. I loved that shit.

My egging career came to an abrupt halt in eighth grade after I egged this kid's house and he beat me up in front of a bunch of people at school. It was the first real fight I'd ever been in, and although I didn't actually get hurt, it was really humiliating. I found the whole thing unbelievably traumatic, probably more so than was appropriate. To this day I'm still terrified of fighting and, despite being a lifelong pain in everybody's ass, I've avoided it at all costs.

I also got pretty into shoplifting in Toronto. A kid named Justin introduced me to it, but then, as was my way with just about everything, I took it to the extreme. I stole stuff all the time, mostly stuff I didn't really need or even want. I got caught only once, for shoplifting a comic book. I wasn't even into comic books, but I was with friends from school who were and felt compelled to impress them. Plus, it was an adrenaline kick. As it turned out, the owner of the store saw me slip a comic inside my school blazer. He grabbed me, pulled me into his back room, and called the cops and my house. I was a little freaked out but Cindy—who at that time was harboring serious dreams about one day becoming an FBI agent—answered the call, showed up, schmoozed the cops, and helped get me off the hook with just a warning.

Around this time, Mom was drinking heavily and my home life was getting more chaotic and unruly. Cindy obviously longed for some law and order, but my reaction was to get more chaotic and unruly myself. The more fucked up things were at home, the less accountability there was for me. I could just drop off the radar.

At one point, I took this idea to its logical extreme and ran away from home. I had been making plans to run away since the year before, when we lived in London. I even remember sitting in class making lists of what I'd need to bring with me: pots, pans, food, money. When I actually got around to doing it though, I brought only my Walkman, some heavy-metal cassettes, and a shitty little tent. I set my tent up in some woods not too far from my school and was actually asleep in it when the cops found me and took me home. I'd told Cindy where I was planning on going, and she ratted me out. I hadn't been gone much more than a few hours, but when the police showed up and shined their flashlight into that tent, I felt kind of badass.

CINDY: We both fantasized about running away. My plan was elaborate and involved getting a fake ID. I was much more aware that if I was going to make it on my own, I was going to have to get a job and an apartment. Steve ran away and pitched his tent in a park by a stream. He'd left a note and my parents were worried. It was getting dark. I don't think they thought to ask me about it, but I waited about two hours before I spilled the beans. Steve was mad at me, but he was also glad to be found because it was getting cold and I don't think he'd packed warm enough stuff.

TED: That probably scared me more than anything else he had ever done. As close as Steve was to his mother, I think this was his way of rebelling against her alcoholism and lack of attention, and against my not being around enough to pick up the pieces. I had no understanding of alcoholism at the time. Eventually, after we'd moved back to London, it reached a point where if she was passed out when I came home, I'd simply carry her to the car and drive her to a rehab facility. However, even if I'd understood alcoholism as a disease, I truly doubt I could've motivated her to combat it successfully. My major regret is the effect my lack of understanding had on the kids, and the extent to which Steve was unsupervised during his early teens.

Between seventh and eighth grade I switched schools, from a highly regarded private school, Bayview Glen, to the local public school. I was convinced this private school was the cause of all my problems. I didn't need to be wearing some posh green blazer to school and hanging out with a bunch of spoiled rich kids. I needed to start over someplace new, someplace *more real*, and was sure this change would solve everything. Once I got to public school though, nothing changed. I'd brought all my problems with me. If anything, things got worse. It was a bigger school and I fit in even less there than I had at Bayview Glen.

The year I changed schools, Cindy became a boarding student at her all-girls high school. It was pretty unusual to go to boarding school in the same city where your family lives, but I suppose that's a measure of just how fed up she was with the situation at home. She basically *got permission* to run away from home. What that meant for me was that I was left at home with Drunk Mom most of the time while Dad traveled.

It's pretty clear that Toronto was where I really upped the ante on my juvenile delinquency. While I was living there, I went from being a wild kid who had some issues at school to being a genuinely troubled kid who was into shoplifting and getting wasted. When I think back now on what caused this change, I'm sure it wasn't really Mötley Crüe, my mom's alcoholism, or my dad's being away all the time. I think after all the moving around we had done, it was finally starting to dawn on me that the problem wasn't where I lived or my school or my teachers or my friends or even my family. It was me.

for example, their decision to let their out-of-control teenage son move into the sprawling basement apartment of that five-story house in London.

I had quite the setup: the basement was originally designed to be the servants' quarters, so in addition to a large bedroom and a bathroom, there was also a kitchen, a laundry room, and a second bedroom that had been converted into a game room with a pool table. I had my own phone line down there and also my own separate door to the outside, so I really had to see the rest of my family only when it suited me. A lot of the time, I'd be in the basement, Mom would be three stories above me doing her drunk thing, and Dad would be out of town. My main companion down there was a pet hamster named Doyle I'd conned my mom into buying for me. She'd said repeatedly that I couldn't get a hamster, but then when she was drunk, I'd brought her purse to her and she groggily handed over the money for it. As you might imagine, this living arrangement was a dream for me, but any sensible person should've recognized it from a mile away as a surefire recipe for teenage disaster.

Initially though, a renewed interest in skateboarding took precedence over my juvenile delinquency. When I got back to London after a year and a half in Toronto, I realized that when I'd quit skating, all my other friends hadn't. Shortly after arriving, I was on the playground at school and saw a kid jump over a backpack on his skateboard. I was absolutely floored. It was the first time I'd ever seen anyone do an ollie, and this was a kid who'd started skating around the same time I did but just never stopped. I realized that I'd blown it by quitting skateboarding. I was going to have to work my ass off to make up for lost time. My first order of business was teaching myself to do an ollie.

I practiced all the time, often in that basement apartment, where I had the luxury of banging around on my skateboard without really disturbing anyone else in the house. It's hard to describe, but there was something so urgent about my *need* to do an ollie. It was really not that different a feeling from the one I'd had four months earlier when I

TRUE LOVE, THY NAME IS . . . JVC VHS-C CAMCORDER

Halfway through eighth grade, Dad became the president of the international division of Nabisco Brands and we moved back to London and into a five-story house in the upscale St. John's Wood section of the city, right across the street from Regent's Park. I reenrolled at the American School in London, but my sister stayed behind at boarding school in Toronto rather than relocate before her senior year. That meant that as we moved into this big, beautiful London home, it was just me, Mom, and Dad, with Dad still traveling for work all the time. It set up a depressing family dynamic: the house was getting bigger while the family was getting smaller.

I know my parents did their best with me but there are a few decisions they made that I look back on now and wonder, *What the hell were they thinking?* Take, decided that I simply *had* to meet Mötley Crüe. This just took longer. I started by turning a soda can on its side, crushing it down, and trying to jump over it on the board. I worked up toward doing it with the soda can uncrushed, then with the can standing up vertically, and then, finally, by the time ninth grade started, I could ollie over a backpack.

Skateboarding was a completely positive influence in my life: I put a ton of hard work into it and got genuine results. All the energy I'd been devoting to getting into trouble in Toronto suddenly was channeled in a more productive direction. I even swore off drinking for a while. For all of tenth grade, I considered myself "straight edge," and skated around for a while with black X's—the international mark of "straight edge" kids—scrawled on my hands. I remember a project I had to do for health class that year about my thoughts on drugs. I wrote, "I prefer to get high off of skate ramps." My teacher, Mr. Randolfi, responded by saying something to the effect of, "We'll see how long that lasts." I was offended. I felt like he was calling me a liar. But thinking about it now, I believe he simply understood addiction and recognized me as an alcoholic just waiting to pop.

I loved living in London. The buses and the subways made it possible to get anywhere I wanted without a car, which meant I had as much freedom by the age of nine as a kid in America would have at sixteen. The city also felt culturally diverse in a way that most places in America only claimed to be. I was a U.S. citizen (I also have British and Canadian citizenship), but years later, at the University of Miami, I was taken aback by the pretty blatant racism that was part of American culture. I remember thinking, *This isn't a melting pot—it's a TV dinner.* The differences between people created real separation. In London, I went all over the city and don't really remember there being bad neighborhoods like you'd find in American cities. I mean, I did get mugged a few times, but even those experiences, while frightening, seem sort of quaint in retrospect. The muggers would demand my money, my watch, my skateboard, whatever, but there was never a threat of gun violence, and it never made me afraid to travel anywhere in London.

WHEN I was fifteen, Dad won a video camera in a corporate golf tournament. He wasn't too into it, so he stuck it in his closet and forgot about it. Not long after, I took it out of his closet and immediately started filming myself and my friends skateboarding all around London.

Skateboarders have always had a special relationship with video cameras. The sport developed and grew through VHS tapes. Back then, there was no YouTube, there were no X Games. The way you saw Tony Hawk, Steve Caballero, or Christian Hosoi was by buying a video from a skate shop or borrowing one from a friend. In just about any other sport, if you want to get noticed, you do it by winning competitions. In skateboarding, if you wanted to get sponsored, you made videos of yourself to show to skate shop owners or to send to skateboard and apparel companies. As video cameras became common household items, skateboarders were already ahead of the curve and uniquely positioned to take television production into their own hands, a fact that would eventually prove significant in the birth of *Jackass*.

Once I had that video camera, I quickly figured out how to hook up two VCRs to edit the footage we'd recorded. I showed one of my first cuts to Dad. Even though it looked like crap, he was thrilled that his usually unmotivated son had been interested enough to not only snatch the camera from that closet but to attempt something useful with it. We called our very first video "I Hate Rain." It had footage of us performing whatever tricks we could manage back then, but it emphasized wiping out almost as much as it did skating. I edited the video to repeat our falls over and over and to show off my bloody wounds. In addition, that first video included footage of me and two of my buddies messing around and singing a song we wrote called "Oh Maggie." It's pretty embarrassing, but also an early indication that I was falling in love harder with the video camera than the skateboard. I wanted it pointed at me all the time.

When we finished that first video, I took it to school hoping to show it off at some point during the day. I told my tenth grade chemistry teacher about it, and for some reason he decided to screen it for the class. I felt like hot shit: a teacher was forcing my classmates to watch a video I'd made *instead* of doing schoolwork.

A lot of the material in those early videos later surfaced on a DVD I released called *Steve-O: The Early Years.* The skating on it doesn't look that impressive now, but for a while there, I actually got pretty good. Street skating was still in its infancy back then, so it wasn't as if the stuff I was doing was too many notches down from what some pros were doing. Which makes it all the more of a bummer that by the end of the summer after tenth grade, I'd quit again.

Skateboarding was more than just a hobby for me at that time—it was my whole identity. I may not have been the coolest kid in the world, but being a skater made me comfortable with being uncool, just like those Little League uniforms had years before. Between ninth and tenth grade though, most of my skater buddies moved away or quit, and by the time eleventh grade started, there were no other skaters left. As a hopelessly insecure teenager, I just wasn't willing to be the only skate rat in my school. So I decided to find a new hobby.

That's why I made the decision at the beginning of eleventh grade to become a pothead. That's right, I *made the decision.* I knew I needed a new identity and quickly figured that smoking pot was something I could get pretty good at. At that point in my life, I'd never even smoked a joint, but I showed up at school that year on the prowl for marijuana. Then one day, after school, a kid named Eric asked me if I wanted to smoke with him. We walked right around the corner from school and smoked some hash out of a pipe.

It wasn't really love at first toke between me and marijuana. That first time, I didn't even get high, although I sure acted like I was, or at least how I thought people were supposed to act if they were high. Even the following day, I was still acting like a douchebag and pretending to be stoned. If I'd been hoping pot would help me become a cool kid, this was a really bad start. Nonetheless, I had decided I was going to be a stoner, so I stuck with it. I immediately began smoking weed on a near-daily basis, kick-starting a habit that continued until 2008, when I finally got clean. Much like with drinking—which I also started doing with more gusto around this time—the initial appeal of pot wasn't chemical: I just loved the fact that I was doing something I wasn't supposed to.

I took to my new pothead persona with zeal. I went in for all the clichés: I stopped cutting my hair, started wearing ridiculous psychedelic clothes, and got really into the Grateful Dead. I'd found my new uniform.

CINDY: When I left for college that year, I left a little brother who had a fairly preppy haircut, loved skateboarding, and would draw black X's on the backs of his hands for "straight edge"—no drugs, no drinking, adrenaline is my high. I came back at Christmas and his hair had grown well past his ears. He was wearing these seventies-style Charles Manson hippie shirts, his skin was sallow, and his posture was terrible. He was a flaming waste case of a pothead. And it happened really fast. It was one semester that I was gone.

Smoking pot led in pretty quick succession to dropping acid. The first time I tried it was in Regent's Park about a month and a half into the school year. One of my new stoner friends had given me a little tab, and I'd been carrying it around in my wallet, eagerly anticipating the weekend, when I would trip for the first time. But I was nervous, so I took only half the hit and gave the other half to a friend. I suppose the LSD had probably absorbed into my wallet, because nothing happened after I took it. Of course, I acted like it had.

A few weeks later, on November 1, 1990, I saw the Grateful Dead at Wembley Arena and had my first real LSD trip. I got home from

I had to strip off my jeans because they were weighing me down, and eventually one of the other guys basically saved me from going under for good. Once we got out, we trudged back toward the apartment. At one point, we were hugging the ground in a parking lot to keep from being blown over by the wind. When we made it back to the apartment, everyone passed out.

As it turned out, I slept through the main thrust of what turned out to be a Category 5 hurricane, the fourth most powerful to make landfall in U.S. history. When I finally woke up the next day, I went outside and saw trees mangled and fallen, power lines down, roofs that had blown off buildings, and tons of shattered windows and debris everywhere. The campus was wrecked. There was more than $13 million worth of damage, and school officials decided to delay the start of the semester by three weeks. I spent that time with Cindy in St. Louis, where she was a junior at Washington University. When I returned to Miami, I finally moved into my dorm room, but not for long.

My roommate was a serious student who was putting himself through school. I was drinking and smoking pot constantly, leaving empty beer cans everywhere, and this guy wanted to do crazy shit like study and occasionally get a decent night's sleep. We'd been living together for two weeks when I came back to my room and found a document from the university taped to the door informing me that I'd been busted for having alcohol and marijuana in the room. I have no doubt my roommate turned me in, and frankly I can't blame him. University officials came by with a huge hamper on wheels and hauled out all the contraband—tons of booze containers, a wooden box filled with weed, and all my rolling papers. I was relocated to another dorm and placed on what they called "final disciplinary probation."

It occurred to me at this point that my drinking had become a problem. I'd been getting loaded pretty consistently for two years and it was obviously wreaking havoc in my life. I resolved to quit drinking for thirty days. Surely, if I could make it thirty days without a drink, it would prove that alcohol wasn't a major issue for me. I made it eleven.

Not drinking made me completely uncomfortable. All I could think about was the fact that I wasn't drinking. When I caved in, I got someone to buy me a 1.75-liter plastic bottle of cheap-ass vodka and poured myself eleven shots. I downed them one at a time and chased them with swigs of Coke. My thinking was that rather than admit I'd failed to make it thirty days without a drink, my eleven shots were a symbolic way of unadmitting I had a problem: one shot for each day I should've been drinking anyway.

My new dorm room was in a twelve-story tower on a floor occupied mostly by upperclassmen. After my brief flirtation with sobriety, I reapplied myself to getting loaded with fresh enthusiasm. When the guys in my new dorm saw how hard I was partying, they told me straight-out that there was no way I could keep carrying on like that and survive in college. They'd seen guys like me flunk out before. In fact, they were so convinced I was a dead man walking that they made me a bet: If I could maintain a 2.0 grade point average for the semester they'd throw me a party.

I'm proud to say I won that bet and did so without curbing my partying one bit. I picked up pretty early on what I figured was the key to keeping your head above water at college without really trying: Go to class. If you go to class, you know when to do the minimum amount of work and can squeak by. I shocked my entire floor in the dorm by getting a 2.7 GPA that first semester.

Things went south from there though. At the end of that first semester, I met a girl named Tracie Smith who lived one floor below me in the dorm. She was a pretty girl from Staten Island who was smart and driven but also really liked to drink and have fun. I was totally into her in a way I'd never been into any of the girls I'd been with in high school. We started dating and when second semester began, I essentially moved into her dorm room with her.

Life was great: Here I was, on this beautiful, sunny college campus, living with this unbelievable girlfriend and getting loaded all the time.

I'd started skateboarding again and found that in the two years that I'd been off the board, skateboards had gotten smaller, lighter, and more maneuverable. Tricks that I'd been frustrated with a few years ago were now a piece of cake. I also spent a lot of time hanging around the diving towers at the university's Olympic pool. I'd always loved the diving board, but at Miami, I had access to these killer springboards where I practiced different flips. Even though my form was atrocious and my landings frequently painful, it was always really satisfying to learn a new trick. The only part of my life at school that seemed to be kind of a bummer was the school part, so I basically just stopped dealing with it. That second semester I quit going to class almost entirely and earned a stunning 0.86 GPA.

The summer following freshman year, I went with Tracie to her parents' house in Staten Island. She got a job as a waitress while I mostly hung around her pool working on my tan. We had jobs lined up as counselors at the same summer camp, but a few days before we were set to leave, she sprung the news on me that she wasn't going. She didn't exactly break up with me, but she made it clear we were going our separate ways for the summer. I was disappointed but decided I might as well go to this camp in upstate New York by myself.

I lasted eight days there before they fired me. I was getting drunk every night and smoking pot all the time, which is apparently frowned upon when you're working with kids. I had nowhere to go, so I took a bus back to Tracie's house. You can imagine how happy she and her parents were to see me. I guess they looked at me as a charity case though, because they didn't shut the door in my face. They let me stay there, but I wasn't allowed to stay in Tracie's room—I had to bunk down on the couch.

I immediately began abusing their hospitality. Her father got me a job with a family friend who had a landscaping business, but I stopped showing up for that after a day or two. Then, just a few days later, came my birthday. We went out to celebrate and Tracie's friends bought me shot after shot. I came back to her house hammered, climbed into her waterbed with her, and passed out. A few hours later, she nudged me awake. We were lying in a pool of water. I thought for a second that maybe the waterbed had sprung a leak, but in fact, I had: I'd peed in her bed and we were now swimming in it.

Tracie was disgusted. She marched into the bathroom and told me to "deal with it." So I gathered up this huge, heavy, piss-soaked duvet and stumbled out of her room, still very drunk, wondering how I was going to clean it in the middle of the night. I managed to find the laundry room and shove this massive thing into the washing machine, but in the process, I broke the washer door, rendering the machine inoperable. At which point I gave up and went back to sleep.

The next morning, Tracie's mother woke up to find a piss-soaked duvet sitting in a broken washing machine and her daughter's recently fired, degenerate boyfriend passed out on a urine-stained waterbed next to their darling daughter. When Tracie took me aside during breakfast and said, "Look, it's really not working out," it was an admirable understatement.

TRACIE SMITH (ex-girlfriend): Steve was incredibly sweet but never had any desire to do anything but party and be rad. My family loved him though. He was really helpful during the day but would just get obliterated at night. I mean, that night was not the first time he'd peed in my bed. There was the time we went camping and he peed in the tent, the time he peed in my dorm room. But it had just gotten to the point where it was like, "Come on! It's one thing doing stupid things in a dorm room but how can you let it all just hang out at my family's house and not realize there is a certain way people are supposed to behave?" I was so angry. It's not that I wasn't in love with the person that I fell for, it was that I was dying for him to change just a little so I could see that it was just a passing phase, like it was for most people in college.

Amazingly, after that incident, Tracie didn't cut me loose completely—at least not the way I understood it—but merely told me I couldn't spend the summer with her in Staten Island. So I packed up and headed to St. Louis to crash with Cindy for the rest of the summer.

When I returned to school in the fall, I arrived to a couple of rude awakenings. First, I showed up at my dorm room to find a welcome sign taped to the door that read: STEPHEN GLOVER, FRESHMAN. At first, I thought it was a mistake, but I had failed so many classes that I didn't have enough credits to be a sophomore.

The second bombshell was the one I should've seen from a mile away but didn't: Tracie dumped me. I was completely devastated. Whatever minimal effort I had been putting into school my first year was completely abandoned. I didn't bother dropping out, I didn't inform my parents, I just stopped going. When Dad would call, I'd lie and say I was going to class and working hard.

I can look back now and see that my relationship with Tracie never stood a chance of lasting, but when she broke up with me it sent me into a very real tailspin. Those first few weeks back at school I was depressed and getting loaded every day. I became obsessed with the idea of somehow getting her back. A few times, I weaseled my way back into her bed, but after we'd have sex she'd say, "No, we're still broken up," and I'd be back to square one.

As it happened, around this same time, my maternal grandmother's second husband, Wayne, died and I inherited his video camera. That gave me the idea and the tools for my plot to win Tracie back: I would videotape myself doing crazy stunts, then show them to her.

I'd been into skateboard tricks and doing flips off diving boards, and now I'd found the natural next step. Along with a few friends, I began going on late-night stunt missions. We'd get wasted, then tie rock-climbing ropes to banisters and go rappelling down the sides of tall buildings. I'd jump off the balconies of apartment complexes into shallow swimming pools. We'd scale local bridges, then jump off. In my mind, I figured when Tracie saw this footage she'd either be so blown away by how rad I was or so concerned that I was going to die that she'd immediately want to get back together with me. Neither of these things happened.

> **TRACIE:** Some part of me realized that he was trying to impress me, but it was so tough to swallow because that was the exact reason I was breaking up with him. His goals in life were to accomplish tricks and to be rad. It was just kind of sad. He was throwing himself off bridges to win me back. I didn't know what to say. He'd say, "Hey, I'm going to jump from a moving car off a bridge. Will you love me?" It was like, "I don't know what to say. Please just don't get hurt."

I continued with the stunts regardless of the consequences—and there *were* consequences. In October 1993, I smashed out the window at the top of the stairwell in my dorm, crawled out of it, and then crossed a balcony-size gap to get onto the roof of this twelve-story building. I climbed a radio tower up there and was spotted from the ground by someone who called the cops. As a result, I was booted from the dorms entirely. They gave me a couple days to clear out my shit, which I did, though I didn't actually leave the campus—I just started crashing with friends.

Ironically enough, it was around this time that my aimless existence began to gain a little shape. Even though that early stunt footage didn't make Tracie fall back in love with me, as I showed it to other people—and make no mistake, I showed it to *everybody* I possibly could—and saw their reactions, I started to formulate the outlines of what might be called my career plan. Whenever I had shown off the skateboarding videos I made in high school, nobody had ever been that impressed. With the footage I'd been filming at UM, I put together a video that got genuine reactions. The skating was better, but it was the footage of me doing things like hanging from the railing of a twelve-story building by my bare hands that really shocked people. The stuff I was doing was genuinely reckless, and the way people reacted to it really made me feel like I was on to something. I knew I wasn't going to make it in college or ever be able to hold down a normal job. But after Tracie dumped me, I realized what I really loved was filming myself doing dangerous stunts with the video camera—*so why not just do that?* If I really had to pinpoint a single event that set me on the path toward what would eventually become *Jackass*, that was definitely it: getting my heart broken for the first time.

WITH THIS new revelation in mind, it quickly became obvious that I was wasting my time at school. A friend named Jamie Haselton had decided to drop out of college and drive to Lake Tahoe, California, to work at a ski resort. A job at a resort, he explained, gets you free lift tickets and you can spend the whole winter snowboarding. I'd never snowboarded in my life, but it sounded like something that would burnish my credentials as a budding stuntman and all-around rad dude, so when Thanksgiving holiday rolled around, I packed my stuff into Jamie's beat-up old van and left the University of Miami. Jamie and I had $600 between us and CALI OR BUST written on the side of the dusty van. I didn't have a driver's license, so Jamie drove the whole way.

The trip out there was not without its mishaps—we ended up having to steal an entire wheel off a similar vintage van to replace one that had flown off Jamie's while we were on the highway—and when we finally got out to the Squaw Valley Resort near Lake Tahoe, we were confronted with two major problems: no snow and no jobs. We met up with a friend of Jamie's named Devon Murelli and reworked the master plan. There was snow in Colorado, so we pointed the van in the direction of Steamboat Springs and headed off with Devon following us in his car.

When we got there we were running short of cash. We met some students from a local college who, for a few days, let us sleep in their dorm rooms, eat in their cafeteria, and smoke their weed. Jamie got hired as a dishwasher at a resort in Steamboat, which got him his beloved free season pass and a room in the employee apartment complex. Devon and I moved into the apartment of two girls who lived there, Kristen and Danika. I found a job bagging groceries and cleaning the meat room at a nearby supermarket, and Devon got hired at a hotel. What little money we made was spent on food and booze, and when that ran out we quickly resorted to various schemes and in some cases outright theft to keep ourselves well fed and liquored up.

Once I got familiar with the supermarket where I worked, we routinely stole cartons of cigarettes and cases of beer from the place. At first we just snatched stuff from the aisles of the store, but after a couple weeks this progressed into well-organized heists, during which someone would pull a car behind the supermarket, and we'd schlep cases and cases of beer right out the back door from the stockroom. It's amazing we never got caught.

I had a great Christmas in Steamboat that year, but Devon and I were disenchanted with our jobs. We heard about a place in Austin, Texas, that paid people to have drugs tested on them, so Devon called them up and found out about a study that would pay good money but required us to apply in person in two days. There was also an intense screening process. We had to be in perfect health and our systems needed to be free of drugs. Undeterred, we hopped in Devon's car and drove twenty-two hours nonstop to Austin, guzzling water and popping goldenseal capsules the whole way to flush the THC out of our systems. We arrived just in time to be interviewed, be examined, give our urine samples, and fill out paperwork promising not to hold anyone liable should we have the misfortune to drop dead during the study. Then we had to wait twelve days to find out if we were accepted.

We knew no one in Austin, and after a couple days, we were completely broke and legitimately homeless. When we got hungry, we had to be crafty. We'd go into a diner and swipe the free saltines off a table, or play "freelance busboy" and bus the tables before the actual busboy did, chowing down on whatever people had left behind on their plates. Sometimes we'd beg on the streets. When we'd get fifty cents together, we'd go to a supermarket, buy a forty-nine-cent loaf of bread and steal some hot dogs. Experience taught me that it was less suspicious to go into a store and buy something—in this case, bread—than to walk around the store and then mysteriously leave without paying for anything. We'd then bring our hot dogs over to a 7-Eleven and use their microwave and condiments to make ourselves a decent little meal.

Devon's car was a two-seater and it was packed with stuff, which made sleeping in it extremely uncomfortable, if not outright impossible. Sleeping in the streets seemed a little dangerous, but we decided if we could get ourselves up onto the roof of a building, nobody would be likely to fuck with us up there. So we found a suitable spot, scaled the side of the building, and bunked down on top. It was January, so it got pretty fucking chilly, but really it wasn't a terrible setup. We even stole flashlights and a few books from the Salvation Army so we could read up there at night.

When it rained or got too cold to hack it up there, we slept under an awning behind an abandoned Chinese restaurant. That was a slightly sketchier situation.

I remember waking up under that awning one day to find two bags filled with fast food. We were stoked and immediately began eating. After a few minutes, a car drove up and a guy rolled down the window.

"Hey, did you get the food I left for you?" he asked.

We told him we did and thanked him for it.

"Listen," he continued. "I have a place where you guys can shower if you want. And then I'll cook you a nice meal."

This guy looked like a very conservative, clean-cut Good Samaritan. We hadn't showered in more than a week and the idea of a home-cooked meal sounded amazing, so we got in Devon's car and followed him to his house. In retrospect, that guy easily could've been a serial killer, so the fact that he just turned out to be a shady gay man cruising for homeless kids really wasn't so bad. We didn't catch on to this fact until we had already showered and eaten at his house. But when he proposed that we "fool around" with him, we politely, though abruptly, got the fuck out of there.

In the midst of living as a street bum, it of course crossed my mind that I could call Mom or Dad and ask them to send me money, but the fact of the matter was, I hadn't talked to either one of them since I bailed from school. I felt like I had wasted enough of their money and really wanted to prove that I could stand on my own two feet. In Austin, it certainly seemed as if I couldn't, but I was too proud to admit it to my parents. Besides, I felt everything I had been up to pretty well qualified me as a disappointment to them, and in light of that fact, I couldn't bring myself to ask them for money.

Fortunately, after twelve days of living on the streets in Austin, Devon and I were accepted into this medical study. We reported to a big laboratory run by a company called Pharmaco LSR.

The way most medical studies work is that participants are paid according to the risks they're willing to subject themselves to. Our study was for a drug called ractopamine hydrochloride. It's a food additive that is given to pigs and cows, which causes them to produce less fat and more muscle. The doctors running the study were quite candid in admitting that beyond this, they didn't know much about the drug or what effects it would have on humans. They expected it would increase our heart rates and the purpose of the study was to determine just how much ractopamine hydrochloride the average human could consume before his or her heart rate would shoot up to a dangerous level. As these sorts of studies go, this one was considered fairly high risk and because of this there were only six participants in it, including me and Devon, and we'd each get paid $2,000.

We were given the drug every other day, then every hour on the hour, doctors watched our hearts on ultrasound machines and checked our heart rates. An average resting heart rate is typically between 60 and 80 beats per minute, and the plan was that we would keep getting increased doses of ractopamine hydrochloride until someone in the study achieved a resting rate of 150 bpm.

As it turned out, the doctors discovered that I had a particularly powerful heart. My normal resting rate was in the high forties, which meant that my heart needed to beat a little more than half as many times in a minute to circulate the same amount of blood through my body as the average Joe. As the study went on, while some of the other participants were sweating and shaking uncontrollably, my heart rate never climbed above one hundred. I was fine.

After twelve long days in that lab, they sent us on our way with $800 each. (The other $1,200 would come in the mail.) Another guy in the study, whose name I seem to recall was Lamar, invited Devon and me back to his place in Killeen, Texas, to celebrate our freedom while we made some necessary repairs to Devon's car.

When we got to Killeen, we hung out with Lamar for a few days. He seemed like an okay guy. He told us he could get us each a pound of weed for $500, which sounded like a good thing to spend our new-found cash on. We drove him to an apartment complex on the outskirts of Killeen and gave him our money. He walked into the apartments and didn't come out. We looked around a little but had no idea where he was. We weren't sure what had happened but managed to find our way back to his place. When we got there, Lamar wasn't there but his roommate let us in.

The next day, Devon was working on his car at a nearby gas station and I was sitting on the sofa by myself when Lamar finally showed up. He was surprised to see me. He quickly left and returned with two other guys. I asked him what happened back at the apartment complex. Nobody answered me. Instead, one of Lamar's buddies punched me and kicked me in the head a few times and told me to give him the rest of my money. I had about $200 left from the medical study earnings, which I handed over. The three of them walked out and told me that I better not still be there when they got back. The whole episode really sucked: in the course of about thirty seconds, I realized Devon and I had been robbed, I got my ass kicked, and then I was robbed again.

I had no choice but to wait for Devon to return and, when he did, I told him what had happened. As stupid as we'd been to trust Lamar and then not even realize we'd been scammed, he wasn't much smarter to leave the two people he'd just robbed alone in his house. Devon and I immediately began running through the house, stealing everything that wasn't bolted down—clothes, shoes, CDs, even a pet python and terrarium that he'd just bought a couple days before. We loaded all the loot into Devon's car and got the hell out of Texas as fast as we could.

5

COPS, DOCTORS, AND DEADHEADS

After hauling ass out of Texas, Devon and I drove back to Steamboat with Lamar's python, which we gave to Kristen and Danika. I called my mom and asked her to wire me money to tide me over until I received the $1,200 check from the medical study. Mom had moved back to Florida after the divorce, hoping for a fresh start, and was living alone in Boca Raton, near Miami, at the time. It sucks that after not talking to Mom for so long, I broke the silence by calling to ask her for money, but she was so happy to hear from me she not only wired me the money, she offered to fly me home to Florida once I received the check.

Once back in Florida, I returned to the University of Miami but not as a student. I'd often crash at friends' places, but when that failed I had to get creative. One of my standard moves was to climb in the windows of empty on-campus apartments and snooze there. Other times, I'd put my Austin experience to use and bunk down on the roof of some university building. One of my favorite spots was a six-story academic building in the middle of the campus with a pretty easily accessible roof. When I'd wake up there, I'd peer down and see the students marching back and forth between classes like ants.

That fall I spent a lot of my time skateboarding. I'd improved a lot and was intent on getting sponsored. I knew I wasn't as good as most sponsored skaters but figured if I got enough footage of myself doing lunatic stunts as well that would help my cause. I took the tricks I'd learned at the UM diving towers and started trying them off apartment complex balconies into shallow pools or off bridges into local waterways. The fact that I lacked any real skill at diving didn't matter—the idea was to appear totally insane.

Around this time, I told anyone who would listen that I was going to be a rad stuntman and was really starting to believe it myself. In truth though, I had no earthly idea how to achieve this goal. So I just kept collecting footage and showing it to everyone I could. I rarely went anywhere in those days without a copy of my latest stunt video.

TED: When he told me on the phone that he wanted to be a stuntman, Sophie and I went to the National Cinema Library in London. Our mission was to find published accounts that confirmed that professional stuntmen were in the process of being replaced by digital photography. After a couple hours, we proudly came home with some photocopies of clippings and jumped on the phone to Steve. We gave him the word and said, "We have documentation!" We put these clippings in the mail so he'd be able to read them himself. After he got them, he very calmly said, "Okay, if there's no room for stuntmen in movies, I'm just going to recruit a bunch of crazy guys, form a circus, and travel around the country doing stunts." Of course, that's effectively what he wound up doing.

As hard as I was working at skateboarding and stunts, I was working just as hard at getting loaded. I spent a lot of nights on my buddy Bill Schnell's couch. I'd met Bill in the dorm during my first freshman year. He had his dorm room set up with an elaborate system of fans designed to prevent marijuana smoke from being detected in the hallways. For Bill, just like me, partying was the top priority at UM, and he didn't last much longer as a student than I did.

After that year in the dorm, Bill moved into an apartment across the street from a gas station that sold beer. One night, we were walking across the street to buy more beer and stopped in the middle of the road to play chicken with the oncoming cars. One of those cars, it turned out, was a police cruiser. When I saw the cop get out of his car, I tried to hide my open beer behind me in the waistband of my pants.

Here's a tip for anyone who is ever approached by a police officer on a dark road at night: do not reach behind you into the waistband of your pants. The cops thought I had a gun and, quite predictably, freaked the fuck out. They spread-eagled my ass on the ground and arrested both Bill and me for drunk and disorderly conduct. The police report summed up the scene quite well: "While on routine patrol we observed the def and co-def walking in the middle of SW 72 St. in the lane of eastbound traffic. Both were waving their arms about and taunting eastbound drivers. Vehicles were slowing and honking as the def and co-def appeared to be laughing and playing in the roadway." We spent the night in jail and then got sentenced to an alcohol education class.

When the school year ended at UM, I flew to St. Louis to join Dad and Sophie in attendance at my sister's college graduation. Mom had been trying to move on after the divorce, and had had a couple of fairly disastrous relationships since then, but wasn't over it by a long shot. She didn't want to be anywhere Sophie was going to be, so she stayed in Florida.

I felt an obvious loyalty to Mom, but I have to admit I liked Sophie from the first time I met her, and not just because she frequently gave me money, beer, and cigarettes. She was born in Morocco, but grew up in Belgium. Dad had met her in 1991, when she'd been working as the food and beverage manager in a Brussels hotel where he frequently stayed on business. She was exotic looking and spoke with a thick accent. To her credit, she made a real effort to become friends with me, instead of just being "Dad's new woman." During my senior year of high school, I'd had a few Kuwaiti friends, and Sophie spent a lot of time teaching me Arabic so I could impress them. She was a good influence on Dad too. He'd definitely mellowed a little since they'd gotten together, which I think helped him deal with me better.

SOPHIE GLOVER (stepmother): When I left Belgium and moved to London, I didn't have any friends. Steve was my friend. We had fun together. When Steve left the University of Miami, Ted was a little aggressive with him in the beginning. I was like Steve's lawyer sometimes trying to defend him. Ted, in the end, accepted it.

That trip to St. Louis was the first time I'd seen Dad in a while. We had a good talk and I told him that despite all appearances to the contrary, I was doing great. "However," I explained to him, "it would be much easier for me to be productive if I had a car."

Not hearing from me for so long had worried him and Sophie sick, and I think they agreed to buy me a car because they felt it would reestablish communication between us. So a few days after Cindy's graduation, we did a tour of St. Louis used car dealerships and eventually found a 1991 Ford Tempo that Sophie hard-balled a salesman into selling us at a good price.

Funnily enough, at that point, I didn't even know how to drive. Spending all four years of high school in London, then going straight to UM, I hadn't ever needed to learn. Through all the traveling I'd done, I'd never once gotten behind the wheel myself. So Dad and Sophie sprung for some driving lessons, after which I went to the DMV, took a driving test, passed, and got a license. I picked up the car on my birthday, June 13, 1994, and with two hundred bucks to my name, drove all the way to Canada without sleeping a wink.

In Toronto, I met up with a high school friend named Meredith and hung out with my cousin Neil, the aspiring mortician whom I'd met only a couple times when we were little kids. I spent about two weeks there—mostly just partying, though for a short spell Meredith got me a job with Greenpeace doing door-to-door begging—then left with Meredith's roommate to follow the Grateful Dead for the summer.

Although my initial interest in the Dead was more about playing the part of a pothead than anything else, I'd grown to genuinely love the music. Plus, the tours were a roving carnival of lost souls doing virtually nothing with their lives but staying loaded, so it was one of the few environments I felt I could fit right into. I had $40 to my name but figured I could make enough to fund the trip by selling beers, grilled cheese, and burgers in the parking lots outside the shows.

I bought forty-eight beers before the first show in Highgate, Vermont, and barely made my money back selling them for $2 apiece. Before some shows, I'd do sketchy back flips off cars in the parking lot for dollar bills. But that first week I struggled to make enough gas money to get from one show to the next. Then a guy at a campground in Indiana offered to pay me to bring people to his van to buy drugs. This was a job I could do. I never actually had drugs on me that night but made about $50.

A few days later at Soldier Field in Chicago, I decided to branch out on my own. I started with $5 in my pocket, spent it on three hits of acid, and sold them each for $5. Then with my $15 I bought a bag of weed and sold it for $30. After selling and buying drugs for a couple hours, I ended up with $80. That became more or less my regular routine for the rest of the summer—well, as regular as any routine can be when you're spending so much of your time stoned or tripping on acid. It was never difficult to turn $5 into $100 in a day, but once I had $100 in my pocket, I was pretty satisfied and would just go skateboard or kick a hacky sack until the show started. Drug dealing for me was strictly about daily subsistence. I was no entrepreneur.

The final night of the tour at the Meadowlands in New Jersey, I was selling acid to some guys in the parking lot when I heard a deep, authoritative voice yell, "Hey!" in my direction. I turned my head and saw that the voice belonged to a cop. *Oh, fuck.* I had heard horror stories of Deadheads getting caught selling acid and landing serious prison sentences. I took off running. I sprinted through the Meadowlands parking lot, weaving through cars and tents, scared shitless. Lucky for me, I was either faster than that cop or he wasn't all that interested in chasing down some twenty-year-old kid over a few hits of acid.

AFTER THE summer, I returned to Miami and got hired as a pizza delivery driver. Although it seems like a pretty easy job, I sucked at it. I didn't know my way around, so on my first day it took me forty-five minutes to get to a house right around the corner. I lasted one shift before I got fired.

Hurting for cash, I applied the skills I'd picked up over the summer and sold drugs around the UM campus, treating it like it was essentially a large Grateful Dead parking lot. I was a pretty crappy drug dealer though. My bags of weed were always underweight, and I smoked too much and sold too little to reinvest in more supply. I think I just lacked the necessary ambition: I never had any interest in getting rich; I just wanted to have enough cash to keep myself loaded.

Drug dealing wasn't exactly steady work for me, so I got a job bussing tables at a seafood restaurant called Cami's. It was a good gig—I'd generally make at least $50 a night. I was relatively flush but still never bothered to get my own place to live. Instead, I made sure I always had a bag of weed on me, which made couch surfing easier. Nobody likes a freeloader, but a freeloader with a bag of weed isn't so bad.

For Thanksgiving in 1994, my buddy Kevin "Kev-O" Biemuller invited me to his mom's house. Kev-O had dropped out of UM about the same time I did as a direct result of the partying we did together. We struggled together as homeless dropouts at UM and always seemed to have a great time doing it.

Kev-O's mom lived on a waterway in Jupiter, Florida, and had a ski boat. The morning after Thanksgiving, we took the boat out with an inner tube tied behind it. I'd been talking endlessly about how I was going to be this kickass stuntman, so when it was my turn on the inner tube, Kev-O decided to see if I could back up all my yapping. He gunned the boat and began driving like a madman. I hung on for dear life. At one point, he whipped me around and my right leg slammed into something hard in the water, maybe a log. I didn't let go, though perhaps I should've because when I finally wiped out, it hurt like a motherfucker. I looked at my leg: the skin wasn't broken but something was very wrong.

When we docked the boat, I made two calls—one to my mom, begging her to take me to the hospital, and the other to Cami's, explaining that I wouldn't be at work for a while. Mom took me to Boca Raton Community Hospital, where a doctor told me my leg wasn't broken and sent me on my way with a prescription for Vicodin. I took a few but was still in serious pain. I returned to the hospital, essentially to ask them for some better drugs, and a doctor examined my leg again. He said the swelling was creating so much pressure within my leg that the muscles were beginning to turn gray. If they didn't do something quickly it would need to be amputated.

They rushed me in for emergency surgery, drained the fluid from my leg, and left the wound open so the pressure wouldn't build up again. For a while, the doctors weren't certain whether there might be permanent damage. Hearing that, I broke down, sobbing uncontrollably at the idea that my future as a stuntman might be in jeopardy. Considering that I had no idea how I was ever going to make any real money doing anything that could be called a stunt, I suppose it's absurd that that's what would make me so upset. But becoming a stuntman was more than a dream to me at that point—it was the only plan I had.

When I found out I'd need a second surgery to clean out my leg one more time and close it up, it seemed too good an opportunity to waste, so I had my buddies bring my video camera to the hospital. During the prep for that second operation, I told a nurse I wanted her to film my leg during surgery. She agreed to do it.

I'm told the first thing I said when I emerged from the fog of general anesthesia after the operation was, "Did I get footage?" The surgeon informed me that the camera wasn't sterile so they couldn't bring it into the operating room. When I heard this, I lost my shit. I had such a temper tantrum that the doctors told Mom I suffered from a rage disorder.

After five days in the hospital, I was released. I needed to spend almost a month in a wheelchair with my leg elevated, but by Christmas I'd healed up enough to be limping around, bussing tables back at Cami's, and a few weeks into the new year I was back to routinely doing incredibly foolish things.

For example: It's January, and I'm at a keg party at UM, standing out on the balcony trying to impress this chick by telling her I'm going to be a stuntman. At the time, I'd developed a stunt where I could fling myself off a second-floor balcony onto the concrete below and walk away with hardly a scratch. The key was I'd put my weight and my abdomen on the balcony rail and, as I went over, I'd use my free hand to grab the ground of that second floor. So I'd end up with one hand on the rail and one hand on the floor while my body went up and over the railing. Then I wouldn't really let go until I was hanging from both hands, which cut down the distance I was falling considerably. I'd then land on my feet and roll out of it. I'd practiced this stunt enough times that it all flowed together smoothly and looked pretty damn impressive.

So there I am, explaining my future line of work to this girl and acting out a fight scene so she can get the appropriate visual accompaniment. I pretend to get punched and then throw myself over the railing of the balcony. Unfortunately, I'm so drunk that I forget to grab the rail or the floor and basically just do a flip and a half and land face-first on the concrete. I don't remember hitting the ground, nor do I remember lying there motionless for fifteen minutes with blood pooling around my head waiting for the paramedics to arrive.

By the time I was scraped off the pavement, about thirty people had gathered around me and most of them assumed I was dead. I wasn't dead but wasn't too far off either: I had a broken cheekbone, seven broken teeth, a broken wrist, a concussion, and a gash in my chin that required ten stitches to close.

The next day I woke up in the hospital very groggy and feeling like a small man with a large sledgehammer was inside my head trying to bash his way out. I told the nurse that I needed to call my mom and she directed me to the phone in the hallway. What I really wanted was to get the fuck out of the hospital. I called my friend Dave Olshansky and asked him to come pick me up. Minutes later, he pulled up in his car, and I walked out of there still wearing my hospital gown. I'd gotten stitches in my chin but had yet to get a cast on my wrist, and my face was a battered, swollen mess.

Dave and I drove back to the UM campus, where I pulled my video camera from the trunk of my car in the parking lot and proudly filmed my injuries. From there, we returned to the scene of the crime, where I tried to drink a beer on the spot I'd face-planted the night before. But my mouth and face were so fucked up that it was too painful to drink. I went by Cami's to tell them, once again, that I couldn't work. They told me I was fired.

The next few weeks were unbelievably unpleasant. My sinuses would routinely fill with blood, so I was walking around constantly hocking up loogies of coagulated blood. My face was so beat up that for days, I couldn't really eat anything. At one point, I mixed tuna and mayonnaise in a blender and tried to drink it. It was even grosser than it sounds.

I eventually went back to the hospital and got a cast for my wrist. I don't know if I even would've bothered, but I was worried it would heal wrong and then I wouldn't be able to walk on my hands anymore. Mom also made me an appointment to get my teeth fixed. The night before that dentist appointment, I was partying again with my friend Bill. He was moving to New York, so we were at his place, putting all his belongings into boxes. At some point, I grabbed my keys and told Bill I was going to meet up with this girl I was trying to hook up with. He took one look at me and said, "If you get behind the wheel of that car you are going to wind up either in jail or in the morgue."

I was defiant.

"I've had exactly nine beers and two Valiums," I told him. "If I wasn't okay to drive, how would I know that?" To me, the fact I could still count meant I was perfectly fine to be operating heavy machinery.

I left, stopped briefly at Taco Bell, and then swerved around the road for who knows how long before finally realizing there was a police car behind me, right on my back bumper, lights flashing and siren blaring, trying to get my attention to pull me over. I stopped the car, and before the cop could even ask me for my license and registration I rolled down the window and loudly proclaimed, "Okay, you got me! You got me fair and square! I will cooperate!"

I was asked to walk a straight line, fell off it, and refused to continue the roadside sobriety test.

"No need," I said. "I'm completely wasted."

When they brought me to the police station, they initially tossed me in a holding cell with all the other dudes who had been picked up that night. Then a pissed-off-looking female cop pulled me out and told me I'd have to be relocated. According to her, the cast on my wrist was a potential weapon and would give me an unfair advantage if I got into a fight. I would've argued that having a broken wrist was a distinct *disadvantage* in a fight, but she wasn't hearing that from the kid who just blew a 0.23 on the Breathalyzer.

I was moved to a different part of the Miami-Dade County Jail and put in a large cell alongside guys who weren't awaiting trial but had already been convicted and were serving their sentences. (Why my cast didn't give me an unfair advantage in a fight against any of these guys wasn't explained.) The cell was a huge, narrow rectangle, with a series of bunk beds on both sides that stretched to a bathroom area in the back. Unlike the holding cell, which was filled mostly with guys sleeping off whatever stupid shit they'd tried to pull when they were wasted, the dudes in this cell looked a lot more at home in jail. The guard pointed me in and told me I needed to take a shower immediately. I can say unequivocally that the very last thing I wanted to be doing after walking into this cell past these hardened criminals was getting naked and taking a shower. But I did and then was given a chance to make a phone call.

I called my mom, who at the time was in a prolonged stretch of sobriety. I distinctly recall her sounding kind of chipper.

"Hey, Stever! How's it going?"

"Not so good, Mom. I'm in jail."

Her mood changed considerably after that. She was fed up with me and I don't blame her. After Mom and Dad got divorced, they each kind of took turns being the primary parent who had to deal with my bullshit, and it had been her turn recently. I was more than just an out-of-control pain in the ass—I was a significant financial burden. In the past year, I'd needed serious medical treatment for my fucked-up leg and mangled face. I'd also been arrested twice. The source of all these problems was simply my desire to be loaded all the time. Mom was very serious about sobriety then, so when she heard I was in jail that was the last straw for her. It was tough love time. She told me, "Have a good time in there because I'm not bailing you out unless you go directly to rehab." I took a quick look around and told her rehab sounded like a pretty good idea.

I spent a day or two in jail, mostly sleeping—and missed that dentist appointment—before Mom picked me up. After a quick stop at Mom's house to pack a bag, she took me directly to Pathways to Recovery, a drug and alcohol rehab center in South Florida.

The place looked like a run-down miniature summer camp, with a gazebo and an incredibly haggard sand volleyball court. I knew I had a drinking problem and, in theory, I wanted to give rehab a fair shot. Realistically, I just wasn't ready for it yet. My priorities were elsewhere. After my orientation, the first thing I did was locate a TV with a VCR in the common room and pop in my latest stunt video. I wanted to make sure everyone in rehab knew they were sharing space with a totally amazing daredevil. About two minutes into the video, one of the counselors at the facility came in, ejected the tape, and confiscated it. That pissed me off something fierce and definitely didn't start me off on the right foot in there. Not that anybody starts off rehab on the *right* foot.

I recall a statistic I heard during my time in rehab from one of the counselors there: Only 5 percent of alcoholics and addicts get sober and stay that way. Ninety-five percent die drunk or high. To me, that just sort of sealed it for me: *If the odds were so low, why even try?* I already knew that I was a pedigreed alcoholic—it was in my genes, passed down to me from Mom and her entire family—and now to find out that even if I was completely committed to sobriety, I'd still have only a five in one hundred chance of actually succeeding was as good a reason as I needed to just say "Fuck it." That statistic kept me from even thinking about trying to get sober for many years. As far as I was concerned, I was hopeless.

Despite this attitude, I did learn a few things during my thirty days at Pathways, though I'm sure they weren't the things I was supposed to learn.

living complex and rent a room from this guy Joe who I worked with at the restaurant. So after about forty-five days in these apartments, I gathered my stuff and climbed over the fence at the side of the complex. I'm sure I could've just walked out the front gate, but I didn't really want to draw any attention to myself or deal with anyone. Plus, I liked the symbolism: I was climbing a wall to escape from sobriety.

We spent a great deal of our time in groups, sitting in a circle talking about our problems and feelings. Whenever new people came in they'd introduce themselves and tell everyone what their drug of choice was. The amount of respect you got from the group was almost always directly proportional to how hardcore your substance abuse problem was. There was a lot of "I spilled more than you ever drank" kind of boasts in that rehab facility. I remember thinking, *This isn't rehab—this is just a pissing match to see who's the biggest fuckup.* When some poor dude came in there and said that his drug of choice was marijuana, the other addicts seemed pissed off at him for being there. I really thought he might get his ass kicked. The consensus was that anyone who'd come to rehab for smoking weed was clearly a pussy.

It was cool to be a waste case but only up to a point. Snorting coke was fine, but if you were a crack addict that was over the line. Everyone thought crackheads were walking corpses who couldn't help but steal shit. If you admitted to a crack problem, people would avoid eye contact with you. Nobody would want to be your roommate. Heroin addicts tended to get carried into rehab. Every single one of them said that they had sworn they'd never shoot up, but all of them did because it became economically unfeasible not to once they'd developed a tolerance to snorting and smoking it.

My takeaway from all this was that as long as I never got into heroin or crack, I'd be fine. In fact, after listening to most of the stories I heard in that place, I felt like I really didn't have a problem at all. Sure I got drunk and smoked pot every day, was very into acid and had tried coke, nitrous oxide, and various other uppers and downers, but I was minor league compared to most of these people.

After my month in rehab, I was placed in a sober living apartment complex in Boca that housed about eighteen other recovering alcoholics. In my head, I'd already given up on sobriety. In fact, I began smoking weed again while I was in "sober living." I got a job as a waiter at Ruby Tuesday, and soon after decided I was going to quit the sober

I'M A PROFESSIONAL NOW

I'd saved up a bit of money when I was in sober living but spent it all quickly once I started drinking again. I got fired from Ruby Tuesday because I was too hungover to show up, and then got a job at T.G.I. Friday's, but got fired before my training period was even over for showing up incoherent, sleep-deprived, and wired on coke. Losing those jobs didn't feel good, and living without money certainly wasn't easy, but as far as I was concerned, what really mattered was doing bigger and better stunts, and I didn't need to be employed to do that.

In those days, I was constantly looking for new bridges and buildings to jump off. One spot I eyed for a long time was my mom's house. To jump from her roof to the pool, you had to clear a cement patio, which took a pretty significant leap. From the ground it looked totally doable, but things have a way of looking very different when you're standing on the edge of a roof looking down. I got up there a bunch of times only to chicken out and climb down. I could stand on the patio and see that logically, with a strong jump, I'd clear it easily. But the part of your brain that makes those calculations isn't always able to override the part that tells you not to wreck yourself on a concrete patio. By that time though, I'd developed a simple mental trick to help override that survival instinct: I'd go over the whole thing in my mind and then count to three on my fingers. Once I'd committed myself to whatever dumbass stunt I was trying and visualized it going okay, I'd put out my first finger. With my second finger, I'd take a deep breath. When my third finger would come out, my body would be ready to follow through with it. Over the years there have been stunts that I've decided against doing for one reason or another, but once that first finger comes out, once I've committed, I never turn back.

Up on Mom's roof, I visualized it, counted off, and cleared the gap. Soon afterward I cleared it headfirst with a pretty sweet swan dive, which was later included on my *Steve-O: The Early Years* DVD.

LIVING AT Joe's house didn't last. On my twenty-first birthday, I got access to $5,000 I'd inherited from a relative I'd never met. I owed Mom $3,600 for medical bills, loans, and bail money, then blew through the rest in a matter of weeks. When I got down to my last $200, I decided buying a new video camera was more important than paying rent, so I moved out of Joe's place and back in with Mom.

Mom's sobriety and my alcoholism were not a winning combination. My whole drunk, unemployed slob act grew tiresome to her very quickly. After I slept through a job interview one morning, she kicked me out.

I floated back to the UM campus and did my usual get-loaded-and-sleep-where-I-can routine for a while. My most consistent home during this period was actually the floor of an apartment shared by the top three collegiate divers in the nation: Bryan Gillooly, Chris Mantilla, and Tyce Routson.

I'd met Bryan at a party. He'd won a record ten consecutive junior national diving titles and been a finalist at the 1992 Olympic Trials when he was only sixteen. In 1994, he'd won the senior nationals and become national diving champion. Naturally, I forced him to watch my stunt video. When he saw the footage of me jumping off the roofs of apartment buildings into shallow pools, he thought I was completely insane. So did Chris and Tyce. These guys were about as good at jumping into water as anyone on Earth, so to have them tell me I was nuts really made me feel like I was making progress.

For months, I was a fairly regular fixture on their living room floor and soaked up any advice or coaching they'd throw my way. I'd been struggling to learn to do a standing back flip on flat ground for more than two years—Bryan taught me to swing my arms into the flip to rotate faster and spotted me until I was able to do it on my own. He also taught me to walk up and down stairs on my hands and to hold a handstand completely still by shifting my weight back and forth between my fingers and the heels of my hands. I'm sure they thought I was a pain in the ass, but I think they were also fascinated by my determination. In turn, I was impressed that—particularly in the cases of Bryan and Chris—it was possible to be a world-class athlete and still party your ass off.

AROUND THANKSGIVING 1995, I was at a keg party that some skateboard buddies of mine were throwing. They had a half-pipe in their backyard, and not far from the half-pipe, some guy was sitting at a table giving out free T-shirts. I started talking to him and he told me he worked for a brand-new skate and surf apparel company called Bizo.

This was all the window I needed to bust out my stunt video. He was impressed with it and told me I needed to talk to the owner of the company about getting sponsored. He was sure they'd want me.

This was huge news. After spending the past few years growing more and more determined to spend my life doing crazy stunts, this was the first hint that maybe, just maybe, someone would actually pay me to act like a lunatic. I left the party that night no longer just an alcoholic dope with a video camera: I was going to be *sponsored*.

The next day, I phoned Dad and told him the news.

"What does that mean?" he asked. "What does it get you?"

He may as well have been speaking Swahili.

"Dad, I'm sponsored!"

"I understand what you're saying," he said. "But what will Bizo *give* you?"

Of course, I had no idea. To me, the goal was just to get "sponsored." I never really gave much thought to what that actually entailed. So Dad and Sophie had me write up a budget to submit to Bizo that would account for my annual expenses. In the end, we added up everything I could possibly need and it came to $30,000. That sounded like a fucking fortune to me.

A few days later, I met the company's owner, a short, balding guy in his forties named Mitchell Jamel. Mitchell had made a bunch of money selling pro sports merchandise and now was looking to break into the skate and surf market. He knew less than nothing about skateboarding, but he was smart, confident, and definitely not about to give me anything resembling $30,000. In fact, I never got much more out of Bizo than a few hundred bucks, some pretty lame merchandise, and business cards that said "Steve-O: Team Rider," which of course I loved.

Even though my arrangement with Bizo was as chintzy as it gets, I still told every single person I knew, met, or ran into that I was a sponsored skateboarder and stuntman. I managed to work this piece of information—often in wildly exaggerated form—into almost every conversation I had.

In January, I drove with the Bizo guys to Orlando for a surf and skate convention. They set up a booth with their gear in the convention hall and hired two models to stand out front to attract business. I was being paid $100 for each of the three days of the convention, which, to me, meant that I was a "pro" skateboarder. Nonetheless, I spent most of the day showing my video to other companies.

After we left the convention that first day, I went out drinking with a few people, including one of the models from the Bizo booth, a girl named Nicole Bello. We ended up at a strip club and I got pretty out of hand. I've never been a huge fan of strip clubs, probably because I've always had a hard time being in any room where I wasn't the center of attention. To remedy this problem, I climbed up on the catwalk area and started walking on my hands. Nobody there appreciated my performance, least of all the bouncers, who threw me out immediately.

Nicole left with me and initially got behind the wheel of my car. She was a little drunk herself but nowhere near the haggard condition I was in by this point. She hadn't driven far when I insisted she pull over.

"You're driving horribly," I told her. "I'll drive. If anybody is going to jail, it's going to be me!" I'd just gotten my license back a month earlier from my first DUI, but I thought offering to drive was the chivalrous thing to do. Once I pulled the car away from the curb, I vaguely recall making an illegal U-turn through a red light, thinking we were lost, coming back to the same red light, then making another illegal U-turn through it and just continuing in this loop for a few minutes before a police car finally pulled me over.

This time when the cop asked me if I was drunk, I denied it. I told him I was just tired. When he asked me to take a roadside sobriety test, I refused. I said I was a pro skateboarder and had hurt my knee, so I couldn't walk in a straight line. I explained that I was exhausted and really just wanted to go take a nap. I was quickly arrested and, as you'll recall from the paragraph that opens this book, the officer actually included this detail—"Defendant declined roadside sobriety tests stating he'd prefer to take a nap"—in the subsequent report.

I spent that night in a freezing-cold holding cell. Nicole grew a guilty conscience over the fact she'd been with me—not that it was her fault—and managed to gather up the $1,000 to spring me from jail the following night.

Once the convention ended, I was in a bind. My car was still impounded. Even if I had had the money to get it out, I wouldn't have been able to because the registration had expired. I had nowhere to go and no way to get there.

Nicole offered to drive me to her place in Boca and let me stay there. She had no real romantic interest in me, and I'm sure she thought of it as a short-term arrangement, but I managed to camp out at her place, rent-free, off and on, for nearly six months. I have no doubt she was merely taking pity on me, but at that point, I was open to any kindness I could get, especially from a hot model.

Kev-O eventually drove me back to Orlando, where I managed to get my car out of impound. I drove it back to Nicole's, but the tags were expired and my license was suspended, so I tried not to drive it much after that. I had to be back in Orlando in March for my court date for the DUI, and when it came around, I scraped together enough money to buy a roundtrip Greyhound bus ticket. When I arrived at the courthouse, I met with the public defender. I told him that I thought we could beat the charge.

"I never took a roadside sobriety test or blew in a Breathalyzer," I told him. "They don't have anything on me."

He laughed.

"They have video of you drunk at the police station, and I've seen it," he said. "You're not going to beat the charge." I absorbed this piece of information and then shifted my strategy.

"In that case, is there any way I can just plead guilty and start serving my sentence immediately?" I asked. "If I need to come back to

Orlando, I don't know how I'll get here." I didn't think I'd have enough money for another bus ticket.

He told me that wouldn't be a problem. During my brief appearance in court, the judge asked me what I had in the way of personal assets. I told him I had a used Ford Tempo, but it was damaged because I'd been skateboarding on it.

"You see, I'm a pro skateboarder," I told the judge proudly. Even the man who was about to lock me up needed to know this fact. He sentenced me to ten days in the Orange County Correctional Facility.

I was loaded into a bus with some other dejected-looking dudes and taken to the jail. At orientation, we were each given a large Tupperware tub for all the supplies we were issued in jail—toothbrush, soap, towel, blanket, that sort of thing—and a guard explained the facility's rules and procedures.

Discipline was enforced largely through fear. Most areas of the jail had surveillance cameras everywhere. You couldn't take a crap without some guard being able to watch you. But if you stepped out of line, you'd be told to pack up your tub and moved to a part of the jail with few cameras and less supervision that was populated by much nastier inmates. Everyone called it the Dungeon. If you were told to pack up your tub, the implication was that you were being thrown to the wolves and it wouldn't be long before you were either beaten senseless or gang-raped in the shower. I have no idea if any of this was actually true or if it was just something they told new inmates to scare them, but in the case of everyone I encountered, it worked. I was scared shitless of the Dungeon and therefore on my best behavior.

At first, I was assigned a spot in a part of the facility that consisted of six pods arrayed around a guard station. Each of those pods had six bunk beds, and downstairs from the pods was a common area with long picnic-style metal tables where inmates spent most of their time.

Once I got over the initial shock of being in jail, it really wasn't that bad. I settled in quickly and began going about my usual business of letting everyone know how rad I was. Within a day or two, there probably wasn't an inmate in my unit who didn't know I was a sponsored stuntman and skateboarder. I did back handsprings for extra desserts. While the other inmates were playing cards or watching TV, I passed the time working on my handstands. In fact, it was actually during the time I was locked up that I finally mastered the standing handstand that Bryan had taught me.

By all reasonable measures, that stay in Orange County Jail should've been one of the low points of my life. I had no job, no money, no girlfriend, no real place to live, and no promising prospects on any of those fronts. I'd dropped out of college, had a serious drinking problem, my teeth were still fucked up from the face-plant I'd done off a balcony a year earlier, and let's not forget, *I was in jail*. Most people would probably call this bottoming out, but the truth is, I felt like I was getting ready to peak. As far as I was concerned, I was this kickass daredevil, living life to the fullest, and it was really just a matter of time before the rest of the world found out how cool I was. I really felt like I was on the cusp of something big. As for jail, *shit*, that was just another notch in my belt. Years later, after the successes of *Jackass* and *Wildboyz*, I had all those signifiers of success—money, girls, acclaim, great career opportunities—but felt depressed and lost. There's a saying about successful people being less happy than those who have nothing: "With nothing, all you have to worry about is your next meal, but once you've made it you have to worry about your last one." I'm not sure if that's got anything to do with how my life wound up years later, but there's something about the way I felt in that Orlando jail that I lost along the way.

After about a week locked up, I was moved from the unit I was in to a large gymnasium-style mega cell that had about fifty bunk beds set up in rows. My final night in there, I asked for some paper and began writing my "memoir," which, as I quoted in the opening passages of this book, began with the dilemma about whether, with fame *rapidly* approaching, I should continue going by the name Steve-O or revert to my given name. I wrote feverishly that night, recounting the adventures of the previous years and passing each page around for the inmates in neighboring bunks to read. There was never a doubt in my mind that they'd want to read this stuff or that soon the whole world would too.

I remember lying in bed that night after lights-out, thinking about all my plans and not being able to sleep. I was just too excited to get out and conquer the world. *I was on fire.*

On the Greyhound ride back to South Florida, I continued writing parts two and three of my memoir. When I got back to what passed for "home" at that point—I was mostly splitting time between Nicole's and sleeping in my car—I started using whatever money I could scrounge to go to Kinko's to Xerox copies of my work. Later, I'd print a cover with the title *True Stories by Steve-O* that had a photo of me catching huge air off a skate ramp (though, of course, it didn't show my subsequent wipeout). I spiral-bound copies and gave one to people I really wanted to impress. A few of them found it interesting, but I'm sure most thought it was just the latest sign that I was officially bat-shit insane.

I don't know if I expected the world to magically open up to me after I got out of jail, but when the excitement of the memoir wore off, I came down to Earth to find my life pretty much the way I'd left it: a mess.

Although Nicole was still tolerating my presence, I'd long since worn out my welcome there. I was driving my car around despite having a suspended license and no registration, knowing full well that if I got pulled over I'd lose my license for good and be thrown back in jail. All the problems that I was able to gloss over when I was locked up—no job, no money, no prospects—suddenly seemed insurmountable. I knew I wanted to be a famous stuntman but was beginning to despair that there was no real path for me to get there. I woke up most mornings with nowhere to go and nothing to do. I had no real reason to get out of bed—or, as was often the case, climb out of my car. I guess a good psychiatrist would probably have categorized that electrifying feeling

I'd had in jail as some kind of mania, and this as the deep, deep depression that followed.

At one point, I recall thinking that the best way forward would be to kill myself. Not only would it solve the problem of figuring out what to do with my life, surely all the video footage of me doing kickass stunts would be appreciated once I was gone. Even though I would've failed in life that footage would be my message in a bottle. I'd be dead but immortal.

The only method of suicide I could bring myself to even consider was inhaling carbon monoxide from my car. I understood that it was a peaceful and painless way to go, just like falling asleep. I don't know that I would've ever really gone through with it, but the moment when I came closest, my willingness became a moot point because my car was out of gas and I was so broke I didn't have enough money to refill the tank. I guess that's kind of funny, although it didn't feel like it at the time.

DURING MY time at Nicole's, I met a guy with a huge nose who lived around the corner from her who went by the nickname Schnozz. I'd just gotten out of jail, and my primary job over the past couple years had been selling drugs, but this dude was *really* shady. Everything I ever heard anyone say about Schnozz gave me the impression that he was just a bad person, through and through. Whenever he came around, he seemed to make everyone uncomfortable. At the time, he had another buddy staying with him whose name I can't remember and who seemed even shadier than Schnozz. I didn't like either of them—in fact, they scared me—but let's face it: we had some similar interests.

One day, Schnozz and his friend invited me to go pick psychedelic mushrooms with them. They knew a place up near Ft. Pierce where mushrooms grew wild but those guys had no car, which is why they needed me. I suppose I knew that this was a bad idea—what with having just gotten out of jail and all—but I had nothing else to do and it seemed like a way to get my hands on some mushrooms and/or money. We drove up there in my Tempo and spent a few hours collecting mushroom caps off piles of cow shit and putting them in grocery bags. There were tons of them out there in this huge field, and when we were finished, we'd each filled a plastic grocery bag about half full. On the ride back, we were eating some mushrooms without even washing them, which sounds a lot more disgusting now than it did back then. When we got back to Nicole's house, Schnozz told me to give him my bag.

"Wait, you want me to give you all these mushrooms I just picked?" I said. "Why? You never said anything about me handing over everything I picked."

"We showed you where this spot was," he said.

"Yeah, but I took all the risk. I just got out of jail, and we went there in my car. You think I came along just for fun?"

I held my ground and managed to get into Nicole's house and lock the door. She was out of town, so I spent the next couple days eating mushrooms there by myself. I was asleep one morning later that week when Schnozz's friend walked into the house and asked if they could borrow my car to go pick more mushrooms. I knew they were still pissed at me but figured letting him borrow my car might smooth things over. I gave him the keys and went back to bed.

I woke up a few hours later and my car wasn't back yet. When I tracked down Schnozz and his buddy, they told me my car wouldn't start so they'd been forced to ditch it out by the cow pasture. Something was definitely fishy. I'd never had a problem with that car starting.

I got a ride out to the field and after much looking found the Tempo. It was trashed. The windows were busted out, and under the hood, everything had been mangled. It was beyond repair.

I grabbed a stunt video from the trunk, then left the car there in the field and headed back to Nicole's. I considered my options and realized I had no good ones: If I confronted Schnozz and his friend, in the best-case scenario they would deny having anything to do with the damage to the car. More likely they'd beat the ever-loving shit out of me, or worse. I wasn't about to go to the cops, so basically any way I sliced it, I was screwed.

Looking back on it now, those guys did me a favor. That car was bad news—hell, had they not trashed it, I would've surely wound up back in jail for driving it, or might've even used it to kill myself. My life at that point in South Florida was at a dead end. I was seriously depressed and desperate for a fresh start. The death of the Tempo was just the kick in the ass I needed.

7

BURNING BOY
FESTIVAL

After the demise of the Tempo, I called my sister.
Cindy was working as a newspaper reporter in Albuquerque, New Mexico, and was lonely out there. I was
homeless and at the end of my rope in Florida, so it
just made sense for me to head out west and move in
with her.

Dad made a deal with me: if I was enrolled in
school and maintaining a 3.0 GPA, he'd pay for tuition
and my half of the rent while I lived with Cindy. I
signed up for summer classes at the University of New
Mexico the same day I arrived. I hadn't given up hope
of becoming a world-famous lunatic stuntman, but
now saw school as a new way to focus my efforts. My
class schedule over the following year reflected this:
Elements of Filmmaking, TV Field Production, Tumbling (yes, I took a college course in gymnastics),
Acting, and Stagecraft.

The change of scenery also did me some good. Albuquerque is two thousand miles from South Florida and looks almost like a different planet. The city sits more than a mile above sea level on the edge of a desert surrounded by the Sandia Mountains. The air is dry and light, and having come from Florida's wet, subtropical stew, even breathing felt different there.

Good things started to happen almost immediately for me in Albuquerque. The first was meeting Ryan Simonetti less than a week after I got there. I walked into a skate park and saw Ryan sitting behind the counter working the cash register. I broke the ice in my usual way: I handed him one of my stunt videos and told him to check it out. He put it right in.

"That's some crazy shit," he told me after the tape finished. Then he thought for a second and said, "Hey, I know some places around here where you could jump off some roofs."

I can't remember whether it was the same day or the following day, but very soon after that first conversation, Ryan and I were in his car cruising around Albuquerque looking at roofs to jump off. The first spot we hit was a two-story motel. We walked past the reception to the pool area, stripped to our boxers, left our clothes in piles, and clambered up onto the roof. I was getting ready to jump when a lady who worked there came outside and began yelling at us. She was holding a cordless phone, telling us she was calling the cops while simultaneously hollering at us to get down off the roof. I waved to her and laughed.

"You want me to get down?" I shouted back. "All right, I'm coming right now!"

With that, I jumped off and did a gainer flip into the pool. Ryan followed right behind me. Unfortunately for him, he didn't have much experience with landing in shallow pools. The thing I'd discovered over the years is you can't land straight on your feet when you launch yourself from that height into five feet of water. When you land, you need to curve in and slide along the bottom of the pool like you're sliding into second base. Ryan just went straight through the water and bashed his heels on the bottom.

After he limped out in considerable pain, we both grabbed our clothes and made a mad dash past the irate lady on the way out. I made it by safely, but she clobbered Ryan on the head with the phone as he ran past.

Ryan and I drove off in our boxers, soaking wet. His heels were fucked up—he wouldn't be able to skate for a few weeks after that—and he had a growing lump on his head from where he got clocked with the phone. A friendship was born.

I HAD figured Ryan worked at that skate park where I met him, but, in fact, he owned it and had built it with his bare hands. He'd been a pro skateboarder for several years and had developed a style all his own. He'd skate anything anywhere—streets, rails, ramps, pools, on top of trucks—the more ridiculous the better. Because of my Bizo sponsorship, I considered myself a pro skater, but Ryan was in a completely different stratosphere from me. On a creative level though, we were a lot alike.

His impact on my stunts and videos cannot be overstated. Plenty of friends had encouraged me in the past and those divers at UM even gave me some coaching, but Ryan and I became like a team. Bryan Gillooly may have taught me to do a decent handstand, but Ryan revved up his car and drove it down the street while I did one on the roof. We'd have "footage nights" every few months, when we'd stay up all night at Cindy's house editing our footage into reels that looked so much better than what I'd been doing before.

Ryan and I fed off each other's enthusiasm. He was always game to help me with whatever ridiculous stunt I was planning and, in turn, my tricks and ideas helped enhance his skateboard footage. Instead of him just doing an ollie down some concrete steps, he'd do one over my legs while I stood on my hands on the concrete steps, balancing a skateboard on my feet. Ryan also played a big part in incorporating fire into my act.

I'd first started trying to breathe fire in Florida. A few weeks before moving to New Mexico, I'd performed at a live talent show put on by a radio station as Steve-O the Alcoholic Gymnast. My act involved shotgunning lots of beers and then doing handstands and back handsprings. I was *really* good at shotgunning beers, and the more I drank, the more the crowd ate it up. In fact, it was when I heard them chanting, "Steve-O! Steve-O! Steve-O!" that I knew I'd never change my "professional" name back to Steve Glover. I also tried to blow my first fireball at that talent show. I'd seen a friend of mine do it by spitting rubbing alcohol at a lighter, but when I tried it onstage, I kept blowing out the lighter and dousing my hand in rubbing alcohol. I finally got it to work, but in doing so set my whole hand on fire and had to shake it furiously to put it out.

When I got to Albuquerque, I was determined to figure out a better way to breathe fire. It didn't take long before I realized that accidentally spitting rubbing alcohol all over my hand wasn't the problem with blowing fireballs, it was the solution. When my hand had been on fire, it burned fairly lightly and I didn't get hurt: it was the alcohol burning, not my skin. What I needed to do was douse my hand with alcohol and ignite it so I could use it as a torch to blow fireballs. When I tried this, it worked like a charm.

Once I figured that out, fire was everything. One day, I showed up at Ryan's skate park and we started lighting my hair on fire. Before long we were blowing fireballs off my head. The standing back flip that I'd only recently mastered now became a fire-breathing standing back flip. I added a midair fireball to my flips off bridges and buildings. I even tried lathering my whole body in Vaseline and rubbing alcohol, setting myself on fire and doing back flips. There was almost nothing in my arsenal that wasn't improved by adding fire.

Combining all these parts of my act made it unique. I knew I wasn't terribly talented at too many things. To this day, the only thing I'll claim to be really world-class at is shotgunning beers. Nobody could ever beat me at that. (It's almost too bad I can no longer show off my greatest gift.) But I really poured myself into innovating new tricks, combining things in ways nobody had ever thought of before. I mean, lots of people can do a standing back flip, but I've yet to find one of them dumb enough to do it while spitting flames off his burning hand.

Another thing Ryan did for me was introduce me to the magazine *Big Brother*. It had been around since the early nineties, but I'd never seen it. *Big Brother* was, in the most basic sense, a skateboarding magazine, though it was really much more than that. The magazine was as much about purposefully being a bad influence on young skateboarders as it was about skating itself. It was all attitude: Along with irreverent interviews with pro skaters, it had articles about how to buy crack, commit suicide, and make fake IDs. It had reviews of bongs and penis pumps, pictures of naked chicks, and lots of inside jokes. It's still my favorite publication ever.

In May 1997, *Big Brother* was doing a tour sponsored by Duffs Shoes that was scheduled to make a stop in Albuquerque. The tour featured the Duffs pro skaters doing their thing while being trailed by a videographer from the shoe company and a couple guys shooting photos for the magazine. Ryan told me they'd be stopping by his skate park when they got to town. I made it my mission to get their attention.

By this time, I'd begun to get some notice in the skate community. In February, I'd gotten my first magazine coverage when a photo of a pro skater named Richard Kirby blowing a fireball off my head appeared in a skateboard magazine called *Thrasher*. A month before that, I'd ditched Bizo and gotten a new sponsorship with a skate wear company called XYZ after meeting one of the company's owners, Tommy Caudill, during my second trip to that surf and skate convention in Orlando. XYZ wasn't some fly-by-night operation run by a guy who wouldn't know a skateboard if it hit him in the face. Tommy started

XYZ with skateboarding legend Danny Way, and even though they never paid me, they flew me out to California to shoot photos and videos, paid for full-page ads featuring me in magazines, distributed videos with me in them, and sent me huge boxes of great gear all the time.

When the *Big Brother* crew showed up at Ryan's skate park, I started following them around. A girl was throwing a keg party that night, and I promised the *Big Brother* guys I'd pull off a stunt there that would be totally rad:

1) **Someone would blow a fireball off my head;**
2) **I'd stick my arm in the flames;**
3) **I'd do a back flip with my hair and arm on fire;**
4) **While in the air, I'd blow a fireball myself.**

I kept talking up this stunt to Dimitry Elyashkevich, a cameraman and writer for *Big Brother* (and later for *Jackass*), and Dimitry kept saying, "All right, whatever. We'll shoot it. Just mellow out."

One of the pro skaters on the tour was a guy named Kris Markovich. I was a big fan of his and when I saw him at the party that night, I asked him if he'd do the honors of blowing the fireball off my head. All he needed to do, I told him, was spit the rubbing alcohol at the flames coming off my hair and I'd do the rest. He was game.

When the time came, I put on a new pair of Duffs shoes, loaded up my hair with hairspray, someone lit it on fire, and Markovich spit the rubbing alcohol at me. Unfortunately, his aim sucked: he blew it directly into my face. Within a split second my entire head, face, arm, and hand were engulfed in flames. This was not supposed to happen.

They say that in accidents it often seems like time suddenly moves very slowly, and although if you watch this stunt on YouTube it all happens in a matter of seconds, I can distinctly remember having the time to think, *Okay, I've got a serious problem.* For most people, their next thought would probably have been, *I'd better stop, drop, and roll and put out this fire.* Mine was, *I better hurry up and do this fire-breathing back flip so I don't disappoint everyone.* So I went ahead and did the stunt.

I landed on my knees and entirely off balance—I was really much better at doing back flips barefoot—which delayed my initial attempt to put out the fire. My entire head and face were still very much in flames as I rose to my feet trying to bat them out with my hands. I flailed across the backyard, finally managing to smother the fire with my Duffs T-shirt. On the video, you can see that after I'd gotten the fire out, I flashed the camera the proudest look I could muster, but, make no mistake, I was in a world of hurt at that point.

I called Cindy and told her I needed a ride to the hospital. But even as I waited in the street outside the party for her to pick me up, I couldn't turn off my ridiculous need to try to impress people: when she pulled up, I was doing back flips in the street, charred face and all.

At the hospital, they had to scrape layers of skin off my face, which fucking sucked. The doctors told me I'd need to stay out of the sun for six months and that the scars might be noticeable for the rest of my life. After a few hours, they sent me home. When I awoke the next day, my face was literally stuck to the pillow with pus that had been oozing from it. I'd have to peel my face from the pillowcase and scrape it clean every morning for weeks after that.

I spent a lot of that next day in bed, sobbing. I was in serious pain and was convinced half my face was going to permanently look like fucking Freddy Krueger. A few people called to see how I was doing, but I told Cindy I didn't want to see or talk to anyone. Ryan came over anyway.

"Dude, this is just another notch in your belt," he told me. "So you burned your face. So what? It's not your knees, it's nothing that's going to get in the way of you being totally rad. All your joints still work. You'll get better. This just makes you more rad."

RYAN SIMONETTI (pro skateboarder, friend): He was on fire for way too long, but I wasn't expecting it to be as bad as it was. I could tell from the first conversation with him, he was pretty devastated. I'd never seen that guy bummed. He was always super stoked. He told me he didn't really want to see anybody. I barged in on him anyhow. I was going to give him a little moral support at least. We had a good "bro down."

There aren't words to describe how much Ryan showing up and giving me that pep talk meant. The burns were still a bummer, it still hurt like shit, and I still hated peeling my face off the pillow and scraping away the pus each morning, but he was right: I'd be okay. Besides, I accomplished my mission. A few months later, there was a small article about the stunt in *Big Brother*, along with a photo of me before, during, and after. It was titled, "The Burning Boy Festival."

CINDY KNEW how serious I was about becoming a stuntman but didn't think I was making any real progress toward that goal. So she was always trying to figure out some sort of reasonable way of focusing my completely unreasonable interests into a sustainable career. In March 1997, two months before my fiery mishap for *Big Brother* and, coincidentally, just a couple weeks after I finally got my broken teeth fixed at an Albuquerque strip mall dentist, Cindy read something about Ringling Bros. and Barnum & Bailey Clown College. Tuition was free, but it was statistically more difficult to get into than Harvard—roughly thirty of about two thousand applicants were accepted each year. She encouraged me to try out, so I called and learned there was an audition in Denver in just a few days. Unfortunately, I had no car and no easy way of getting to Denver.

That night fate intervened: I met a girl at a party who was visiting Albuquerque from Colorado during her spring break. She could give me a ride the next day as far as Colorado Springs. That was a step in the right direction. She dropped me off at a Denny's there and, armed with a portfolio of my best stunt photos, I managed to convince a waitress to drive me the rest of the way to Denver.

I made an impression at that audition. There were about sixty people trying out, and the first thing we had to do was get in front of a camera and introduce ourselves. I did so with gusto:

"My name is Steve Glover. I'm an aspiring stuntman from Albuquerque, New Mexico, and I just hitchhiked all the way to Denver from Albuquerque because I don't want to spend the rest of my life wondering if I would've missed out on the biggest opportunity I ever had." Okay, maybe I didn't exactly hitchhike, but I wasn't going to quibble over details. After my spiel, I did a perfect back flip.

The rest of the audition consisted of a bunch of exercises aimed at determining who among us had the least inhibition. That was a contest I rarely lost.

At the end of the day, they sat us all down and the guy running the audition held up a stack of Clown College applications. He told us not to even bother taking one unless we were really serious about doing this. Tuition was free, but there was a pretty substantial "materials fee" for anyone who enrolled. The position we were fighting for as a Ringling Bros. clown paid $235 a week with accommodations on a circus train in a room that measures six feet by three feet. And it was hard work. He said if any of these facts were giving us second thoughts about Clown College, we shouldn't waste anyone's time by filling out an application. I was having second thoughts but took an application anyway.

A couple weeks later, I got a call from someone at the Clown College saying that they were waiting for my application. He also hinted that I could potentially get a scholarship to cover the materials fee if that was an issue. That was all the encouragement I needed.

It wasn't long after I burned my face off for *Big Brother* that I got the call that I'd been accepted to Clown College and that they'd waived my materials fee. The doctors had said to avoid the sun, but I wasn't going to let a little thing like sunlight keep me down. Besides, I was a quick healer. When the time came to head to Sarasota, on the west coast of Florida, for Clown College in July, my face looked much better. The scars I was supposed to have for years were hardly noticeable and would be covered easily by the greasepaint I'd soon be wearing.

CLOWN COLLEGE would've made a great reality show. There were thirty-three students and we were competing for ten contracts with the circus. We all lived together for eight weeks in an apartment building just down the street from the Sarasota Opera House, where we did our training and performances. There weren't reality TV–style eliminations each week, but there was plenty of the kind of ass kissing, showing off, and screwing other people over to make yourself look good that those shows thrive on. It was just like *Rock of Love* except instead of professing our love for Bret Michaels, we were doing it for the circus.

The daily schedule was grueling. Every morning we started at 8 a.m. with a morning workout—stretches, push-ups, that kind of stuff. We'd have one-hour classes all day—makeup, acrobatics, dance, improv, skills, circus history, and so on—with an hour off for lunch. The classes would finish at 6 p.m., then we'd have another hour for dinner and three hours after dinner for working on our own tricks, bits, and gags. We'd finally take off our makeup and head back to our apartments at 10 p.m., at which point I'd spend the next four hours or so drinking.

I didn't get as fucked up at Clown College as I did in my day-to-day life, but that's not to say my boozing didn't cause me problems there. One night during my first week in Sarasota, I was drunk and skateboarding around the apartment complex, and tried to jump down a flight of stairs. I misjudged it and bashed my head into the corner of a cement support beam protruding from the ceiling. Blood was gushing.

I didn't want to go to the emergency room, but I really needed to and some of the other students insisted on taking me. The doctor said I'd need surgical staples to close the wound, so he was going to give me a local anesthetic. I told him I didn't have time for an anesthetic. I knew I was already making a bad impression at Clown College and didn't want to make it any worse by keeping the other students hanging around a hospital waiting room late at night. The doctor thought I was nuts but after some initial resistance went ahead and stapled me up. It actually didn't hurt too badly.

I was told I'd have to come back in two to three weeks to have the staples removed. "Do not, under any circumstances, try to remove them yourself," the doctor told me. "It's impossible without this special staple remover we have."

To me, that sounded like a challenge. So once the gash healed up, I spent every night for a week getting drunk and trying to pull the staples out of my head with the help of some of my fellow clowns-in-training. In the end, I'm happy to report that the emergency room doc was wrong: it *is* possible to pull out surgical staples yourself—you just need to clip them in half with a wire cutter first.

ONE DAY at Clown College they broke with the regular format for a long seminar with a public relations team from Ringling Bros. It was supposed to be a workshop on dealing with the media, but most of the lecture focused on one topic: animal abuse. For years, the circus has battled animal rights activists over charges that they mistreat animals, but I never really had a strong opinion on it until that day.

Essentially, if asked about it by a reporter, we were to say nothing at all on the subject. We were clowns: we were paid to fall down and make people laugh. When it came to animal abuse, we had no opinion. We were to shut the fuck up.

The PR people also made the point that on an annual basis, more than ten million people came to see the circus. If one of their elephants was injured or abused there would be ten million witnesses to it. That immediately sounded like bullshit to me. An elephant's skin wouldn't bruise. If the PR team hadn't made such a big deal of it, I probably never would've thought twice about it back then. But instead, they inadvertently opened my eyes to a real problem that I've only gotten more and more energized about over time.

Years later, I was on Tom Green's Internet TV show and went on a nitrous-fueled rant about animal abuse in the circus. A woman from PETA tracked me down after that and asked whether I'd say something similar for them to post on their Web site. I said I would, though by that point in my life, the righteousness of the cause—which I do completely believe in—was less of a motivation for me than my shameless, self-serving desire to get publicity any way I possibly could. Recently, the same woman from PETA sent me something an ex–Ringling Bros. clown wrote about animal cruelty in the circus and his essay was so much classier than what I had done, so much more humble and self-effacing, that it felt all the more persuasive. Ultimately, I'm grateful for everything I got from Clown College, including the seed of awareness that eventually blossomed into the belief that the way we treat other living things has very real consequences toward how we feel about ourselves.

The animal cruelty stuff aside, Clown College was an unbelievable experience. We were each given our own custom-designed clown costumes. They cost about $2,000 apiece and were pretty rad. I learned to juggle clubs, walk on stilts, ride a unicycle, balance all kinds of stuff on my chin, and do a really great bar trick that involved balancing a beer on my forehead and eventually drinking it down without using my hands. All these things became useful additions to my arsenal. A few of my *Jackass* skits were actually born out of stuff I picked up at Clown College: leaping from an Olympic high-dive platform on stilts and unicycling into a Dumpster simply never would've been possible if I hadn't learned to actually walk on stilts or ride a unicycle.

As the days passed at Clown College, I got increasingly invested in the idea of actually becoming a Ringling Bros. clown. But I had two basic problems. First, I was more interested in showing off the tricks I could already do than in learning anything new. Second, I wasn't trying to be funny. I was all about pulling off these kickass stunts and forgot the whole point of clowns is to make people laugh. I was more likely to make a kid cry. Anything they were teaching us there that I couldn't apply to what I was already doing as a stuntman got ignored. I refused to put much effort into dance class because I sucked at dancing and had no use for it as a stuntman. But I was totally missing the point: I was a *clown*. Instead of seeing the potential humor in being a shitty dancer, I was concerned I wasn't getting the steps right and looked like a fool.

When the eight weeks were up, all the student clowns traveled together up to Washington, D.C., and performed at the International Children's Festival. I was starting to realize that my chance of winning a contract with Ringling Bros. was not that good, but after the festival, when I boarded a Greyhound from D.C. back to Albuquerque, I was still holding out hope.

THE CALL from Ringling never came. When I got back, I'd missed registration at UNM and Cindy had moved a half hour outside of town, so I moved in with two skateboard buddies, hung that $2,000 clown costume in my closet, and started selling underweight bags of pot to make the rent. How quickly things turn.

I mostly sold pot at Ryan's skate park and at a bar across the street from it called Sonny's, where I hung out a lot. After years of practice, I finally started to get pretty good at it. I also started to get really into cocaine. Coke was expensive and I was usually broke, but there was always some of it around at Sonny's. I'd also started dating a stripper named Aimee. She made good money and spent plenty of it on coke, which I helped myself to.

Working for Ringling Bros. hadn't been a lifelong dream, but not getting that clown gig bummed me out. I think more than the job itself, I missed the promise that those days in Clown College seemed to hold. While I was there, it was easy to see a bright future on the horizon and a well-marked path to it. Now, when I looked ahead, it was once again all gray and murky.

Ever the rational planner, Cindy convinced me to go around to a few of the two-bit talent agencies in town and let them know if they ever needed a professional clown to give me a call. To my great surprise, I got a call one day from one of these agents with an offer to appear in a Coppola film. No, not Francis Ford Coppola or even Sofia Coppola, but Christopher Coppola, Francis's nephew.

The name of the movie was *Palmer's Pick-Up*. They were filming in Albuquerque and needed a clown to get his ass kicked in one scene, which was obviously perfect for me. The movie starred Christopher's aunt, Talia Shire, and that guy from *Revenge of the Nerds*, Robert Carradine. I wore my clown costume and made the most of my one scene. I even convinced them to let me do a back flip off a car and blow a fireball in the course of getting the shit kicked out of me. I was paid $350 and got eligibility for the Screen Actors Guild, though by far the biggest boon I got from the experience was a new thing to brag to people about: I'd starred in a Hollywood movie. (Even if it went straight to video.)

Beyond that, the only other clown gig I got was from a girl I had a crush on who worked at a daycare center. She gave me a six-pack of beer to entertain the kids there. I was rotten at it. The kids didn't like me and in the end, neither did she. I'd also occasionally get dressed up in my clown gear and go drinking in downtown Albuquerque—just like I used to go running around in my Little League uniform—but nobody was paying me to do that.

Despite my status as an out-of-work, drug-dealing, cokehead circus clown, by the summer of 1998, I actually had quite a lot of reasons to be optimistic about my career. The Duffs promo video of me on fire had come out and a full-page XYZ ad of me blowing a fireball at Ryan had appeared in a handful of magazines. That summer, *Big Brother* came through town again and I pulled off some kickass stunts—including a gainer flip off a three-story building into four feet of water—that got me another appearance in the magazine, this time without sending me to the hospital. I don't know if I'd go so far as to say that my life was exactly as I wanted it yet, but I felt like I was making some progress. Compared to my days living out of my car in South Florida, life was really good. Little did I know that was all about to change.

THIS CHAPTER IS NOT FUNNY BUT YOU NEED TO READ IT ANYWAY

The night of October 9, 1998, I went out and, as was my usual custom, got loaded. I'd recently moved back in with Cindy, but that night, I ended up crashing with Aimee, the stripper I was dating. Early the next morning, I woke up to the sound of one of my friends, Ron Burns, knocking on her window. He told me something had happened. I needed to call Cindy.

Cindy had grim news: Mom had suffered a massive brain aneurysm and was in the hospital in critical condition. Cindy had already booked us on the next flight back to Florida.

CINDY: I'd gotten the call at 6:45 on Saturday morning. By 8:15 I had us both on the plane. Between 6:45 and 8:15, there was this absolutely manic frenzy of packing suitcases, booking plane tickets, getting a rental car sorted out, and calling the hospital to find out how Mom was doing, because she was not expected to survive very long. I picked Steve up, and we drove straight to the airport and got on the plane. I was okay while I had stuff to do, but as soon as we got on that plane and had three hours with nothing to do but think, I completely fell apart. At that point, Steve put his arm around me and he was the strong one and I was the mess. It was a reversal of our normal roles.

When we arrived at Boca Raton Community Hospital, the scene was completely horrifying. Mom was hooked up to all these machines and still convulsing from the aneurysm. Her brain was hemorrhaging and the doctors were not optimistic about her chances for survival. I remember she had this fucked-up look in her eyes: She was scared and shaking and somehow "not there" all at the same time. It was like she was awake enough and aware enough to be afraid, but not coherent enough to comprehend what was happening. That look on her face was one of the most awful things I've ever seen and it still haunts me to this day. Not to trivialize it, but when we were filming the first *Jackass* movie and Knoxville got knocked out cold by four-hundred-pound pro boxer Butterbean, he had a similar look on his face. I could never watch that footage without getting upset, because it reminded me of my mom.

Mom was fifty-one years old at the time and had gotten remarried a few years earlier to a guy I'll call Roger, who owned his own business. I didn't really know the guy but when he and Mom had come out to visit us in Albuquerque, I took advantage of him trying to be nice and convinced him to buy me a video camera. I remember holding up the box before I opened it and telling him, with total seriousness, "The entire world is in this box." That was pretty much the extent of our relationship.

Mom and Roger had met in sobriety, but it wasn't long before they both relapsed and started drinking together. I don't know who fell off the wagon first, but I distinctly remember them both showing up for move her, she'd die, though she might die anyway. He said if we were going to move Mom, she should go to Jackson Memorial Hospital in Miami. They had twenty neurosurgeons on staff and a special neurosurgical intensive care unit. His colleague disagreed and said if we moved her against his medical advice, she'd die and it would be our fault. Steve and I made the decision and there was no hesitation. The forty-five-minute ambulance ride to Miami was terrifying, but Mom survived.

As it turned out, that surgery in Miami probably saved Mom's life, but she was by no means out of the woods. She underwent several more surgeries and soon slipped into a coma. The basic prognosis at that point was that it was possible Mom was going to survive, but she'd likely be a vegetable. There was no "recovering" from this: if we kept her alive, that's exactly what we'd be doing—*keeping* her alive.

I distinctly remember those first few weeks feeling like it was Cindy and me versus the doctors. They kept telling us things like, "There's nothing left to save." Our attitude was "Fuck you. We're not giving up on her." I wouldn't be surprised if my memory has oversimplified this dynamic—many of her doctors and nurses were genuinely great—but that's certainly how it felt. Regardless, we began dealing with the very real possibility that there might be a decision to make soon: Do we pull the plug on Mom?

CINDY: Ultimately, as the older, somewhat more responsible child, I was the decision maker with the durable power of attorney. But as I told Steve, as long as we were on the same team making every decision and could look at each other and be okay with it, this was going to be all right. We could tune out the rest of the world.

Mom's sister Janice came down to Florida shortly after the aneurysm and made it very clear that she felt Mom wouldn't want to be alive my Clown College graduation noticeably drunk. She and Roger had actually divorced several months earlier but were in the process o reconciling.

Roger was already at the hospital when Cindy and I showed up, and he relayed what had happened: The day before, Mom had played eighteen holes of golf and cooked a three-course meal. Apparently, she'd been drunk but not on a really ugly bender or anything like that. That morning when she'd woken up, her body was shaking but Roger thought it wasn't that serious. Later, he broke down in tears and admitted that he'd waited ten minutes to call the ambulance, even though she was convulsing. I don't know exactly how costly that ten-minute delay turned out to be, but the impression I got from the doctors was that it was pretty significant. I stayed with Mom at the hospital that first night while Cindy went back to Mom's house and spent the entire night on the computer reading medical journals.

CINDY: Once we got to the hospital, Steve wasn't leaving. He spread out on the waiting room floor, ignored stares from other visitors, and managed to get some sleep. In lighter moments, we used to tease Steve that there was no crisis he couldn't sleep through, but I was desperately grateful to have him there because that was the only way I could've left. I stayed up all night reading ten years' worth of articles on aneurysms. I found that there was an alternative to traditional surgery that had better survival rates. The next morning, I cornered one of the two neurosurgeons the hospital had on call and asked if Boca Raton Community Hospital had the capacity to perform this alternative procedure. They didn't. I asked him where the nearest hospital was that did. He was offended and said something to the effect of "I went to medical school so you wouldn't have to." The second neurosurgeon seemed more honest and open to questions. He told us point-blank that the hospital wasn't equipped to deal with Mom's situation, and if we didn't in this situation. If there was a switch to turn off, Janice was all about turning it off. The thing is, for better or worse, there was no switch. Mom needed twenty-four-hour assistance. She needed help to breathe, to eat, to drink, to move—but she always had brain activity, so we were never faced with the decision to pull the plug. In retrospect, I'm grateful, because I'm not sure how I could've lived with either choice.

Strangely enough, the last serious conversation I'd had with Mom was about death. When I'd been in Florida several months earlier, she'd sat me down and told me she was planning on changing her will. The details of the discussion aren't that important—she knew how irresponsible I was with money and wanted to set up her will in a way that would keep me from inheriting a lump sum that I'd likely piss away—but her head was clearly in a dark place at that point. I don't know if she felt sick but she was clearly drinking again. As it turns out, studies have shown alcoholism to be a significant contributing risk factor in brain aneurysms, and I have little doubt that it was in hers.

For six weeks, Mom was in a coma. Cindy and I were living at Mom's house in Boca, so every night we'd drive down to Miami and spend a few hours with her in her room. There were often medical issues to deal with and doctors to speak to, but for the most part, we just sat and talked to Mom. It was important to us to be with her but also really fucking hard. Looking down at her in that hospital bed attached to cold, lifeless machines monitoring her vital signs, it was impossible to keep from thinking, *That's* my mom *lying there like that.*

CINDY: After Mom had been at the hospital in Miami for a while, she was completely immobile. People like that need to be turned every two hours so they don't get bedsores. One night, there was this nurse changing Mom's diaper and rolling her over who was being really rough. She was handling Mom like baggage carriers at the airport handle suitcases. When I saw that, I was on the brink of committing a violent felony. At the very least, I wanted to chew this woman out or go to her boss and make sure that bitch never touched Mom again. Steve looked at me and said, "No. That's not the way you're going to handle it and I'll tell you why. We're not here twenty-two hours of the day. If you do that, when we're not here, she's going to take it out on Mom, and then you're going to feel like crap about that." One thing most people would never guess about Steve is that he has the greatest people skills. He can be very diplomatic. So he talked me down off that ledge and then sweet-talked this nurse. And damned if Mom didn't get first-class treatment the rest of the time she was there.

Dad and Sophie flew in from London almost immediately after the aneurysm. Dad had already put us in touch with Pepsi's former medical director, who had been offering some useful advice, and having Dad and Sophie there really gave Cindy and me some much needed support. One day, I went to lunch with Dad and talk turned—as it often did—to what I was going to do with the rest of my life. But when we came to the point in the conversation when he'd normally tell me I needed to get my act together, finish school, and figure out something practical to do, he surprised me.

"I feel like I've done a major disservice to you by not supporting you in this career you've chosen," he said. "It's not a traditional path but you're obviously committed to it, so I want you to be the best you can be at it, and I want to help you out however I can." It's worth remembering that at this point in my "career," I hadn't really made any money doing crazy stunts: I was an unemployed clown who'd appeared in a few skateboard magazines. So my father's pledge of support felt pretty extraordinary. For a guy like Dad, who is firmly grounded and logical, to sign on to my flight of fancy showed tremendous faith in me, and in many ways made it feel more real. *This was really what I was doing with my life.*

As it became clear that Mom's condition wasn't going to change in the short term, Cindy and I began rearranging our lives to cope. Thanksgiving weekend, we flew back to Albuquerque to pack our stuff into a U-Haul and drive it all back to Florida. After having been in Florida dealing night and day with Mom's condition for nearly six weeks, New Mexico felt like a brief reprieve. In my spare time that weekend, Ryan and I got back to doing stunts. The main one I remember was balancing one of the legs of a lit barbecue grill on my chin so Ryan could jump over the flames on his skateboard. It was a great idea, although the lighter fluid kept dripping on my face and the photos of the stunt proved a little underwhelming.

When we'd finally packed up, I went to say good-bye to Ryan and the rest of my skateboard buddies. As a parting gift, they gave me a bunch of magic mushrooms. I promptly gobbled them up and then climbed into the U-Haul with my sister. *What a fucking dumb idea.* We were confined to this miserable little truck cab for a cross-country trip to go resettle in Florida so we could take care of my comatose mother, and I was tripping my ass off. Mushrooms always made me uncomfortably self-aware: if I didn't have something to do, I'd just pick myself apart. I couldn't bring myself to tell Cindy what I'd done, so I just stared out the window, hating myself and trying to hold it together. Not a fun day.

Mom was moved from Jackson Memorial to a specialized facility in Ft. Lauderdale for people on ventilators, and then to a smaller care center in Delray Beach. She had emerged from her coma and eventually her condition stabilized enough that the doctors told us it was time for her to go home. But the Mom who was ready to leave the hospital was nearly unrecognizable. Although she would have surprising moments of coherence, she was severely mentally and physically disabled. Her speech was feeble to the point of being mostly incomprehensible. She was going to need round-the-clock assistance.

In a somewhat surprising turn of events, Roger insisted that she move into his house. I think he still felt guilty about waiting ten minutes to call that ambulance and this was his way of performing some sort of penance. He had also asked Mom to remarry him while at the care center in Delray Beach. Although it sounds romantic and Roger's presence often seemed to improve Mom's mood, Cindy and I were worried about his motives.

> **CINDY:** He proposed at her bedside and actually wanted to have a ceremony at this incredibly depressing nursing home. There was no question in my mind that he was after her money. I was horrified and really felt Mom wasn't in any condition to make big decisions. If she wanted to move back into his house, I wouldn't stand in the way. But I didn't trust Roger at all and still held power of attorney over her affairs. I was ready to go to court to block a wedding if he tried to move too fast and I let him know that.

The care Mom got at Roger's house wasn't very good. To his credit, Roger hired a full-time caregiver named Carline who was a saint. But Carline later confided to me about some of the things that happened at Roger's house, and even recounting them now makes me feel violently angry.

Contrary to the doctors' initial prognosis, Mom wasn't a vegetable, but she had little or no control over her body or mind. Roger either didn't understand this or simply couldn't handle it. When Mom would drool or wail, he'd get mad at her, and apparently he once told Carline to leave without changing her diaper as punishment for what he perceived as Mom's disrespectful behavior toward him.

I also blame Roger for the horrific bedsores that Mom first got around this time and that never went away. Cindy insists she already had them when she moved into Roger's place, but I'm not so sure. Most people don't really understand how fucking awful bedsores are, but I don't know of any medical condition that can cause more horrible suffering. The fact that the people who get bedsores are already helpless really fucked with my sense of righteousness in the universe. *How could a loving God inflict such intense suffering on those who were already in such dire shape?* I could deal with Mom being physically and mentally disabled, but her cries of pain from those bedsores quite literally fucked me up for life. Over the years, I've tried to let go of the resentment I feel toward Roger because of all this, but I'd be lying if I said I was entirely successful at that.

After a couple of months at Roger's, we decided to move Mom back into her own house in Boca. Cindy had gotten a job as a reporter at the *South Florida Sun-Sentinel* and I'd reenrolled in school at UM. We hired Carline to take care of Mom during the day and Cindy became her full-time caregiver at night and on the weekends. I rented a room down near the Miami campus and tried to make it back once a week or so to help out with Mom. Realistically, though, this meant that Cindy was saddled with the lion's share of the work.

CINDY: Somebody had to be there every second. Mom was wearing diapers, drooling, had a feeding tube, needed to be turned every four hours, and I had a full-time job. At night, I set the alarm for 1 a.m. and 5 a.m., so I could get up to turn her and feed her. She had bedsores by then and one of them had gotten really bad. Sometimes, she'd just wail in pain because of it. She had surgery on it, and afterward I was very hands-on, involved in cleaning it and packing it with gauze. Steve, partly because of his personality, partly because there were naked parts involved, and partly because he wasn't around as much, wasn't really on the front lines in the same way.

Cindy is right about all that. Even back when it was happening, I realized that Cindy was doing something extremely selfless—not just for Mom, but for me. On paper, I had nothing really going on in my life—no job, no attachments—so it might have made some sense for me to become Mom's primary caregiver. I just don't know that I could've handled it. It tore me up inside to see Mom like that. If I'd been there every day, I can't see how it would've been good for any of us. Either way, there was never really a discussion about it—Cindy just started making arrangements and that was that. She eventually gave up her job as a reporter and went back to school to become a schoolteacher, partially because the schedule made more sense with her new responsibilities toward Mom.

IN JANUARY 1999, before Mom was even out of the coma, the *Big Brother* crew came through Florida on one of their periodic tours. Mom was still in the hospital and I hadn't yet moved down to UM to start the semester, so I invited everyone to meet me over at her house in Boca. This was the first time I met Jeff Tremaine.

Tremaine was the editor in chief of *Big Brother* and would later become one of the creators of *Jackass*. He came off as a pretty smooth dude with a real knack for minimizing the amount of time it took to accomplish what he wanted. I'm sure he thought I was a pain in the ass, because he didn't do a very good job masking his irritation.

I had told Tremaine I was going to do a double front flip off a bridge. I think their plan was to film that, maybe do a few other crazy things with me at my mom's house, and then bid me adieu. But that wasn't enough for me. I latched on to them and wouldn't let go. When they left to go to Miami, I invited myself along and slept on the floor of a hotel room they'd gotten for some of the skaters on the tour.

JEFF TREMAINE (editor in chief of *Big Brother*, co-creator/ executive producer of *Jackass*, *Wildboyz*): We originally invited him to come with us to Miami, but after we were at his house for a little while and shot a funny picture of him blowing a back flip fireball in his mom's living room, I was sort of annoyed with him, so I got everybody into our car and we tried to ditch him on the way to Miami. But there was no way he was going to be ditched. He was not going to let this chance to get in the magazine pass. Then he did this front flip off the bridge—it was probably a fifty-foot bridge and we didn't even know what the water was like. He just blindly did it. That was awesome. He started winning me back over. I started to appreciate him because he was really giving us more content than anyone else. I learned on that trip that he's pretty lovable even though he's annoying.

When the new issue of the magazine came out a few months later, I was all over it. For starters, a photo of me walking down some stairs on my hands with a skateboard balanced on my feet was on the magazine's cover. This was my first magazine cover and it was a *big fucking deal* to me. I was also on the introduction page doing a fire-breathing back flip. Then there was a story about me that had at least three more pages' worth of photos. Unfortunately, the story itself kind of shat all over me.

It didn't bother me too much that the writer wrote about how the *Big Brother* crew was constantly trying to ditch me—that was probably true—but the story claimed I was disrespecting my mom by using her house to stage stunts while she was in a coma. That really fucking stung. This writer was in no position to be making judgments about the situation with my mom. Plus, I thought it was hypocritical of *Big Brother* to plaster photos of me all over the magazine and then rip on me in the story. I mean how much could they have hated me if they were putting me on the cover of the magazine?

In retrospect, I'm sure I was way more offended by that story than was really warranted. It was just a few passages that took me to task, but those psychic wounds from Mom's aneurysm were fresh and deep and certainly didn't need any salt poured in them.

To be fair, that cover story did me plenty of good too. For one, it got me a job. Sort of. By the time the issue came out, I'd moved down to Miami. One night I was at a club called the Chili Pepper and the manager came up to me and asked, "Are you Steve-O from *Big Brother*?" That was probably the first time anyone ever recognized me in public.

She then told me she was a huge *Big Brother* fan and wanted to hire me to do fucked-up shit at the club.

I didn't even wait for her to offer me money before I said, "Hell yeah!" So every Friday and Saturday night, they'd put a spotlight on me and I'd do fire-breathing back flips in my clown gear or the drink-on-the-forehead trick or whatever else I could get away with. In return, I'd get $70 a night plus free drinks. I had already been doing tricks at the club for free drinks, so I felt like I was making out like a bandit.

A few months after I'd started doing my thing at the Chili Pepper, I got a call from a former Ringling Bros. clown. He and a few other clowns had left Ringling and were putting a troupe together to perform on Royal Caribbean cruise ships. They were looking for one more clown and had seen a video of me that I'd sent to classmates from Clown College.

Initially, I was pretty lukewarm to the whole endeavor. I already had my Chili Pepper gig, but more than that, taking this job would mean spending months away from Florida. That would mean dropping out of college (again) and more or less abandoning Mom and Cindy. I told this clown, "Look, I'm performing professionally in a night club"—I did my best to make my bar-tricks-for-peanuts gig sound like some big deal—"so why don't you come down when I'm performing, check out my act, and we can talk about it."

So these veteran circus clowns come to the Chili Pepper, see me do my thing, and decide they definitely want me in their troupe. I'm pretty flattered but tell them I'm not sure if it's for me. Then I'm told I'd start at $625 a week.

Holy shit! I'd been stoked on $70 a night and free drinks. This changed the story altogether. I told them I was in.

I was psyched that I'd be getting paid real money for the first time in my life, but as I started training for that cruise ship job in June 1999, I had mixed feelings. Mom was in bed, permanently disabled and in severe physical pain. Cindy was waking up every few hours at night to turn Mom, feed her, change her diaper, and clean out her bedsores, and then working a full-time job during the day. I was running away to go cruise around the Caribbean doing back flips for fat tourists.

Although part of me felt like I was abandoning my family right when they needed me most, another part felt like the best thing I could do was to go out into the world and do something with my life that would make Mom proud. I knew that sitting around the house in Boca, eating all the food in the fridge and getting depressed, certainly wasn't going to help anyone.

Mom understood me better than anyone in the world: she may have laughed about me going to Clown College and made fun of my stunts, but deep down she knew I could never be some guy sitting in an office for forty hours a week. But real-world success was important to her too, and so far there hadn't been much of that for me. Now here was a legitimate opportunity—this wasn't some skate company that was going to pay me in free schwag. This was a chance to prove that all the fucking up, all the years of devoting my time and energy to jumping off buildings and playing with fire, all the hospital bills and bail money, hadn't been a complete waste. Here was a chance for me to finally stand on my own two feet. Perhaps I'm just trying to justify doing what *I* wanted to do, but Cindy had already rearranged her entire life to take care of Mom, so my feeling was, *This aneurysm has already imposed its will on two lives, I'm not going to let it destroy me.*

So I didn't.

CLOWN ON A MISSION

Being a clown on a cruise ship was pretty much a
dream job for me. We warmed up the crowd each night
in the ship's main theater and the rest of the time we
were supposed to wander around the ship as "inter-
active performers." Essentially, I was getting paid to
fuck with people. I'd goof around, show off, annoy
passengers, and do all the same sorts of bar tricks
I'd always done—back flips, juggling, balancing things
on my nose, drinking from glasses without using my
hands. And for this I was paid what seemed like a
fucking fortune.

I roomed with one of the other clowns in my troupe,
a guy named Mike Daugherty. He was an okay guy and
deserves special mention for showing me two tricks
that would soon become regular features of my act.
The first was chewing glass. He'd break a lightbulb,
then take one of the pieces of broken glass, pop it in

his mouth, chew it up, and swallow it. I thought that was fucking bad-ass. It turns out that there's not much to it: When you chew glass enough, it turns to sand and then you can just swallow it. It's horrible for your teeth, but otherwise no problem. Once I got pretty comfort-able with chewing glass, it occurred to me there was something I'd learned as a kid that would make the whole stunt look even crazier.

When I was about eight years old, I was messing around in my par-ents' bathroom and accidentally squeezed a bunch of toothpaste onto the counter. It was a mess and I was worried that I was going to get in trou-ble, so I grabbed the first thing I saw—a Bic razor—and began scraping up the toothpaste with it. That didn't really do much to clean up the mess, and now there was toothpaste all over the razor too. So I tried *lick-ing* the toothpaste off the razor. My tongue started bleeding profusely. I quickly grabbed some toilet paper, bunched it up on my tongue, and ap-plied pressure. Much to my surprise, the bleeding stopped almost im-mediately. It turns out that a tongue bleeds a lot but also heals itself faster than any other part of the body.

With this in mind, I soon added my own special twist to Mike's glass-chewing: I'd break a lightbulb, use one of the shards of glass to cut my tongue, and then start chewing on it, while blood dripped from my mouth. A couple years later, after I'd gained some notoriety from *Jackass*, I started doing a live stage show, and this was usually one of my opening stunts. After the blood started flowing, I'd smear it across my face and let it drip all over my chest, which really set the appropriate tone for the show.

Another thing Mike showed me became an even more integral part of my act. One day while we were writing up our weekly reports in the ship's office, Mike suddenly grabbed a stapler and pumped a staple into his forearm. I was floored. Again, it turned out to be less horrifying than it appeared—it hurt a bit, but you could just pop the staple out and it didn't leave much of a mark.

I took this idea and really ran with it. Royal Caribbean paid us in cash every two weeks. The first time I ever stapled myself, I took ten

$100 bills from my pay envelope and stapled them to my arms and chest. I called that video clip "The Thousand Dollar Man."

That was just the beginning. On my first day of filming for *Jackass*, I stapled the letters "J-A-C-K-A-S-S" across my butt cheeks. (Anything you can do to your arms is way funnier if you do it to your butt.) Before long, a regular office stapler wasn't crazy enough, so I stepped up to an industrial staple gun. That came with much larger, longer staples and hurt way more, but it got a much better reaction. After using that thing a few times, I got the idea to staple my scrotum to my leg. That would become one of my signature stunts. Despite winding up with occasional infected, bruised staple holes in my nut sack, I was surprised to find that it's generally more painful for the leg than the scrotum.

I didn't pull any of that shit on the cruises though. My antics had to be considerably more G-rated. Still, they went over well with the passengers. My fellow clowns were less amused. They were constantly trying to write skits and come up with new bits, none of which I thought were all that funny or cool. I felt like I already had my own bag of crowd-pleasing tricks, so why should I bother collaborating on the lame stuff they were coming up with? Whenever they were working on new material, I'd just put on my headphones and do my own thing. Whatever my reasons might've been, I was a total dick about it.

It's no surprise then, I guess, that the other three clowns in my troupe went behind my back and basically got me fired. I had a six-month contract, but after about four months, they went to the Royal Caribbean brass and made a threat: if Steve's contract is renewed we're all quitting. I wasn't supposed to know this had happened, but one of the company's head clowns found out and told me I'd soon be out of a job. I appreciated his telling me, but I couldn't let on that I knew— otherwise *he'd* get fired. So for two months I had to work with these backstabbing clowns and pretend everything was fine. It was especially shitty because for the last month or so, we were training to perform on the maiden journey of the *Voyager of the Seas*.

The *Voyager* would be the largest cruise ship in the world and the jewel in Royal Caribbean's crown. We had a more elaborate show planned for that trip, so I spent two months training, memorizing scripts, and learning new routines, knowing the whole time that I'd be let go before I ever got to do any of the stuff in front of a real audience.

Knowing that I'd be out of work by the end of November, I was desperate to figure out what to do next. The cruise ship had given me my first taste of career accomplishment and I was not anxious to return to bussing tables, selling pot, or sleeping on couches. Ever since meeting Tremaine in Florida, I'd stayed in touch with him, calling him frequently, and sending a steady barrage of e-mails. Now I figured I needed to make some shit happen, so I told Tremaine that I'd be coming out to California just before Y2K to do a stunt so huge that he'd be an idiot to miss it. I figured if I cooked up something rad enough, it could possibly get me back on the cover of *Big Brother* and into another one of their videos.

A month and a half before my contract ended, we went to Finland, where we lived on the *Voyager* while the construction of the ship was being finished. Most days, I'd go to an Internet café and fire off e-mails making the arrangements for my Y2K stunt. I knew I'd need stilts, stilt pants, Ryan Simonetti, a unicycle, and someone who could ride it.

Once the *Voyager* was fully constructed, the whole staff rode on it across the Atlantic to Florida, where I was officially informed of my dismissal. I left the boat with $9,000 in cash. I bought a 1991 Mercury Grand Marquis, stilts, juggling gear, and a plane ticket.

I got out to California the last week of December 1999, where I met up with Simonetti and Jim Hahn, a dude I'd found online who told me he could ride a unicycle. When we rendezvoused with the *Big Brother* contingent a few days later in Encinitas, Tremaine had news to report: they weren't collecting footage for *Big Brother* anymore; they were working on a pilot for MTV.

I wasn't very savvy in the ways of television, but I knew enough to know that making a pilot for MTV was a far bigger deal than doing

Dad's college graduation photo, 1964.

Mom's nursing college graduation photo, 1968.

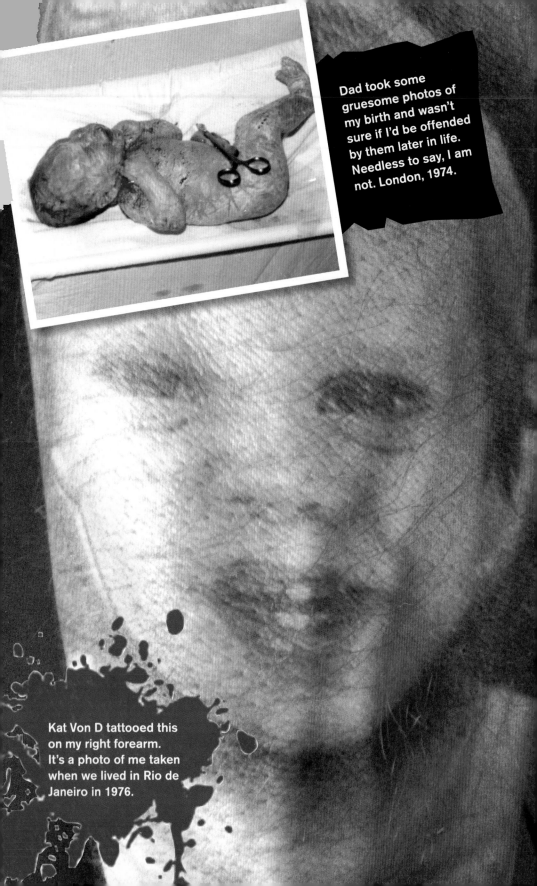

Dad took some gruesome photos of my birth and wasn't sure if I'd be offended by them later in life. Needless to say, I am not. London, 1974.

Kat Von D tattooed this on my right forearm. It's a photo of me taken when we lived in Rio de Janeiro in 1976.

Wearing my bib backward as a cape, like a real superhero. Darien, CT, 1978.

Government of Canada   Gouvernement du Canada

STEPHEN GILCHRIST GLOVER

D.O.B. - D de N D-J M Y-A	SEX SEXE	HEIGHT-TAILL CM
13 06 74	M	135

YP-AP	EYES-YEUX
83	BROWN

Steve Glover

In full football uniform and pads at the passport photo office. I'm sure I didn't even have a game that day. Miami, 1983.

With Nikki Sixx and Tommy Lee backstage at Maple Leaf Gardens in Toronto, 1987.

Skateboarding in London during my brief "straight edge" phase, 1989.

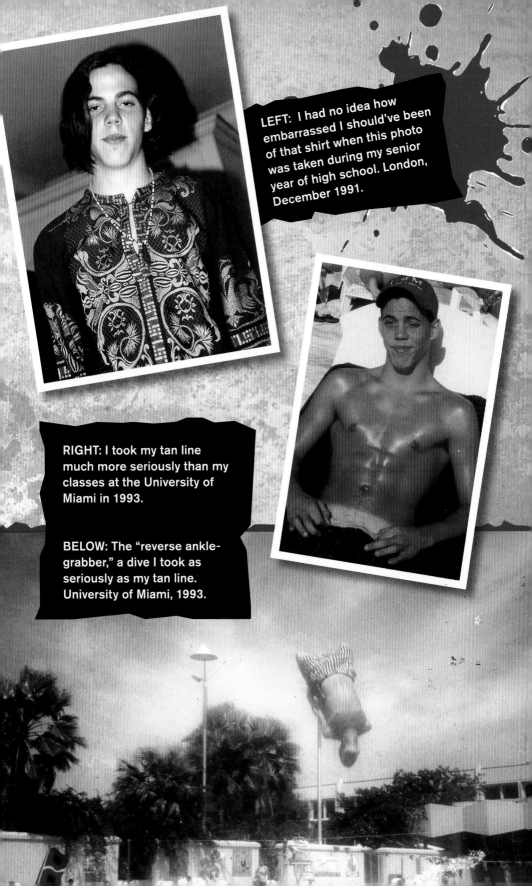

LEFT: I had no idea how embarrassed I should've been of that shirt when this photo was taken during my senior year of high school. London, December 1991.

RIGHT: I took my tan line much more seriously than my classes at the University of Miami in 1993.

BELOW: The "reverse ankle-grabber," a dive I took as seriously as my tan line. University of Miami, 1993.

LEFT: Me jumping off Mom's house, over the patio, into the pool. What's so rad about this photo is that Mom took it. Boca Raton, FL, 1994.

BELOW: From 1995–1997 I had this one full tooth with broken ones on each side of it. I looked ridiculous, but I don't remember being terribly bothered by it. Florida, 1996.

It wasn't long after I perfected my standing backflip that I learned to light my left hand on fire and simultaneously blow a fireball off it as I flipped. This became a trademark maneuver. Albuquerque, 1997.

Photos of my burns after setting myself on fire for *Big Brother*. Albuquerque, 1997.

ABOVE: Mom and me at my Clown College graduation. 1997.

RIGHT: Doing flips from the roofs of three-story buildings was my specialty, and this was one of my favorites. This is a gainer flip into less than five feet of water. Albuquerque, 1998.

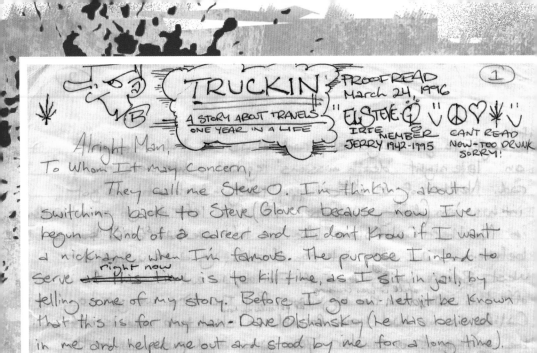

TRUCKIN'
A STORY ABOUT TRAVELS
ONE YEAR IN A LIFE

PROOFREAD
March 24, 1996
"EL STEVE O" ♥☮♡☣♥
IRIE
MEMBER   CANT READ
JERRY 1942-1995   NOW-TOO DRUNK
SORRY!

Alright Man,

To Whom It may Concern,

    They call me Steve-O. I'm thinking about switching back to Steve (Glover because now) I've begun kind of a career and I don't know if I want a nickname when I'm famous. The purpose I intend to serve ~~it this time~~ right now is to kill time, as I sit in jail, by telling some of my story. Before I go on-let it be known that this is for my man- Dave Olshansky (he has believed in me and helped me out and stood by me for a long time).

    When I met Dave I was a feeble representation of a ~~student at University of Miami~~. Dave's a second year freshman and Dave was a true freshman. The school year had just begun and I was heartbroken by my girlfriend of the year before. I gave up on everything- drank harder than usual (which was a task) and released my frustrations by endangering my life in numerous ways. I still don't know why. I think it was a last ditch ~~attempt~~ at feeling good about myself and getting back at this girl by making her worry. I became an independent stuntman.

    It was basically inevetable I guess - I've been in and out of hardcore skateboarding since 1985 (age 11), and took up diving as soon as I arrived at UM (the pool saw more of me than my teachers - combined). I met this guy named Jamie Haselton - not long after I met Dave. He was a snowboarder from Vermont. It wasn't easy for Jamie to be in a "sunshine state" but he was under the duress of his South Floridian father. Jamie had as much

It could be said that I began working on this book while I was in jail in Orlando in March of 1996. This is the original first page from my jailhouse memoir.

stunts for *Big Brother*. For me, the feeling was kind of like auditioning for Clown College: it was still a long shot that anything would really come of it, but just the possibility seemed to change everything for the better. If MTV was even entertaining the idea of buying a program that consisted of a bunch of idiots doing crazy shit, then potentially the reckless dream I'd been chasing could one day be fulfilled. I was fucking stoked.

Tremaine introduced me to a tall, lanky guy named PJ Clapp, who I recognized immediately from his appearances in *Big Brother* videos under the name Johnny Knoxville. I was already star-struck by Knoxville, just based on the insane shit he'd pulled off in those *Big Brother* videos—getting Tasered, shooting himself with a .38, willingly being hit by a car. He was funny and charismatic, and like everyone else who met me, I'm sure he was annoyed by my never-ending need to show off.

KNOXVILLE: I didn't find Steve as annoying as some of the other people. He didn't seem like a bad guy, he was just so hyperexcitable. At first, it really got on people's nerves, but he's such a sweet guy and that came through.

My stunt had a lot of moving parts. The idea was for me to get up on stilts, light my pants on fire, then blow a fireball from my mouth at Simonetti as he ollied over my head from the roof of a house on his skateboard while Hahn rode through my flaming legs on a unicycle at the same time. Then I'd fall over on the stilts and be extinguished. I had only three sets of stilt pants to burn, so I had just three tries to get this thing right on camera. The first two attempts went okay, but the third was perfect. Everything happened at the exact moment it should have.

Tremaine and Knoxville hadn't yet worked out the format of *Jackass*, and at that point it seemed like Knoxville might be more like a host. We actually did a sit-down interview on camera before the stunt, which was obviously an element of the show that would be dropped when it finally aired. In fact, my entire stunt never ended up airing on MTV or anywhere else for that matter—though you can find it on YouTube if you look hard enough. But Tremaine and Knoxville were impressed not only with the intricacy and creativity of what I'd done, but also the initiative I'd taken to make it happen. I'd flown across the country on my own dime, lugging my stilts with me, and managed to get Simonetti and Hahn there too. They could see I was hungry.

KNOXVILLE: Steve did everything in his power to make that bit usable but it didn't make it. We didn't really know what *Jackass* was at that point. We were just taking a lot of shots in the dark.

TREMAINE: At that point we weren't really clearing every-thing we were shooting with MTV. We were just doing it how we'd do *Big Brother*, where any idea that sounded good we'd just do. We had a half-assed safety crew and didn't really have a big plan on how to put Steve-O out once he was on fire other than just buckets of water and maybe one fire extinguisher. The long pants turned out to be extremely flammable and it became this sort of panic situation once his legs were on fire. But we got the fire out and he didn't get burned up too badly. The stunt was cool. We weren't allowed to ever air it because MTV had some real bad experience with fire with *Beavis and Butt-head*. Fire was a big no-no on the network.

Over the years, I've thought a lot about how much I owe this huge break to dumb luck. After all, had I not gotten the boot from Royal Caribbean, I would've been juggling oranges aboard the *Voyager of the Seas* instead of dragging my ass across the country to impress Tre-maine. Had those other clowns not gone behind my back and con-spired to have me fired, I never would've been a part of *Jackass*.

I RETURNED to Florida after New Year's to a sobering reality. I may have been part of making a pilot for MTV, but at the moment I was still an unemployed drunk. After I got off the cruise ship, I moved in with Cindy and Mom at Mom's house in Boca. Mom's condition hadn't improved, but I told her the news about my stunt in California and the MTV pilot. In a rare moment of clarity, she understood what I was talking about well enough to laugh and make a joke about it at my expense, which made me incredibly happy.

I didn't want to sit around and wait to hear about a TV show that might never happen, so I tried to be proactive by sending out packets of photos with videotapes to every single talent agent I could find in Florida. None of them wanted shit to do with me. I was starting to feel like the pilot would evaporate as quickly as it had materialized. By March, I was spending a lot of time sitting around Mom's house doing fuck-all but getting depressed.

Cindy insisted I get off my ass and do something. She was appalled that I'd sunk so much time, money, and energy into being a clown and now had nothing to show for it but a closet full of expensive gear. She told me about a circus at a flea market in nearby Ft. Lauderdale, and suggested I apply for a job there. I was skeptical, but we went and checked out their show. I thought it was actually pretty killer.

After the show, I talked to one of the showgirls and she introduced me to an old guy named George Hanneford II who ran the whole thing. No sooner had I told him that I'd graduated from Ringling Bros. and Barnum & Bailey Clown College than he asked me if I could start the next day. He told me he'd pay me $500 a week.

The Hanneford Family Circus was an old-school big-top circus run by a famed circus family, but by 2000, it was a little down on its luck. There was a family of acrobats, a Russian lady with trained dogs and cats, and another woman who could spin sixty hula hoops at one time. They even had three elephants and a tiger, though the ringmaster, George Hanneford III, always seemed to have one eye peering over his shoulder, on the lookout for animal rights activists. When I showed up, they didn't have any full-time clowns and were really hurting for one. As such, they let me do pretty much whatever I wanted. I'd blow fire, balance ladders on my chin, all my usual tricks.

We'd do about ten shows a week, so it was pretty grueling, but I regularly kept myself fueled up with a steady diet of cocaine. I would peel off my clown nose backstage and snort lines in my makeshift, tarped-off dressing room while still in full clown makeup. I suppose the whole scene was morbidly hilarious, but thankfully I wouldn't be in it for much longer.

10

I'M GOING TO GET BITTEN BY A SHARK IN THIS CHAPTER

June 13. That was the day my life really changed for good. I have no trouble remembering the date because it's my birthday. I remember feeling pretty down that day—I was twenty-six years old and as stupid as it sounds, I was starting to feel old. I decided to call Tremaine to tell him it was my birthday (as if he'd care) and make sure he hadn't forgotten about me. I remember his exact words when he got on the phone: "It's not a pilot anymore."

I knew exactly what that meant. Tremaine told me to start writing ideas because they'd be coming through Florida in August to film. He also told me to box up all my stunt videos and send them to him, so they could license the footage to use on the show. (As it would turn out, none of my footage that was good enough for the show made it past MTV's standards and practices department.) *Jackass* was happening and I was going to be a part of it.

It's hard to describe how I felt upon hearing this news. For nearly ten years I'd been chasing a dream that was—let's face it—fucking ridiculous. Ever since Tracie Smith dumped my ass, I'd been convincing myself that it was possible to become famous for doing crazy shit in front of a camera. My confidence in this idea had wavered over the years. There were moments, like when I was sitting in jail writing my "memoir," that I was absolutely certain that it was inevitable. Then there were times, like when I was standing in that field of cow shit staring at the ruins of my Ford Tempo, when it seemed completely impossible.

Most of the time, I just couldn't really picture what success would even look like. So I ended up at skateboard conventions and Clown College and many, many bars peddling my act for free booze. Often it felt almost like a religious quest, because I had little more than blind faith leading the way. I mean, really, who in the whole world could I have pointed to and said, "He's doing what I want to be doing"? There wasn't any precedent for it. I'm not saying I invented all the reckless stunts I was doing or that I was the only one out there doing them, but once MTV picked up the pilot it felt like this grand validation. Not that I had really proved anything yet, but everything was now telling me that my instincts had been right and that all the work I'd done was going to pay off.

Two and a half months later, the *Jackass* crew rolled into the circus to pick me up. Knoxville and Chris Pontius were the only other cast members who made the trip, but most of the main players from the crew—Tremaine, Dimitry, co-producer Trip Taylor, cameraman Rick Kosick—were there too.

PONTIUS: This flea market circus was like nothing I'd seen before. We were just walking through this crazy place and it was filthy. You could buy switchblades, nunchucks, and throwing stars, and it also had the biggest drive-in movie theater in the world. After Steve's act was over, while he was still in clown makeup, he came over and said something like, "Hey, dude! Did you watch my act?" And I was like, *Oh, god*. He was just so out of hand.

KNOXVILLE: It was the most rinky-dink budget circus you could ever imagine. We walk into Steve-O's dressing room and there are all these lines of coke everywhere. He's actually a very talented clown, but he comes out with that Steve-O voice and kids are running behind their moms' legs. It was just unbelievably odd and, looking back, extremely funny. Aside from John Wayne Gacy, he's probably the scariest clown I ever saw.

That was the first time I met Pontius. I thought he was just cool as shit. Everything that came out of his mouth was hysterical. In fact, I was envious of him because being funny and entertaining seemed to come so easily to him. I had to work so hard and force it all the time, but he just had this natural talent. I know I annoyed him but we bonded pretty quickly, and in a strange way he became a mentor to me in those early days. I was clearly on the fringe of the entire operation, but he'd worked at *Big Brother* out in California, so he helped me understand who everyone was and the way everything was going to go down.

After my act finished, I washed off my clown makeup, jumped in the Grand Marquis with Tremaine, and we set off, with everyone else following in the production van. We hadn't gotten more than a mile before my car sputtered and died right in the middle of this sketchy Haitian ghetto. I couldn't believe it. This is my big fucking break and my car conks out with the show's creator in it. I honestly thought they were going to leave me right there in the middle of the road, but I guess I was more distressed about it than anyone else was. We got out of the car and pushed it into a strip mall parking lot.

One of the stunt ideas I'd submitted to Tremaine was called "The

Goldfish Trick." I was going to swallow a goldfish and then puke it back into a bowl, still alive. Once we'd gotten my car off the road, Tremaine didn't want to waste time, so he sent someone to a nearby pet store to buy a goldfish. I'd been thinking about this idea for a while but had never actually tried it. I'd figured if I drank enough water beforehand, I'd puke easily and the goldfish would survive the ride without a problem. But when the goldfish showed up a few minutes later, I hadn't had anything to drink and felt totally unprepared. With my car breaking down though, I sensed that I was on thin ice with these guys as it was, so I couldn't back out. This show was everything I'd been working toward since I was a teenager. I didn't want to fuck it up.

I was supposed to introduce myself and my trick on camera but was too nervous to speak, so Knoxville had to do it.

"Hi, I'm Johnny Knoxville and this is Steve-O, and he's getting ready to do the Goldfish Trick."

Swallowing the fish was a piece of cake, but throwing him back up was rough. I spent more than a full minute—an eternity in TV time—crouched on my knees over the fishbowl in that parking lot, sticking my finger down my throat and occasionally gulping from a water jug before that little dude popped out of my mouth and back into the bowl looking none the worse for the wear. I suppose if he'd come back up my throat the wrong way, he really could've ripped up my esophagus, but the moment I saw him swimming around that bowl, I was so stoked I'm not sure I would've even minded. In fact, all my struggling to get that fish back up is what made the sketch work—if he'd popped right out, it wouldn't have been nearly as dramatic. I remember Knoxville came up to me after we'd finished the bit and said, "Well, Steve-O, if you weren't famous before, I'd say you're gonna be famous now."

I spent five days in South Florida with the *Jackass* crew filming all my clips for the first season of the show. The whole trip was incredible. Everything was happening so quickly and it was all so fucking exciting. That first night, I had the word "Jackass" stapled to my butt, then, later on at the bar, I pulled out one of my bar tricks, wrapping my mouth around the rim of a glass and downing it without using my hands. Both stunts ended up on the show. After I was pretty plastered, they also filmed me shooting a bottle rocket out of my ass. That never played on *Jackass* but later wound up on the Internet.

I partied pretty hard on that trip, but everyone was getting out of hand. The mix of adrenaline, testosterone, and booze was potent and really served to bond us together quickly. One night I took things too far and did a whole bunch of ecstasy and blow. There's a short clip of me passed out buck-naked in a hotel room that was shown on the fourth episode of the first season. That was from the day after my binge.

Mostly, though, I was on a natural high during that trip and didn't feel as desperate to keep myself as fucked up as I usually did. For the first time in my life, I felt like I was surrounded by guys who understood me. I mean, I'm sure they all thought I was a little much to handle, but after years of struggling to explain my life's mission to everyone around me, I was now part of a team with the same mission, backed by a network betting on us to pull it off.

For most people, *Jackass* seemed to come out of nowhere, but really Tremaine and Knoxville didn't create all the lunacy, they just found a home for it. Knoxville, Pontius, Tremaine, and Jason "Wee-Man" Acuña all were based in California and had been filming outrageous footage for *Big Brother*. Bam Margera was a pro skateboarder who had been filming similar stuff with Ryan Dunn and a few others (like Brandon DiCamillo and Rake Yohn, both of whom made frequent appearances on *Jackass*) simultaneously in Pennsylvania. Dave England and "Danger" Ehren McGhehey were snowboarders from Oregon, who'd been creating their own cache of crazy footage. *Big Brother* had been a magnet for the exploits of all these misfit daredevil freaks, then *Jackass* honed the best of it into a show.

TREMAINE: In the early days, we weren't thinking there was going to be a steady cast. We were just going to film guys as they come and go. But I knew Steve-O would be a good source of content. He's a gold mine. He's so funny. In those days though, he couldn't talk to the camera. He really struggled. He was so nervous and hyper. That was true with a lot of our guys early on. They were great for physical gags but talking was a struggle.

All of the stunts I did on that Florida trip worked at least as well as I'd hoped. One day, we filled a baby pool with elephant crap that I'd spent a week collecting from the circus and putting into these huge Tupperware bins. My original plan had been to light my whole body on fire, then do a back flip off a ladder into the pile of crap, at which point I'd roll around and put out the flames. Tremaine knew MTV wouldn't approve any fire-related skits, so he suggested skipping that part: doing a back flip into elephant shit off a tall ladder would be enough. We filmed that one in the yard at my mom's house.

We also reshot a bit that I had originally filmed on my own with Ryan called "Bum Fishing." (MTV aired it under the slightly more sensitive title "Street Fishing.") It involved attaching a dollar to the end of a fishing line and then reeling it in as people on the street chase it. I remember that when I'd originally filmed it with Ryan, I was almost certainly more broke than the "bums" we were fishing for. It felt like a real investment for me to put a dollar on the end of that fishing line.

The gnarliest thing I did while shooting that first season never actually aired. We were filming "Shark Hugs," which was exactly what it sounds like. Tremaine found a tour operator who took tourists to swim with nurse sharks. Pontius and I planned on getting close enough to give them some loving. I had no experience whatsoever with sharks, but the guides said nurse sharks were very docile and hardly ever bite. Just don't wave your hands around in front of their faces and you'll be fine, I was told.

Pontius and I donned our scuba gear and jumped in the water, which was fairly shallow. Initially, the sharks did seem friendly. We petted them, hugged them, and pretended to hump them. Then I forgot the one instruction I'd gotten before entering the water and waved my hands in front of one shark's face. *Snap!* The bite was more shocking than painful, but when I swam to the surface my finger was bloody and mangled.

The guy who ran the tour company was horrified—not at my injury but that it was going to make his company look bad. He immediately told Tremaine that MTV couldn't show the footage of me getting bitten. So when the segment aired, it showed us swimming with and humping the sharks, but not the bite. Years later, the full segment, bite and all, surfaced on a DVD called *Jackass: The Lost Tapes*.

A few weeks after the filming, some guy from MTV called to tell me to send over my hospital bills from the shark bite. I proudly told him I never actually went to the hospital, even though I probably needed stitches. After I hung up, it occurred to me that if MTV was going to reimburse me for all my medical expenses that meant I could get as fucked up as I wanted to while I did *Jackass*. This seemed an important realization.

AFTER MY five-day excursion for *Jackass*, I returned to the flea market circus to find out I'd been fired. They told me there was no longer enough room in the budget for me. My sister was also pretty unhappy with me. It seems that when we'd finished the elephant poo diving sketch in Mom's backyard, I hadn't bothered to clean it up. The funny thing is that Trip had actually offered to have it cleaned up right after we finished filming, but I hadn't wanted to bother him with that. After we left the scene, it rained all night and a river of watery elephant crap had run from Mom's yard into the neighbor's. Cindy was fielding angry complaints, which she then passed along to me at increased volume.

"Do you think you're really going to get famous for jumping in a pile of shit?" she asked me. "Do you really think something productive is going to come out of that?" Actually, I did.

After a few more arguments with Cindy—mostly about me being an unreliable slob who was contributing nothing to the household—she kicked me out. I was once again back to my couch surfing/car sleeping routine.

Jackass premiered on October 1, 2000, and was an immediate hit. I had only one little appearance in that first episode—the bit where I down the drink without using my hands—but I was stoked. I had really been worried that MTV was going to water everything down and make it into some sort of family-friendly *America's Funniest Home Videos* type of bullshit. But Tremaine, Knoxville, and Spike Jonze—the *Being John Malkovich* director who was one of *Jackass*'s producers—deserve a lot of credit for navigating the show through a minefield of rules and standards without losing any of what made it cool. To this day, I have a hard time believing they let us put all of that fucked-up shit on basic cable. The ratings were great too; in fact, by week two, we were the highest-rated half-hour show in MTV history. Almost immediately, people started recognizing me in public, asking for my autograph or wanting me to pose for photos with them. Getting free drinks in bars no longer required doing anything more than showing up.

I made a grand total of $1,500 for my work on the entire first season of *Jackass*. I guess that's called paying your dues. Between booze, drugs, and whatever other bad shit I was blowing money on in those days, that cash didn't last long. Within a week or two of *Jackass*'s premiere, my life was officially absurd: I was broke, unemployed, homeless, and a star of a hit show on MTV. How many people can ever say that?

I TOLD YOU I WAS
GOING TO BE FAMOUS

MTV ordered sixteen more episodes—two more seasons—of *Jackass* just a few weeks after the show had premiered. The pay was a big step up: $2,000 per episode. Coming off the poverty line existence I'd been leading, I suddenly felt like a rich man.

In November, Knoxville, Tremaine, and the crew returned to Florida, ready for another five days of shooting. Outside the hotel in Miami that first night, Knoxville gave me what amounted to a friendly warning.

"This isn't looking like Season One," he said. "Get ready for a really rough time."

The first morning, I found out what Knoxville meant when he and I got pelted with oranges by professional jai alai players. Later the same day, I snorted an earthworm up my nose and pulled it out my mouth, still alive and wriggling around. Next, I rode a unicycle into a swamp, landing right next to an alligator.

After a day or two around Miami and the Everglades, we headed up toward Orlando. The final episode of Season One was airing that night on MTV, and someone thought it might be funny if we knocked on a stranger's door and asked if we could come in and watch the show. We pulled into a trailer park around West Palm Beach, and after getting turned away from two doorsteps, Knoxville walked up to a third and said, "Hi, I'm Johnny Knoxville, and I have a TV show that's about to come on. Is it okay if we watch with you?"

The husband and wife who lived in this trailer had no idea who we were but were happy to have us, especially when we brought in several cases of beer. We all settled in and then the husband said, "Hey, my lady does tattoos. Any of you guys want a tattoo?"

Immediately, I raised my hand and yelled out, "Satan Fish!"

For me, a "Jesus Fish" facing the wrong direction with the word "Satan" in it seemed like the perfect tattoo. I've never been a fan of organized religion—I have a hard time being interested in a heaven that would exclude family and friends because they were Jewish, Muslim, atheist, or anything else—and collecting silly tattoos had become a bit of a hobby.

I'd gotten my first back in high school. I purposely picked the cheapest, least manly tattoo the shop had—a little flower—and got it on my hip. When I showed my dad, I thought he'd be really shocked, but his only comment was "Awww, isn't that nice?"

After Tracie Smith dumped me, I tried to get a serious-looking tattoo that would somehow reflect my inner turmoil and picked this Celtic-looking tribal bat thing. It ended up being one of my funniest tattoos simply because it's so lame. It's lopsided, and it's not symmetrical or in the center of my back where it's supposed to be. Even if it had been done well, it still would've been lame. It looks like Batman's bat signal as drawn by a complete douchebag suffering from vertigo.

After that experience, I started to get tattoos that were funny on purpose. In Albuquerque, I had "your name" tattooed on my ass cheek and "I Love to Bone" spelled out in symbols—an eye, a heart, the roman numeral II, and a bone—on my arm. Tattoos became like stunts to me in that they were designed and acquired mainly to get a reaction out of people. The Satan Fish certainly fell into that category.

Unfortunately, the woman in this trailer was nervous to be on camera, and the lines on my Satan Fish were coming out so shaky that they looked like EKGs. Eventually Tremaine had to step in and finish the job. Knoxville was convinced I'd get my ass kicked at least once a month for that tattoo, but to this day, nobody has ever really confronted me about it.

Up in Orlando, I had a plan to do a flip off a ten-meter diving platform while wearing stilts. When I got up there, it was pretty fucking terrifying to be balancing on those things thirty-plus feet above the pool. I couldn't even start the count on my fingers. I wussed out and just jumped off instead of flipping. I was bummed but no one else was, thanks in part to the unique look I was sporting when I did it.

The night before, I'd been filmed getting my entire body waxed—bikini line, armpits, chest, eyebrows, the works. I had my head shaved down to the scalp too, so I looked like a sideshow freak when I leaped off that high dive. It was also in this hairless state that I first learned a wonderful and valuable lesson about the power of celebrity.

Shortly before the guys had come down to Florida to film for Season Two, I'd hooked up with the hottest chick I'd ever been with in my entire life. *By far.* She was some sort of model with ludicrously big fake boobs and an unbelievable body. I can't remember her name to save my life, but I met her in some nightclub and she decided she wanted to fuck me. That in itself blew me away because, let's face it, girls this hot generally aren't that into broke, homeless, insecure ex-clowns with a propensity for premature ejaculation. But I was on TV! Still, I figured once I returned from Orlando looking like a hairless mole rat, she'd want nothing more to do with me. In fact, it was quite the opposite. Not only was she still completely down with having sex with me, she actually started to get really clingy. At one point, she made the unilateral decla-ration that she and I were "exclusive" and couldn't date other people. Which was my cue to stop calling her.

I'd always heard that girls want to sleep with famous dudes, but I really had no idea how true it would be. Not only did I score this in-credibly gorgeous chick *and keep her* despite my freakish lack of eye-brows, but now *I* was blowing *her* off. All because I was on MTV. I suppose there might be some guys who'd see a dark side to all this and feel hollow because women were interested in them only for their ce-lebrity status, not the person they were on the inside. I was not one of those guys.

THE MONEY for the second and third seasons of *Jackass* hadn't come through from MTV yet, so after that filming trip, I was back in South Florida, hurting for cash. I thought I could maybe make some money doing my thing in nightclubs again but had no real idea how to go about getting work. I called around to some clubs and somehow man-aged to get myself booked to appear at a place called Lola in South Beach on New Year's Eve. I showed up in full clown makeup and did my whole act—chewing lightbulbs, walking on stilts, back flips, everything—and got paid $200. That's right, two hundred bucks for a star of a hit TV show to risk serious injury in a packed nightclub on New Year's Eve. In fact, I got wasted that night, took way too much ecstasy to be doing a back flip off the bar, and needed six stitches to close up the cut that resulted from my face hitting the ground. All for two hundred bucks.

I know now that I should have demanded to be paid ten times that, if not more, but the bottom line was I simply had no idea what I was doing. I had no manager, no agent, no nobody to tell me that I was sell-ing myself way short, and there was no lack of people out there happy to take advantage of my naïveté. My main business advisor was my dad, who was extremely helpful but had no background in entertainment.

I can't imagine this is an unusual dilemma for people in my shoes. Between TV, movies, and the Internet, new celebrities are being minted on a daily basis, and there is an entire industry of shady managers, agents, promoters, lawyers, and others that has grown up around exploiting them.

In this particular case though, I wasn't really all that upset about how things turned out. Early the next morning, the manager of Lola took me back to her place. I had sex with her—still in my clown makeup and sporting a bloody lip—then downed a few Bloody Marys and cruised over to the hospital to get my lip stitched up. That felt like a pretty good way to spend New Year's.

One other minor moneymaking opportunity fell into my lap around this time. An Internet company called Alltrue flew me to New York City to film some hidden camera videos that they could post on their site. They paid me $500 per clip, and a few of the videos were actually pretty funny. In one, I wrapped myself in Saran Wrap and paid a hooker to piss on me. In another, I jogged around Greenwich, Connecticut, in a tracksuit with chocolate pudding in my pants, telling passersby that I'd accidentally shit myself, and then asking if I could come into their homes to clean up. I also went around to three different used-car dealerships and, as I peed in my pants, asked them to let me test-drive a car. That idea actually grew from personal embarrassment, after I'd gotten insanely drunk one night and pissed in the guest bed at my great-uncle's house.

IN JANUARY, just after I got the stitches out of my lip, the *Jackass* guys were back in Florida for another round of filming. Immediately after they got off the plane, I took Dimitry with me to go get my butt cheeks pierced together. The following day, Pontius and I were scheduled to swim with great hammerhead sharks, accompanied by Manny Puig, the wildlife expert who became a regular on *Jackass* and, later, *Wildboyz*. With the butt piercing wound still fresh, swimming with sharks might not have been very smart, but Manny wasn't worried about it.

As far as the MTV lawyers were concerned, it was okay for us to do dangerous stunts, but only if we had an acclaimed expert overseeing our activity. We'd met Manny a couple months earlier. After my Season One shark bite had to be left on the cutting room floor due to skittish tour operators, Tremaine was dead set on finding someone really badass to help us with our animal bits. At the time, Manny already had a show on Animal Planet and was well known for filming his extremely close encounters with dangerous predators. Tremaine and Pontius saw Manny on TV wrestling alligators and riding sharks, all while wearing a Speedo. Of course, the alligator wrestling and shark riding was important, but Tremaine will tell you it was the Speedo that got Manny the job.

Manny looked the part too. He was tall, with long, wild hair, a bushy graying beard, and a shark tooth necklace. He perpetually appears as if he just arrived from spending three weeks sleeping happily in a swamp.

Once we started working with Manny, I felt more comfortable in the presence of wild animals than was probably wise. In retrospect, the fact that Manny was the arbiter of what was safe and reasonable is hilarious. He hatched and okayed plenty of ideas that were clearly *not okay*. So you knew if he said no to something, that meant "FUCK NO!" On that previous Florida trip, Knoxville desperately wanted to get intentionally bitten by a rattlesnake, but Manny nixed it. Getting bit by a rattlesnake never came up again.

As it happened, Manny had no problem sending us swimming with great hammerheads. As a matter of fact, he strapped huge, bloody chunks of barracuda to me for part of the stunt. That footage came out great, but what you don't see in it is that Pontius and I spent most of that day lying on the boat, sleeping off our hangovers. Manny, meanwhile, was in the ocean, wearing only his Speedo and a diving knife, chumming up the water. The man was out there for six straight hours, treading water and slicing up fish to attract sharks. When they finally appeared, Manny yelled "Shark!" and Pontius and I raced to get in the water. The scene was totally ridiculous: normally, when someone yells "Shark!" people race to get *out* of the water.

After the shark swim, we all drove up to Orlando, where the entire cast was together for the first time. Despite the fact that we were well into filming the second season, I hadn't met Bam, Ryan Dunn, Preston Lacy, Dave, or Ehren yet. Once we were all together, it was impossible to do anything without it turning into mayhem. It didn't matter if we were in a restaurant, a titty bar, or the middle of an empty field, somebody was always "hot," which was our term for being in the state of mind where nothing can stop you from doing insane shit that someone else really ought to be filming.

TREMAINE: We found this hotel that would let us do whatever we wanted so we had the whole cast there and we were just acting really badly. That's when we really felt like we were on to something. We almost had a gang. There were just so many big personalities that gelled. It was sort of miraculous in that way. There was just so much camaraderie and mayhem going on nonstop. You almost didn't know where to look. It was difficult to film because everybody was red hot.

I could tell right away that Bam and Ryan both found me pretty hard to take. By that time, Bam had emerged as the second big breakout star of the show, and to be totally honest, I was very jealous of him. He was younger than me, better looking than me, and was a professional skateboarder as well as a *Jackass*. Thanks to the show, his skateboards were selling as well as Tony Hawk's. Bam also had put out his own videos that he'd shot in Pennsylvania with his buddies, who were known as the CKY (Camp Kill Yourself) crew. I thought his footage was genius: It was genuinely funny in a way that I usually couldn't pull off. I mean, my stuff was shocking for sure, impressive sometimes, and definitely idiotic, but rarely humorous in the way his was.

Just a month or so earlier, I'd watched Bam's *CKY2K* video, while tripping on liquid acid at my friend Jeffro's house. (Incidentally, Jeffro was in his bedroom at the time filming homemade porn with some girl.) Sitting there watching Bam's footage, I was seething with envy. I really wanted to have my own project, and here was Bam, already so far ahead of me. He had produced this video himself and gotten it distributed, and I was sitting on my ass, doing drugs and watching it.

I decided I had to do something about this. *Immediately.* I marched into Jeffro's room, interrupted his porn shoot, and told him to get in the car and bring his video camera. We drove to a local bridge. I strapped on my stilts, then walked toward the railing and tossed myself over the side, doing a flip on the way down. *On acid.* With my legs strapped to the stilts, I could've easily blown out my knee, but instead it all went really well and the footage looked awesome.

In Orlando, I also met Brandon DiCamillo, who was part of the *Jackass* cast at that point. I really liked him. Like Pontius, he had a natural talent for being insanely funny. He didn't need to hurt himself—he could just make great footage out of nothing. Brandon eventually bowed out of *Jackass* before the first movie because, as I understood it, he felt like, at a corporate level, the people behind it were greedy jerks and he didn't want to make money for them. I totally respect that opinion and I'm sure there's truth to it, though in the end, I'm not sure what his principled stand achieved: the greedy jerks still made money without him.

WHILE WE were in Orlando, we went back to the Olympic pool where I'd wimped out of doing the stilt flip off the ten-meter platform two months earlier. I was determined to go through with it this time, and having the whole cast there really gave me the extra kick in the ass I needed. Bam did an awesome ollie off the high dive within ten minutes of us getting there, then all the guys took turns doing their own goofy jumps off the platform—on a scooter, holding a beach umbrella, naked, that sort of thing. Finally, at the end of the day, I strapped on my stilts, dressed up in this absurd Uncle Sam getup—shiny blue jacket, red-and-white-striped stilt pants—counted to three, and did the flip. I made it only three-quarters of the way around, but landing flat on my back in the water with a smack looked way better on TV than a perfect flip ever would have.

Those days in Orlando were intense. We did the majority of filming at a spot by a lake. They had a gigantic ramp built for us to launch ourselves off into the water in whatever creative ways we could think of. I tried to negotiate the ramp in a little red wagon and failed miserably, wiping out off the side before I even reached the lake. In doing so, I scraped the hell out of my butt cheek.

People always ask me what's the most painful thing I've ever done to myself on *Jackass*, and strange as it may sound, that scrape bothered me more than anything else that happened during the television series. (The movies took the pain to a whole new level.) I'll take horrible pain that ends quickly (like, say, a butt-piercing) anytime over something that will bother me for two weeks straight. After the wagon incident, every time I sat down and got up, I had to peel my underwear off that wound.

I remember lying in my hotel room feeling sorry for myself because of this scrape on my butt, and then thinking about my mom at home in Boca with an apple-size hole in her ass from a bedsore. *What a fucking bitch I was.* Here I was running around doing everything I wanted to do, whining about a little bullshit abrasion, while my mother was home in bed crying in pain all the time. *Forever.* Since *Jackass* started, I had become pretty good at distracting myself from Mom's situation, stuffing it all down and ignoring it, but when it backed up on me, it did so with a vengeance.

I called Cindy that night and sat in the hallway of the hotel on the phone with her, crying hysterically. I knew I wasn't dealing with Mom's situation in any sort of remotely healthy way, but I just didn't know what else to do. I was angry at any god that would let this happen. Mom wasn't perfect, but she didn't deserve this life. No one did. I felt guilty that I'd run away from her but would justify what I did by convincing myself she was my motivation—that I needed to succeed, to become famous, in order to make her proud. I don't know if all that actually made me more driven to succeed, but the idea that it did helped quell those feelings of guilt.

NOT LONG after wrapping that second round of filming Season Two in Florida, I got a call from a party promoter in Cleveland named Nick Dunlap. He wanted to fly me, Bam, and Wee-Man to Cleveland to appear at a nightclub there.

"I know you're busy," he told me. "I'll get you in the night of the party and get you out the next morning, so it's not even going to be twenty-four hours of your time. And I'll pay you seven hundred dollars."

I'd been getting paid $500 per video clip from Alltrue, but this guy was talking about $700 to go to a party and not even be filmed.

"Seven hundred dollars?" I responded. "Are you kidding me? For seven hundred dollars I'll fucking chew and swallow glass! I'll light my fucking head on fire!"

That party in Cleveland is kind of a blur. I did all kinds of drugs and got predictably out of hand. At one point, I got two ecstasy pills, gave Bam half of one, and took the rest myself. Bam was still a pretty sweet, innocent kid back then. The ecstasy was doing a number on him and he was floored that I'd had a pill and a half. I'm not sure whether he realized I was also jacked up on coke and meth.

The party itself ended up getting shut down by the cops pretty early in the night. Later, I had sex with some random girl under Dunlap's kitchen table and then fell asleep. I was still there under the table the next day, when Dunlap woke me up.

"Hey, your flight is in an hour," he said. "Do you even want to try to make it?"

I did not. I rolled over and went back to sleep.

NICK DUNLAP (former manager): The day after that party I said, "Steve, I gotta get you to the airport or you're going to miss your flight." He was like, "Dude, Dunlap, man, you need to know one thing: I don't give a fuck about shit." Later, I said, "Hey, when do you want me to get you this plane ticket back?" And he was like, "There's this girl I'm kind of diggin' in Florida so I really want to be back by Valentine's Day, but I got like twelve or thirteen hundred dollars in my back account, so whatever." It was the middle of *January* at this point. To me, the fact that he thought less than $2,000 was enough money that he could go on an open-ended vacation was awesome. Being twenty-three-years-old, I thought that was about as rock and roll as it's gonna get.

Dunlap was an ambitious wheeler-dealer who was always completely up front about the fact that his sole motivation was money and that he'd sell his grandmother to make it. He seemed to have an angle on everything. I found out that he'd cleared about $35,000 on the party that he'd paid me, Bam, and Wee-Man $700 each to show up at.

I ended up spending seven days with Dunlap in Cleveland and it was an important seven days. We talked for hours on end about me and my career, and it was there that he hatched a plot for us to take over the world. He told me he could easily get me a few thousand dollars a weekend to make appearances in March at some spring break spot in Panama City, Florida. I told him I had a bunch of footage MTV would never air that I was hoping to release as a "Too Hot for TV" video. He immediately began trying to convince me to let him figure out how to distribute it.

The second night I was in Cleveland, we walked across a bridge over the Cuyahoga River to a restaurant. When I looked down from the bridge, I noticed the river was partially frozen. In some spots the ice was frosty and dry, in others, thin and wet. As soon as I saw that I announced that I wouldn't leave Cleveland until I put on ice skates and a skimpy tutu and fell through that ice while Dunlap filmed me. I was as good as my word. I actually wound up doing it twice because the first batch of footage wasn't as rad as it could've been. This "Extreme Ice Skating" sketch would eventually lead off my first DVD, *Don't Try This at Home.*

ONCE I finally got the first of the checks from MTV deposited into my account, I decided it was time for me to leave Florida behind and take my act to the West Coast. I was enjoying my newfound fame and knew I needed to get my ass out to Los Angeles to nurture and take full advantage of it.

Dunlap had booked me to make a couple spring break appearances at the biggest nightclub in America, a sprawling monument to cheesy excess in Panama City called Club La Vela. I planned to drive there, do what I needed to do, and then simply keep driving west until I got to Hollywood. Tremaine told me that as long as I came up with a list of stunts to film for Season Three in each and every state between Florida and California, he would fly a camera crew out to meet me in Panama City and follow me cross-country.

The visit to Club La Vela was a revelation. I was really hired only to make an "appearance." That basically amounted to hanging out, signing autographs, and drinking for free. But the club had a stage so it seemed like a waste not to use it. I got up there, busted out all my tricks, and did a lot of drunken rambling into the microphone. The crowd gathered around the stage and stayed there. It quickly dawned on both me and Dunlap that we had the makings of something here. That night we began talking about doing more stage shows.

I did my thing for two debauched nights in Panama City, and Dunlap booked me to come back there a week or two later. Then I set off for California in the Grand Marquis with Dimitry in the passenger seat while the others followed in a rented production van. That was quite a road trip: I got a heart-shaped brand on my chest with a molten-hot coat hanger in Alabama, was horse whipped by a voodoo priestess in New Orleans, dropped crawfish into my pants in Louisiana, tried (and failed) to eat a seventy-two-ounce steak in Texas, and walked around a shopping center in Albuquerque, dressed as a security guard, fucking with people. That security guard bit wasn't the greatest in the world, but the fact that I managed to get some laughs was heartening: it was the first time I'd done something on *Jackass* that was pure comedy and didn't involve something gross or my risking or abusing my body in some way.

I also spent hours behind the wheel of the car on that drive, pontificating on life into the lens of Dimitry's camera. I guess I thought that I had everything pretty much figured out. I was on a hit TV show doing what I loved, I was flush with money, Dunlap and I had begun plotting our world takeover, and I was moving out to the land of opportunity to make big things happen. What could possibly go wrong?

12

I'M NOT LEAVING

"Strike while the iron is hot."

That was the advice I heard over and over again, usually unsolicited, once I arrived in L.A., and it pissed me off. Here I was, fresh to California, my new career finally taking flight after years of struggle, and every person I ran into was telling me that it was all about to be over so I better make the most of it while I could. Well, *fuck that*. My attitude was I'll strike whenever I want to because I'll just make the iron hot whenever I damn well please. I really believed I was in control.

Arriving in Southern California felt in a strange way like a homecoming for me. I'd been there only a few times, but as a kid who grew up loving nothing so much as the attention of others, Hollywood was kind of my spiritual homeland. I remember pulling into town and actually getting tingly when I spotted that iconic

HOLLYWOOD sign perched in the gray-brown foothills of the Santa Monica Mountains.

I'd arrived in California without any sort of practical plan as to what I was going to do once I got there. I had no place to live, and beyond periodic filming days for *Jackass*, no place I really needed to be on a daily basis.

I wasn't the only homeless *Jackass* cast member. Pontius was calling his Toyota Tacoma home, so Tremaine proposed turning our homelessness into a sport. Rather than find a place to live, we'd have a contest to see who could stay homeless longer. The rules were vague, but basically we were supposed to remain without a fixed address for as long as possible, while doing our best to find girls who'd take us home with them each and every night. Considering this wasn't all that different from the existence I'd been leading for the previous seven or eight years, I figured I'd win this little competition without breaking a sweat.

TREMAINE: Pontius was always a couch surfer but did it in such a lovable way. Steve-O came out and he sort of buddied up with Pontius. Steve-O was really good at meeting a girl, staying with her a few days, and moving on to the next. I don't know why I thought it would be funny that they should compete. But I liked the fact that they were homeless. I just thought it was so ridiculous.

Those first few weeks around L.A. were surreal. I just drove around in my big-ass Grand Marquis without much clue as to where I was. It would take me forever to get anyplace because I was constantly getting lost. When I planned on drinking—which was basically every day—I'd usually park my car at the *Jackass* offices. I spent a lot of time in bars around West Hollywood, frequently alone, searching for two things: drugs and girls who'd take me home. As I'd already discovered in Florida, the fact that chicks recognized me from TV made it pretty easy to convince them to sleep with me. Barney's Beanery, a touristy joint on

Santa Monica Boulevard famous for serving Janis Joplin her last meal, was a frequent and fertile stomping ground in those early days.

I had no shame about being a total slut. I even kept track of my sexual conquests on a list I called my Slay Sheet. If I couldn't remember a chick's name—as was occasionally the case—designations like "girl from Oregon" or "chick in back of car" would suffice. It wouldn't have taken a skilled psychologist to tell me that the Slay Sheet was a way of dealing with my insecurities as a man and my inadequacies in bed. But it was also kind of funny. I figured if I was willing to laugh about my own sexual shortcomings—after all, I've got a tattoo that reads "I Have a Small Weiner" (side note: it took me three days to realize "wiener" was misspelled) and have always been candid about my issues with premature ejaculation—I could also joke about how hard I was working to raise my SPA, or Slay Point Average.

All the bars close at 2 a.m. in California, which sucked royally for me because at 2 a.m. I was rarely done partying. It took me a little while, but eventually I discovered an after-hours scene and became a regular at this sushi place on Santa Monica Boulevard. It was a sushi place during normal hours, but once the bars closed it became a hangout for all the shadiest characters around Hollywood. You couldn't drink there but you could score and do just about any drug under the sun. People would snort coke and ketamine pretty openly, take ecstasy, swig caps of GHB, and smoke lots of weed. I partook in all of it. I'd typically roll in there alone a little after two and leave around five or six in the morning as the sun was coming up. The fact that I had no home to go to only made the place more appealing.

Every once in a while, when I couldn't find a place to crash, I'd cheat in my contest with Pontius and pony up $50 for a room at this supremely dingy motel on Hollywood Boulevard called the Hollywood Center. At this point, I had some money from *Jackass*, as well as from shows I'd done with Dunlap—I actually used to drive around with thousands of dollars in cash in the trunk of my car until I started stashing it over at Tremaine's house—but it was a point of pride that I'd get a room only at the most disgusting motel around. A sign in the lobby of the place reminded patrons that prostitution on the premises was strictly prohibited—as sure a sign as any that it was crawling with hookers.

I felt like a failure every time I plunked down cash for a room at the Hollywood Center. I'd typically get a whole bunch of nitrous oxide and hole up there huffing it until it was gone. I'd been doing nitrous occasionally since I was nineteen, but when I arrived in California it became a regular indulgence.

Nitrous, for those who don't know, comes in little cartridges that can be loaded up to six at a time into a canister designed for making whipped cream. When you break the seal on the cartridges, the gas goes into the canister and then comes out when you push down on the canister's lever. When you suck it in, you get a brief flash of dizzy euphoria, and if you do enough of it you'll pass out. For me, passing out was always the goal. When I did, I'd be in this dreamy state—sort of halfway between consciousness and unconsciousness—that I found wildly appealing.

I'd go through about a hundred cartridges of nitrous a night at the Hollywood Center. It was a really creepy scene. If someone had been watching on a surveillance camera, they'd have seen me in this room alone, huffing nitrous until my lips turned blue, passing out, flopping around in convulsions, coming to, then huffing some more. Even the sketchiest of characters who hung around that place would've probably found it disturbing to watch.

I FILMED more bits for the third season of *Jackass* in California, and we also flew up to Mount Hood in Oregon early in the spring of 2001 and filmed up there. That trip became most notable because Stephanie Hodge, a model who'd been previously involved in a bunch of *Jackass* skits, broke her back filming a stunt with Dave England.

They were both meant to sled down the mountain on an air mattress, but when they hit a massive jump, Stephanie landed hard and wrong. At the time, nobody realized the extent of her injury. She was carted off on the back of a snowmobile, but that seemed mostly a precaution. When we later heard that she'd fractured her vertebrae and pelvis, it knocked the wind out of all of us.

To that point, Stephanie was almost like an auxiliary member of the *Jackass* fraternity, but that incident drilled home an important point about what we did: Nobody wants to see a chick get hurt. I don't know if that statement is chivalrous or chauvinist, but I'm sure it's true. It's worth noting that Stephanie made a full recovery and remained a close friend of all of ours. In fact, her apartment became a frequent crash pad for both Pontius and me during our homeless era.

With two seasons of the show already under our belts, *Jackass* had gained cultural resonance that extended far beyond the skateboarding community that had birthed it. That made for some strange opportunities, many of which we indulged in simply for their strangeness. I'd probably put our music video shoot with Shaquille O'Neal into that category.

Shaq was a fan of the show and wanted us in his new rap video, so we showed up and spent the day goofing around with him. To his credit, he was game for our antics. Well, sort of: I broke a candy-glass bottle filled with fake piss on his head, he wrestled with everyone and spent quite a lot of the day dry humping Wee-Man. His video never came out, but we used some of the footage for a segment in *Jackass*'s third season.

Shaq also tried to sign me to some sort of bullshit management deal that day. He pulled me aside and called me into a meeting with a business associate of his. They proposed something along the lines of getting 80 percent of all my earnings for the work I did for the rest of my life. I will be the first to admit I'm not the savviest businessman in the world, but this had to be one of the most ludicrous contracts ever written up. Needless to say, I passed.

In April, Knoxville, Pontius, Tremaine, Dimitry, and I took part in the Gumball Rally, a five-day car race from London to Russia and back that was filmed as an hour-long MTV special. The rally is an annual event and most of the competitors are rich dudes with fancy cars. I'd been looking forward to it—we'd been told there would be crazy parties every night—but mostly I remember being trapped in the back of a car with Pontius for five days.

He and I decided to pass the time with another contest: to see who could jerk off more times in a car full of guys while we were driving. We called it "Carjacking." So as we pulled out of Hyde Park in London in this parade of really expensive cars, the two of us were in the backseat furiously tugging at our dicks. In the end, I believe this competition ended in a draw at four loads apiece. That doesn't sound too impressive over five days, but really there are few things less arousing than being stuck in a small car with a bunch of dudes, so I consider it a worthy accomplishment. Beyond that, I did a bunch of coke, slept a whole lot, and at one point shit in a plastic bag in the backseat of the car. In other words, nothing too out of the ordinary.

When I got back to London after the trip, I spent some time partying with these rich guys I'd met on the rally. One night, they ordered me a high-end Russian hooker. She was pretty decent looking—dark hair, great body—but I've never been into the idea of paying for sex and felt awkward sitting with her in my hotel room. I asked her to give me a back rub, but after she started to, she said, "This is one expensive back rub." This Russian hooker was actually making fun of me. At that point, I just said, "Fuck it," strapped on a rubber, and humped her. Afterward, we snuggled. Really.

DESPITE HATING to hear everyone tell me to "strike while the iron is hot," I knew there was some truth to what they were saying. I'd always thought of video footage as my eternal legacy—I'd die one day, but my footage would last forever. But in reality, footage became less like an immortal monument cast in bronze and more like a carton of milk: There was a definite expiration date on it. There would come a time when *Jackass* was yesterday's news. I needed to make something new happen quickly and the only plan I had was to keep filming stuff that wouldn't be allowed on television, then release it myself. So wherever I went, I'd pack my own camera and a bunch of tapes in a backpack.

That spring, Tremaine, Knoxville, Pontius, and I went to Chicago to appear at some big radio station concert there. I brought along the hospital gown that I'd taken from the hospital in Miami years earlier after doing that face-plant off the balcony, figuring it could come in handy for some filming.

When we got there, we partied all night, and at 10 a.m. the next morning, Pontius and I were sitting in a bar, drinking again. I was brainstorming ideas for what I could do with my gown. I remembered a story I'd heard about Mötley Crüe injecting Jack Daniel's when they ran out of drugs and decided it would be really gnarly if I "drank" alcohol through an IV. A woman sitting near us at the bar overheard this and mentioned that her sister-in-law was a registered nurse who'd just lost her job at a hospital. I got on the phone with this unemployed nurse and a few hours later was lying in my hotel bed in the hospital gown, filming as an IV was stuck into my arm. I initially poured only a single shot of vodka into the bag with the saline solution but when that didn't seem to have much effect on me, I moseyed down to the hotel bar—in my gown, dragging my IV stand—and ordered two shots of Grey Goose. I added those to the bag but still didn't feel much. I returned to the bar, got two more shots, poured them in, and then watched the remains of the bag drain into my arm. I still felt more or less fine, so I wheeled my IV stand down the street to another bar and did a bunch more shots the old-fashioned way until I was good and drunk. People have told me that shooting booze directly into your veins can be insanely dangerous, but to me it felt like just another night of getting loaded.

At the airport on the way home from Chicago, I carried a big bottle of whiskey with me through security. This was pre-9/11 but, strangely, I remember they made me swig from it to prove it wasn't some kind of dangerous liquid. I did so happily and continued through the checkpoint with the bottle. On the plane, the flight attendant took the bottle away from me and I made a drunken scene, screaming at him and calling him a "faggot." Knoxville slunk down in his seat next to me, mortified.

KNOXVILLE: In hindsight, it makes me giggle, but it wasn't fun sitting next to him. For years, I didn't like sitting next to him on planes. He and Pontius both used to act up on planes, but his acting up was different from Pontius's. Pontius gets loaded and doesn't know what he's doing. He thinks he's in the bathroom but is actually in the middle of the aisle peeing. He has no clue. Steve-O had a little anger behind him. I wasn't super psyched when he'd get drunk and yell at people. I often felt like Steve was *trying* to act up. He wasn't just oblivious.

After doing those two weekends' worth of spring break shows in Panama City, Dunlap booked a bunch more shows in Cancún in June. I didn't think many people vacationed in Mexico in the heat of the summer, but it turns out I was very wrong. We sold out the largest nightclub in the country three weekends in a row.

Pontius came down for the shows one weekend, and Wee-Man came down another weekend, but Dunlap and I stayed there for more than two weeks straight. The whole trip was just a blizzard of cocaine and ass. As easy as it was getting laid around L.A., in Cancún the combination of booze, drugs, and foreign travel seemed to eliminate any and all inhibitions in the female population. I must've had sex with at least ten different girls while I was down there. Then after two weeks, I left with $12,000 in cash and went home.

The success of the Cancún excursion really solidified my relationship with Dunlap. It was also around this time that another business associate entered the picture, a guy I'd known from the University of Miami named Jason Berk. We were party buddies in college, but since then, he'd become a lawyer and was living in Cleveland, not far from Dunlap. I introduced the two and they hit it off. I was getting close to finishing the filming for my first DVD, and they decided to form a company together, J&N Media, to put it out. Berk would deal with the contracts, the deals, and all the legal stuff, Dunlap with postproduction, graphic and Web design, schmoozing, and whatever else came up. In retrospect, I didn't put a whole lot of thought into whether Berk was really the kind of guy I should be teaming up with to guide my career. I just did it.

THAT AUGUST, I went back to Florida, ostensibly to sort out some problems with the DMV there. Before moving to California, I'd gotten a ticket for driving with a broken windshield—I'd kicked it out while I was drunk, just after filming the "Bobbing for Jellyfish" stunt for Season Two—but never bothered to deal with it. As a result my license was suspended. Plus, my registration had expired. But rather than deal with these very fixable problems, upon arriving in Florida I made a beeline for my buddy Jeffro's house and started doing coke with him and a few other friends.

Our coke binge lasted through that night, the next day, and the next night. The following morning, I balked again at a trip to the DMV, instead deciding that it was far more pressing to go do a flip off a bridge from a moving car. I'd been talking about this stunt for close to five years and had the perfect bridge picked out on Islamorada in the Florida Keys.

When we got down there, we rented some Jet Skis so Jeffro could film from the vantage point of the water. I climbed up on the car and it got going about thirty miles per hour before I leaped off, flipped, and landed hard on the water. That hurt like a motherfucker, but the footage looked good. When we went to return the Jet Skis, I showed the owner of the rental company the video of the bridge flip. He was impressed and had an idea for another stunt. He owned a little sea glider airplane and really wanted to see me jump out of it into the ocean without a parachute. It sounded fucking crazy.

This guy admitted he was worried that I might get chewed up by the propeller and cause the plane to crash; I was more worried that the plane would be so high up and moving so fast that when I hit the water, it would be like landing on concrete. The whole prospect was downright terrifying, but I figured I wasn't likely to get another chance at something like this.

"Fuck it," I said. "Let's do it."

When we got up in the air, we had to be going at least forty or fifty miles per hour. Out there, soaring over the ocean, it occurred to me how ill-conceived this whole stunt was: I was on day three of a coke bender, as was my completely nonprofessional cameraman down in the water on a Jet Ski. Meanwhile, the pilot was operating the second of our video cameras with one hand, filming backward over his shoulder, while flying with the other hand. I was risking my life and I couldn't even be sure I would get any footage out of it, let alone good footage. But there was no turning back now.

I knew that to be in the shot, I had to jump right as we were passing over the Jet Skis. As we came around, we were probably close to fifty feet in the air when I threw myself out of the plane. I cleared the propeller without a problem, then flailed my arms and legs the whole way down and landed on my back. *Holy shit, did it hurt.* That is one of a handful of what I refer to as "I'm not okay" moments when my initial thought was just that.

Slamming into the water knocked the wind out of me, and for a few seconds I couldn't breathe. Once I caught my breath, I was convinced that I must have organ damage. But the sting wore off and, except for some serious soreness, I was okay. What's more, by some miracle my coked-up cameraman and the one-handed pilot both managed to get the shot perfectly.

I never did make it to the DMV that weekend, a fact that would come back to haunt me in April 2002, when I got pulled over in California for driving with expired tags. Because my license was suspended and my insurance was no good, the cop told me it was a criminal matter rather than a traffic violation. He got permission to "catch-and-release" me—essentially booking me and serving me with a court summons without bringing me to jail—but wouldn't let me drive away. The Grand Marquis was towed, with all my clown gear—costume, juggling pins, stilts—still in the trunk. As it was towed away, I made a conscious decision that I'd let the tow yard keep it. I figured that car and that clown gear belonged to a part of my life that was over.

I never made any attempt to show up in court to deal with the ticket either. A bench warrant was issued for my arrest. I ignored that warrant for nearly six years, during which time I had numerous run-ins with cops who also chose to ignore it. In 2007, I was walking down a street in L.A. drunk when some sheriffs asked me to take a photo with them. For some reason, I mentioned the warrant, and they asked me my real last name so they could look it up in their system. I paused and asked, "Won't you have to arrest me if you find my warrant?" Their answer was a resounding, "Fuck no!" When they checked their computers, they confirmed it: "Yup. You're hot for ten G's," which meant that if those cops had done their job, I would've been taken to jail and had my bail set at $10,000. Instead, they just let me go. It wasn't until after I got sober in 2008 that I finally dealt with that warrant. It was a year after that that I finally got a California driver's license and a car again.

IN THE fall of 2001, Dunlap had set up what amounted to a tour of a bunch of college campuses that began at my sister's alma mater,

Washington University in St. Louis. The best way to understand this tour is to imagine the wildest, most out of control rock band on tour and then take away the music.

A lot of the other *Jackass* guys took turns doing stints with me on this tour. We'd typically roll into town already wasted, get paid (Dunlap, wisely, wouldn't ever let us go onstage without collecting our money up front), then proceed to bleed, piss, and puke all over a stage, often taking time out to rag on whatever university officials had approved this lunacy. Students would come onstage to chug tequila, strip off their clothes, get kicked in the nuts, whatever—and then, after the show, we'd continue boozing, do more drugs, and fuck whatever girls were willing. The fact that this went on at supposed institutes of higher learning still boggles my mind.

At the time, I was reading the Mötley Crüe biography *The Dirt*. The band had been a bad influence on me in my youth, but now I was in the unique position—on tour, newly famous—to really emulate my heroes at their absolute worst. That book really inspired me to reach new lows in my own personal depravity. In Boston, I met a girl at a party who came back to my hotel. When we got to fooling around, she told me it was a "bad time of the month." I didn't believe there were any bad times of the month, so we yanked out her tampon and starting having sex. Then, after a few pumps, I pulled out and went for a different hole, inaugurating what became known as "the Chocolate-Covered Red Rocket."

PONTIUS: The Kansas trip was the first time Steve and I shared a girl. She was a person who set up the talent for the university. Steve-O actually was a gentleman. He left the room and first I had sex with her. Right afterward, there was a bang on the door and I'm like, "How did he know I was done?" I opened the door and he walked right past me and lay down on the girl, probably in a bunch of cum. I was happy, because I was ready for bed. Eventually, he took her off to his room. He liked to cuddle and stuff, so he was with her all night. Then we had a fun ride to the airport the next day. Her mom was driving us and we kept alluding to things. We signed something for this girl and I wrote, "You were the best I ever had." He wrote, "I was way better than Pontius, huh?"

It was also during this first college tour that I met Dee, who for a while became a semipermanent groupie. She was a beautiful little brunette with a flawless body and no inhibitions whatsoever. I first saw her while I was onstage in Columbus, Ohio. She was right down in the front row, showing her tits to anyone who would look at them. I brought her onstage and within seconds she was flashing her boobs and thong at the audience. I then encouraged Wee-Man to lick her butt crack onstage (he really didn't object), and declared to the audience, "She's coming with us tonight." And she did.

The next stop on the itinerary was Cleveland. On the way there, I was trying to think of a stunt I could film with Dee and settled on blowing a fireball off her tits. We went to Dunlap's apartment and lubed up her chest with Vaseline and rubbing alcohol. The plan was that I'd blow the fireball, then Preston and Wee-Man would smother her flaming boobs with wet towels to put out the fire. The fireball went fine but Preston threw the towel past her and Wee-Man kind of froze and didn't do much. Dee was flailing around on fire for *way* too long. She ended up burning a bunch of skin off her side, leaving a patch under her right tit looking just like my face had looked in that backyard in Albuquerque years earlier.

Berk was there in Dunlap's apartment when this happened, and he immediately went over to the computer and typed up a waiver form for Dee to sign promising that she wouldn't hold any of us liable for what had just happened. The footage itself looked great, but when we were finalizing the edits on the DVD later that year and I showed a cut to Tremaine to get his opinion, he immediately said I should get rid of the scene where Dee got burned. He had a real problem with it and I guess I understood where he was coming from. I'd forgotten the Stephanie Hodge rule: nobody wants to see a chick get hurt.

TREMAINE: Anytime he would show me footage, I'd speak my mind on it. I was psyched that Steve was being productive in doing these tours but in the same sense I wasn't onboard with everything they were doing. Some of it seemed a little dark, especially in some of the video stuff they would shoot. I didn't want that to represent *Jackass*. I always felt like I was sort of on the hook, even though I had nothing to do with it.

I took Tremaine's advice and pulled the footage from what turned out to be my first DVD, *Don't Try This at Home: The Steve-O Video*, which was released early in 2002. It seemed like the right thing to do. That said, when I put out my second DVD the following year, I put the footage back in. What can I say? It was really gnarly.

As for Dee, she was fine. She hung around our little entourage for a while after that and was with me the first time I appeared on *The Howard Stern Show* in April 2002. If I remember correctly, I went in there and swallowed ten goldfish to see how many I could puke up alive. Howard seemed a little concerned and was telling me that I didn't need to do that, but I told him, "I didn't come here to waste anybody's time." I think that quote really endeared me to both Howard and Artie Lange. I seem to recall Artie quoting it back to me multiple times in the coming years. Dee also dropped a pool ball that we'd stolen from a bar from between her boobs onto my head. It wasn't really much of a stunt, but since it involved a topless chick, I figured Howard would like it, and he did.

The other thing I remember from that first appearance on *Stern* is that I talked a whole bunch of shit about Henry Rollins. Dee, it turned out, had a history with him. Before hooking up with me, she used to come out to Los Angeles semiregularly to be with Rollins. I ran my mouth about stealing his girl or some such nonsense, and made Dee confirm that he grunted a lot during sex.

I'd actually been a big Rollins fan when I was younger. I loved Black Flag, and the Rollins Band was one of the first concerts I went to on my own, back in 1989. But a few years after that, he'd come to do his spoken word thing at a campus bar at the University of Miami, and one of the conditions he'd insisted upon was that they couldn't serve booze that night. This was the lamest thing I'd ever heard. Naturally, I showed up to his performance completely loaded and created enough of a scene that Rollins made a crack about me from the stage: "Somebody get this guy a wheelchair." I loved the attention but that didn't change the fact that, to me, Rollins was a fallen hero. This whole Dee thing just gave me a chance to pick on him.

AS THE third season of *Jackass* was drawing to a close, the show had become the target of intense criticism. In early 2001, a thirteen-year-old kid had burned himself supposedly trying to emulate Knoxville's "Human BBQ" stunt, and in the aftermath, Joe Lieberman, the Connecticut senator and former vice presidential candidate, had launched a moral crusade against the show. In response, MTV pushed the show back an hour to 10 p.m. and also started to impose heavy-handed rules about what we could and couldn't do. No stunts could be "imitate-able," which proved to be a very ambiguous sword with which they began to hack away at our existing footage and plans. At one point they instituted a no vomiting rule, which outraged me, since that would kill so much of my airtime.

Most of the pressure from MTV fell on Tremaine and Knoxville, who had to negotiate with the standards department and various lawyers to get every single segment on TV.

KNOXVILLE: That was very frustrating. The whole unfortunate mess with the kid burning himself caused MTV to suddenly have an OSHA [Occupational Safety and Health

Administration] rep telling us we can't jump off things more than four feet high. The hammer came down and when the hammer came down like that we couldn't do the show like we had always done it. We had been doing it for only nine months, but it meant something to all of us, and it meant something to me. I wasn't going to do a watered-down version of *Jackass*, so I gave an interview to my hometown newspaper and said, "I quit. I'm done with *Jackass*."

In August 2001, the cast was informed that Season Three would be the final one. There was some general shock and discomfort at the news but everyone seemed to understand. Better to go out on top than continue to do some bullshit version of *Jackass*. Knoxville and Tremaine softened the blow a little by mentioning that they were working on the possibility of making a feature film instead. It was by no means a sure thing, but the idea was out there.

The wrap party for Season Three took place at a bar in Los Angeles called the Mayan. At 2 a.m. when the bar closed, Tremaine initiated his favorite late-night drunken game: I'm Not Leaving. He'd first introduced me to this game a few months earlier in Chicago. Basically, the bar closes and Tremaine announces, "I'm not leaving." The entire *Jackass* crew then informs the bouncers that we too are not leaving. We'd make the bouncers literally drag us out.

That night, we all linked arms and got really stubborn. There was a real standoff that went on for a while. Finally, one of our guys—I can't remember who—threw a punch at one of the bouncers. That kind of ruined the game.

TREMAINE: The rules are pretty specific. You just have to say you're not leaving but you can't be a dick. You can't fight back. You just turn into dead weight and make the bouncer throw you out. I started playing that game before *Jackass*. It used to bother me that I'd see these giant doormen and bouncers who just sat there and checked IDs and never really had to do their job. What's the point of being huge men if they're not bouncing anything? At the end of the night, I'd just sit there and make the bouncer do his job. I remember telling Knoxville, so he wanted to play it, and it sort of became a *Jackass* game.

We'd play I'm Not Leaving at all the wrap parties for whatever *Jackass* or *Wildboyz* project we were working on. It's ridiculous and comical, but there was something deeper and more significant about it too. Usually, when we were playing it, it was the end of a chapter in our lives. We didn't want to leave that bar, because leaving that bar meant finishing up a job that could very well have been our last. It meant lurching into the great unknown. Every time we've finished a TV show or a film, we've done so not knowing whether we'd ever be back together with this same group of guys doing another one. Each one of those endings had a note of finality to them. As silly as it is, I'm Not Leaving was pretty emotional: it was a way of acknowledging how much we loved what we got to do, and how much we wanted to hold on to it.

YOU CAN'T DO THAT
ON TELEVISION

I'd been homeless out in California for more than six months and what had begun as a funny contest with Pontius was starting to grow a little old. Always looking for a place to be a guest is exhausting. Trying to consume the ridiculous amounts of drugs that I wanted to without a home base is a downright pain in the ass. It was time to get an apartment.

For my whole life, I'd always felt completely incapable of doing the most basic tasks. I'd never even bothered to figure out how to run a dishwasher, so apartment hunting, setting up phone service, and paying bills was completely out of the question. When I met an ex-marine–turned-male stripper named Steve "Schliz" Schleinitz who told me he'd take care of all that stuff if I wanted to get a place with him, it was a no-brainer. Schliz found us an apartment in West Hollywood, on the corner of Sunset and Fuller, almost literally spitting distance from the Seventh Veil, the all-nude strip club that Mötley Crüe name-check in "Girls, Girls, Girls," and a short distance from tons of other bars and clubs on the Sunset Strip.

I got the keys to the place in October. The first time I walked in there, my cell phone rang and it was Tremaine.

"You feel like making a movie?" he asked. I most certainly did. I was fucking pumped.

We began shooting *Jackass: The Movie* in early 2002. My experience working on it is colored by the fact that I was coked up nearly the whole time. I'd always loved cocaine but now things started spiraling out of control. My occasional multiday sleepless coke binges became a regular thing. I was an annoying loudmouth naturally; wired on coke, I wouldn't shut up for days. I snorted lines—or snooters, as I liked to call them—out in the open and without shame. Although a few of the other guys would occasionally do a little with me, they never really took to it. I was the only committed cokehead in the cast.

Not that anyone seemed too concerned. If anything, it was a source of amusement. When Tremaine saw me with a brand-new laptop computer, he laughed and commented, "That's a really expensive snooter tray." One of my stunts in the movie was even titled "Wasabi Snooters," a sly reference to my drug habit.

Ironically, the wasabi snorting came during the only part of the filming when I wasn't jacked up on coke. We were in Japan at the time, where the drug laws are notoriously strict, so I had to get by for the ten days there mostly on booze and magic mushrooms, which, by some quirk of Japanese law, were actually legal and available in tourist shops back then.

While we were in Japan, Pontius and I had a plan to swim with whale sharks off the coast of Okinawa wearing only see-through bathing suits filled with shrimp. Whale sharks are the largest fish on Earth but they really aren't dangerous—their teeth are just nubs, little more than glorified gums. The whole point of the segment was for us to get ourselves bitten by these massive fish.

I needed to get scuba certified in order to go diving with the sharks, so I'd taken a crash course before leaving for Japan. Unfortunately, I was coked to the gills during all the classes and the certification test and retained absolutely nothing. Once we were filming off Okinawa, as I went deeper into the water and realized I could never get back to the surface in a single breath, I began to freak out. I was seized by a fear of drowning. I managed to pull myself together enough to get to the whale shark, hump it a little, and be gently nibbled on, but barely. Then I got the fuck back on the boat. I always thought it was ironic that the things that made me most uncomfortable while filming *Jackass* and *Wildboyz* were generally the safest stuff we did.

The title of that sketch, "Whale Shark Gummer," was another nod to my personal life. The year before, during my homeless days, I'd gotten a blowjob from a girl who'd been in a bad accident when she was younger. I didn't know this until we were fooling around, but she'd had all of her upper front teeth knocked out and replaced with a denture plate. As the action heated up, she pulled out my wiener and said, "Get ready to have a good time." With that, she popped out her front teeth and went to town. I immediately reported the news to the *Jackass* guys. "I didn't get a hummer," I told them, "I got a gummer!" The term "gummer" became an inside joke among us.

BY THE time of the first film, my love affair with dumb tattoos was in full bloom, and the first idea I submitted to Tremaine for the movie was to get a portrait of myself tattooed on my back. It took more than sixteen hours in four sessions to get it done, and I whined pretty much the whole time. The legendary artist who did it, Jack Rudy, absolutely hated working on me because I was such a pussy. I don't think anything I've ever done for work was harder to get through than that. In the end though, it looked amazing and literally larger than life: every part of the portrait is bigger than its corresponding body part.

My other tattoo-related stunt was the "Off Road Tattoo." The idea was I'd be sitting in the backseat of a Jeep getting tattooed while we drove through a motocross track in the California desert.

Everyone thought it would be cool to get a celebrity to drive the Jeep, and after some negotiations, word came down from Tremaine that Nikki Sixx was going to do it. I was completely fucking stoked. I'd idolized Mötley Crüe since I was a kid, and Nikki Sixx was the biggest badass of the bunch. The man had OD'd, flatlined, then returned from the dead to do more drugs. That day, we drove out to the desert and I brought my framed picture of me and Nikki from when I was thirteen and met him backstage in Toronto. As I waited in the white production van for him to arrive, I snorted line after line after line of coke off that framed picture. I felt like that was the greatest honor I could bestow on him. It was as if my life had come full circle: my childhood hero was coming to do a cameo in *my* movie.

As an SUV pulled up, Dimitry filmed me and said, "There he is. There's your hero. Go greet him." I hurried toward the car and the door opened. It wasn't Nikki Sixx. It was Henry fucking Rollins. *Oh, shit*. I figured I was about to get my ass kicked.

I had no doubt my trash-talking a couple months earlier on *Howard Stern* had gotten back to Rollins—and that wasn't the only place I'd been bad-mouthing him, only the most public. I'm sure for the *Jackass* guys, my getting roughed up by Rollins would've only added to the stunt, but he just shook my hand and said nothing about it. He was nice as could be and if he had any pent-up anger toward me, he took it out behind the wheel of that Hummer. He gunned it so hard over that jagged, dusty terrain that he broke one of the axles. Meanwhile, I bounced around furiously in the back and got painfully inked with a blurry, mangled smiley face. It's still one of my favorite tattoos.

TREMAINE: Nikki Sixx had agreed to do it and then at the last minute, he just sort of flaked out on us, so we had to scramble. Someone suggested Rollins because Steve-O was antago-

nizing him. But we told Steve-O it was going to be Nikki Sixx. So Steve walked out of the van with the picture of him as a little kid with Mötley Crüe and then Rollins pops up. In a perfect world, we were hoping Rollins would smack him or something, but I don't know if Rollins was even aware of all the nonsense that Steve-O was up to.

HENRY ROLLINS (ex-frontman for Black Flag, solo artist): I wasn't aware Steve-O had ever said anything about me to anyone. I remember him being somewhat hesitant to meet me, but he seemed friendly enough. Even if I had known, I wouldn't have hit the guy. If I chose to hit every man who spoke poorly of me, I'd need a few pair of extra arms. Besides, I don't know much about those *Jackass* guys but, honestly, I admire them. The commitment to some of those scenes is as intense as you ever want to be, outside of being deployed in Iraq or Afghanistan. As I remember it, Steve-O looked like he took a lot of pain when we got in the vehicle and did the shot.

Filming the movie wasn't really much different from filming the TV show. It was still low-budget, guerrilla-style production, with two real exceptions: the opening and closing scenes. We wanted to start and finish the movie with a bang, so setting up and shooting those segments became a completely different process from what we were used to.

The opening sequence involved packing the entire cast into an over-size shopping cart and rolling us downhill on a bridge in downtown L.A. It may sound like fun, but in order to get the scene right, we had to shoot the thing over and over and over. This went on for two days. Spike Jonze was in charge instead of Tremaine, and getting it the way he wanted required repetition. We must have rolled down that bridge sixty fucking times. That was probably the first time *Jackass* ever felt like actual work to any of us.

The closing sequence was even more involved. All of us were made

up to look like ninety-year-old men still trying to film *Jackass* in the year 2063. The shoot required the cast to show up at 5 or 6 a.m. to undergo hours of makeup and prosthetics. It was a pricey three-day shoot—I think they blew through about $750,000 on it, which by cheapskate *Jackass* standards is a lot. To protect their investment, the studio wanted the entire cast quarantined in a hotel down near the shoot the night before, so nobody could fuck things up by getting too wasted to turn up on time.

The day before the shoot, the cast loaded into a van to drive down to this hotel. I'd just finished filming *Cribs* for MTV and was on day two or three of one of my usual sleepless coke benders. Dunlap was with me. We were constantly collecting footage for my DVDs, so in order to give him something to film I began pounding on the van's ceiling. Soon this escalated into Bam, Dunn, Wee-Man, Preston, Dave, and me tearing this van to pieces. We ripped up the seats, tore out the wiring, kicked out the windows, and laid waste to nearly every inch of that vehicle, while Dunlap recorded the whole thing.

We'd assumed the van was a rental, but as it turned out, it belonged to a local Teamsters union and they were fucking pissed. Trip Taylor, one of the film's executive producers, confronted us and chewed our asses out. Apparently, it was going to cost $30,000 to replace this van. What was so funny about it was that by the time Trip unleashed this shitstorm on us, the entire cast had already been transformed into ninety-year-old men, courtesy of the very talented makeup staff. So if anyone had walked by they would've seen Trip furiously berating a bunch of decrepit old men.

Trip also had an ugly confrontation with Dunlap at the hotel over this incident. He insisted Dunlap hand over the footage of the van's destruction. Dunlap, ever the sneaky bastard, had anticipated this demand and had already hidden two of the three videotapes. He turned the remaining one over to Trip, but we ended up using the footage Dunlap had hidden on my second DVD.

I'm sure this episode did nothing to improve Dunlap's reputation among the *Jackass* higher-ups. For Tremaine, *Jackass* was his baby and Dunlap was a scavenger, circling around the edges of the operation, making money off the scraps. All the cast members, except for Knoxville and Ehren, joined one of Dunlap's tours at one point or another, but legally, these events could never be billed as live *Jackass* shows. They had to be billed as "the stars of *Jackass* live onstage." It was a subtle difference that satisfied the lawyers but I'm sure annoyed the fuck out of Tremaine.

TREMAINE: I never really trusted Dunlap. He just came off like he was going to cash in on our name and put it out there. I wasn't that into that. I wanted the guys to do well, and I was psyched that Steve was taking the *Jackass* thing and making something of it, but I didn't want anything representing *Jackass* to not be affiliated with me and Knoxville.

I understood his feelings about Dunlap, but Tremaine and Knoxville were in a much different position than the rest of the cast. As producers and creators of *Jackass*, they were getting paid well on every dollar the franchise made, whereas most of the rest of us were compensated on a far more modest scale. I don't begrudge them the money— they earned it and deserved it—but they never really encouraged the rest of us to do anything that didn't directly benefit them. Certainly Tremaine and Knoxville weren't going to get me paid thousands of dollars to go get loaded, score chicks, and have a great time. Dunlap did. In fact, by this time, I was making at least as much money from the tours and the sales of the first video as I was from the movie and TV series combined. And, in retrospect, all the work I did with Dunlap helped make me a bigger star than I would've been through *Jackass* alone. If you look at the TV series, I'm not really all that heavily featured in it. The tours and videos raised my profile in a way that ultimately made me much more valuable to the *Jackass* brand.

When the movie came out that fall, it was a hit. I remember Knox-ville calling me the day after the release and telling me we were number one at the box office. The studio was particularly overjoyed: the movie had been made for about $6 million and ended up grossing more than $75 million worldwide.

My deal for the film was worse than crappy, but I was completely ignorant about all that stuff at the time. I didn't have an agent negotiating for me, and the lawyer I was using was incompetent. Considering I was one of the stars of a number one movie, I still lived like a pauper. This was drilled home to me after I watched my episode of *Cribs* on MTV. At the end of the episode, they previewed the following week's show, which would include the home of Sevendust drummer Morgan Rose. I shared a trashed two-bedroom apartment with a male stripper while the drummer from some middling nu-metal band I'd never heard of was living in what looked like a goddamn palace and driving a Ferrari. Go figure.

THE TOURS had begun as stunt shows filled with booze-and-drug-fueled mayhem, but it didn't take long for them to degenerate into shows of booze-and-drug-fueled mayhem with much less emphasis on the stunts. I'd saunter onstage already wasted, then spend my time up there drinking more and occasionally having audience members come up to get kicked in the nuts, punched in the face, or show their tits. It was no longer about the cool tricks I'd do—the whole point was just to see how fucked up I could get. It should come as no great shock that this had some negative consequences.

In July 2002, I had a show at a place called the Abyss in Houma, Louisiana, a small city in the bayou country south of New Orleans. I was onstage that night, doing my usual coke-addled rambling and swigging from a huge bottle of tequila I kept at the foot of the stage. At one point, some kid down front jumped onstage and tried to swipe the tequila but was swiftly neutralized by the bouncers. I was pretty impressed, so I challenged the audience: "Who wants to come up here and see if they can run past the bouncers?"

A scrawny nineteen-year-old guy a few rows back from the stage was jumping up and down, waving his arms in the air. I felt like I had to give him a shot. He came up onstage and I counted "One . . . two . . . three!" He ran into the line of bouncers and was stopped dead in his tracks. The whole thing seemed like it was going to be really anticlimactic, but then one of the bouncers picked the kid up and slammed him down, spiking his head onto the stage. The kid was out cold, twitching. It was an ugly, ugly scene.

An ambulance came and carted him away. I knew it was bad, and for just a few seconds, I froze up onstage, staring out into the audience. But then the old maxim "The show must go on" kicked in, and I picked up right where we'd left off. We even had a second guy do the same stunt (fortunately with less dire results). But when the show finished a few minutes later, I was worried. I didn't know what kind of shape that poor kid was in, but he hadn't looked good at all. Even the morally slippery Dunlap seemed shaken. After the show, he told me, "You're gonna hear about that again." The kid had signed a release form, but I had no confidence that it would shield us from responsibility.

For a little while though, I didn't hear anything about it. We finished two more tour dates and returned to California. Then, about two weeks later, I was back in my apartment in West Hollywood, sleeping off a bender, when Schliz banged on my door and woke me up.

"Steve, you've really got to get up," he said. "This is important." I stumbled out of bed to find three LAPD officers at my apartment door.

"Stephen Glover," one of them said. "We've got to arrest you."

There was a warrant out of Louisiana for me that carried with it a staggering $1.12 million bail. That whopping sum had landed me at the top of the LAPD fugitive division's Most Wanted List. The charges were principal to second-degree battery for the kid getting spiked on his head, and felony obscenity for stapling my nut sack to my leg, which

I did quite regularly. Strangely enough, it was the obscenity charge that appeared to be more serious. It carried a $1 million bail, whereas the bail for the battery was a mere $120,000. I was also facing up to eight years in prison if I was found guilty on both charges.

The LAPD officers were cool with me. I remember one of them telling me, "My son is going to be so bummed that I had to do this. He's a huge fan." Frankly, it was a miracle those cops walked in while I was in hibernation mode and not when I had my face buried in a mountain of blow.

I was taken to the Twin Towers Correctional Facility in downtown L.A. and put into protective custody, which is essentially reserved for celebrities or anyone else who might get hassled in the regular prison population. They called it the Robert Downey Jr. Block.

This was my first experience with protective custody and it had its perks. There was a TV visible from my cell and I had privacy enough to be able to jerk off whenever I wanted. On the other hand, all that solitude doesn't make the time go any quicker. And being that my bail was more than a million dollars, I wasn't going anywhere anytime soon.

Jail sucked. I was scared shitless that I might be going to prison for a long time. I was also having this weird problem with claustrophobia. I'm not sure what caused it, but it may have had something to do with all the ketamine I'd been snorting. I'd get inside my own head and start thinking, *Oh no, what if I can't breathe?* As soon as I thought that, I'd start getting really paranoid about it. I'd be overcome with the sense that I *actually* couldn't breathe. It was the same way I felt when I was swimming with those whale sharks, but instead of being sixty feet below the surface of the ocean, it was the bars and cement that were sending me into a panic. It was pure hell.

After five days in jail—it felt like longer—an attorney that Berk hired got my bail reduced to $150,000. I didn't have that much money either, but I borrowed it from a shady accountant Berk set me up with and posted bail. Rather than trade my prison-issue clothes and shoes back for my own stuff, I decided to walk out of jail onto the streets of downtown L.A. wearing my light blue "L.A. County" prison smock and black "L.A. County" slippers. I hadn't brought my wallet with me when I was arrested and hadn't arranged for anyone to pick me up, so I had to hitch a ride back to my apartment with some kids I met on the street outside the jail.

I had a month between my release and when I'd need to return to Louisiana to turn myself in and be arraigned. Berk said it was entirely possible that they would drug-test me when I did, so he warned me to keep my nose clean. No drugs, no strip clubs, no trouble. I quit everything, except for booze, which was still allowed. It was during this unusual month of drug-free living that Berk suggested I get insured.

"This is probably the only window of time when you'll ever be able to pass a drug test," he told me. "So we're going to get you insured— health insurance, life insurance, the whole deal."

I was down with health insurance but wasn't sure why I needed life insurance. Berk convinced me that with my lifestyle I'd be crazy not to get it. I agreed, but only on two specific conditions. The first was that my niece, Cindy's then newborn daughter, Cassie, would be the sole beneficiary. The second condition was that I didn't want to know the results of any of the medical exams I'd have to take. Whether I was totally healthy or deathly ill, I didn't want to know anything about it. My reasoning was that if I was in perfect health I'd suddenly have something to lose, and if I had some horrible disease like AIDS— which seemed within the realm of possibility considering that I'd had plenty of unprotected sex with sketchy strangers over the previous few years—I'd be cripplingly depressed. Either way, ignorance seemed like bliss to me. Essentially, I'd apply for life insurance but I never wanted to know if I actually got it.

Not too long after, I got a call from the insurance company asking me to do a follow-up interview.

"Follow-up what?" I asked. "Are you telling me I passed the physical for life insurance?"

I had. Then I asked for confirmation that Cassie was the policy's sole beneficiary. She was not: Berk and Dunlap had made themselves beneficiaries of two-thirds of this $3 million policy. Apparently, Berk and Dunlap always saw this more as insurance for their business than my life. This life insurance thing grew into a big problem. After all, the guys whose entire business revolved around getting me to engage in incredibly dangerous, often life-threatening behavior put themselves in a position to profit handsomely should any of that behavior result in my untimely death. They claim I knew about this arrangement and knowingly signed off on it. I didn't.

As it happened, turning myself in to authorities in Louisiana for the arraignment ended up being no big deal. There was no drug test. I merely showed up, had a quick hearing in which I pleaded not guilty on both charges, got fingerprinted, had my mug shot taken, turned over a little more than $5,000 in bail money, and was released. Never even saw the inside of a cell there. All the cops and even the prosecutors were exceedingly cool to me. The impression I got was that the district attorney goosed up the whole case to get some free publicity to boost his election campaign to become a district judge.

The D.A. wasn't the only one who got free publicity out of this. As a guy who was getting paid to be outrageous, I fully believed that for me there was no such thing as negative publicity. After my arraignment, I sent out an e-mail to family and friends crowing about the coverage the arrest had gotten me: "To consider every newspaper article to be a print ad, every mention on television (It's official I was on CNN Headline News) to be a television commercial, likewise for radio," I wrote, "one could consider me to be the most effective purchaser of media attention in the country."

In the end, the whole thing never went to trial. The obscenity charge was dismissed, and I got the other charge knocked down to a misdemeanor. I was sentenced to a year of probation and had to make a $5,000 donation to a local women's shelter.

Meanwhile, the kid who got slammed on his head had some minor injuries but ended up being okay. In fact, I didn't hear much from him until late 2004, when I found out he'd filed a civil suit against me almost two years earlier. Berk had hired a lawyer in Louisiana to deal with it. So I was served in absentia down in Louisiana and remained absent at each proceeding through 2003 and 2004. Eventually my business manager got a bill from the lawyer in Louisiana and called her to find out what it was all about. At that point, depositions were supposed to begin in two weeks, so it was pretty late in the game to be finding all this out.

I was initially told that I stood to lose either "a whole lot" or "everything." I'm not at liberty to reveal the terms of the settlement that we eventually reached, but I think it's safe to say it didn't turn out to be quite that bad.

My relationship with Dunlap and Berk was never the same because of my feelings about how they handled this Louisiana incident. Looking back now, it's shocking to me that I didn't sever all ties with them right there and then, but I guess between the tours and the videos, our business had grown so tangled that I wouldn't have known where to start peeling us apart. Besides, even after *Jackass: The Movie* had debuted at number one, I didn't really have any reputable managers or agents banging down my door. I stuck with Dunlap and Berk for nearly two years after the mess in Louisiana, but the seeds of our dissolution were planted and growing.

14

HOW DO YOU SAY "POO RUBBER" IN SWEDISH?

Despite my abundant legal problems and my issues with Dunlap and Berk, by late 2002 I felt great about the direction in which my life was headed. It was apparent that whatever fallout there still could be from the Louisiana incident, I was definitely not going to prison over it, and that was a relief. Although I'd never wanted to know the results of my medical exams, my clean bill of health gave me a fresh lease on life. All the highly risky, objectionable behavior I'd engaged in had done me no lasting harm. Also, for the first time in my life—or at least the first time since I'd left home—I felt like I had financial security. *Jackass: The Movie* had been a hit, my first DVD, *Don't Try This at Home,* sold well, and the second, *Don't Try This at Home, Volume II: The Tour*, would be out by the end of the year. The tours were consistently playing to packed houses, and Pontius, Tremaine, and I were pitching MTV a new show, *Wildboyz*, that looked promising. I could reliably go to an ATM and withdraw hundreds of dollars without breaking a sweat.

This newfound financial stability also changed my relationship with my dad for the better. While I was roaming the country as a fuckup, Dad and I could never really connect. Everything was always tense. It wasn't as if he didn't love me or wasn't supportive, but I just wasn't available for a good relationship with him. I wasn't proud of myself, so how could I expect him to be proud of me? Now I felt like I was really standing on my own two feet. I was twenty-eight and finally could talk to my dad like a man, not a little boy. That was better for both of us.

The other thing contributing to my overall happiness was my new girlfriend, Candy. I'd met her in August at a bar in New York City. She was only eighteen at the time and had just graduated from high school a few months earlier. I got onstage at a bar and showed off my then freshly inked back tattoo. Afterward, Candy came over and asked me if I wanted to smoke a joint with her. She knew the path to my heart.

We went and smoked together and I couldn't stop staring at her. She was so young and sweet and beautiful. She gave me her number that night and I called the next day. After that, we started spending a lot of time together. Dunlap and Berk had an apartment in New York City, and she would stay with me there all the time. She'd frequently travel with me too, and when she didn't we'd talk on the phone every day. We were genuinely in love.

Candy was innocent but open and eager for new experiences. I was far from the most responsible guide. In December of that year, she was with me for most of the five straight days I spent holed up at the Ramada on Lexington Avenue in New York, smoking PCP. PCP is as powerful as any drug I've ever done. It's in the same class as ketamine, but more unpredictable. Your emotions become magnified. You might have trouble speaking, or become uncoordinated or affectionate or angry or psychotic, or some combination of all these things. It's almost like having an out-of-body experience, and it can go on for days and days after you finish smoking it. Candy and I were having such a fucked-up trip that on the fifth day we actually threw the rest of the PCP out the hotel window. For all the bad experiences I've had on ketamine, I never once threw any away.

I felt the effects of that PCP for at least a week afterward. It's all chronicled in a video called *PCP Saved My Life* that was eventually packaged along with my third DVD, *Out on Bail.* In this PCP video, I run around, talking a mile a minute about how much I love everybody, how I make people happy for a living, and all the "miracles" that are happening all around me. Whenever people I meet mention *PCP Saved My Life*, I can't help but wonder why they are so psyched to meet me.

At a certain point during this PCP episode, everything turned dark. I began thinking about my mom. Her condition had been steadily worsening over the years. She was on a regimen of antibiotics to fight off various infections, but she'd gradually build up immunity to them, so it was a constant struggle to find new ones. I was home only three or four times a year and horrible as it may sound, when I wasn't, I did everything I could to keep from thinking about her. All the drugs were a great distraction, a great way of staying out of my own head, but in the end those emotions were too powerful to ignore forever.

On that *PCP Saved My Life* video, there is footage of a phone conversation I had with my sister just before going onstage one night in New Hampshire. I'm speaking so fast that it's dizzying, but amid all the babbling, drug-addled nonsense is a picture of where my head, heart, and soul were at back then that's probably more honest and accurate than anything I could say about it now:

CINDY: I'm worried about you. But I've been worried about you pretty much every day since . . .
ME: WellIwasworriedaboutMomandnowI'vemademillionsof dollarstomakesurethatshe'shappy. Soyoudon'thavetobitchtome abouthermoneyrunningoutbecauseit'snotgoingtorunout,Cindy!

Sodon'tbitchaboutthatanymoreortalktomeanymoreabouthow muchweloveeachother.

CINDY: Okay, let me tell you what I'm worried about—

ME: Allright,Imightactuallyhanguponyou.

CINDY: I just want to make sure you're okay—

ME: Iamokay,Cindy! Ifyoucan'tfigurethatoutthroughallthe correspondencethenI'mreallygoingtohanguponyou. Sothelast thingI'mgoingtosaytoyouCindyisIloveyoualot. I'mabouttoget onstageatasold-outshowwhereeverybodythinksI'mreallycool. ThankyouforyourconcernandtellDadandCindyandfuckin'Mom andfuckin'yourbabythatIloveyoualландI'mgonnagokickassand bereallyfamousrightnowandmakealotofmoneytotakecareof Momandifthat'saproblemandifyou'refuckin'concernedabout thatCindthenI'msorry.

CINDY: That's good, Squirt . . .

ME: Allright. ThenI'mgoingtogokickbuttonstage.We'remaking thousandsofdollarstogetwastedandmakepeoplehappy.

After that conversation I walked onstage, grabbed the microphone, and yelled, "Tonight's show is for my fuckin' mother and I want you all to scream louder than that for her!" I was a mess.

ALMOST EVERY spare minute I had in those days Dunlap filled with touring. We went all around the country, and to Canada, Mexico, the Caribbean, Australia, New Zealand, and throughout Europe. The shows themselves continued their general slide toward debauchery for its own sake, but that only made them more fun for me. Well, "fun" might not be the exact right word, but for a long time I felt like if I had to live six months of my life on a permanent loop, those first six months of 2003 wouldn't be a bad place to be stuck. The fact that I remember the lifestyle I had back then so fondly qualifies me as one truly messed up son of a bitch. Sure, I was happy to be healthy, financially stable, and in love, but what I was putting my body through with drugs and stunts on that tour was borderline suicidal. Days into one of my coke benders, I decided to let Ryan Dunn choke me unconscious six times in a row. (Search for "Steve-O chokes" on YouTube to see it yourself.) That was unbelievably dumb and dangerous but hardly an unusual example of what was going on during this time period.

I was doing dumb and dangerous stuff all the time. That spring, I decided it'd be really funny to film myself trying to smuggle drugs from Norway to Sweden while we were on tour. The idea had been brewing for a long time. A couple years earlier, when Pontius and I were still neck deep in our homeless contest, one of our frequent crash pads was Stephanie Hodge's apartment. At some point, she went out of town and left us to house-sit and take care of her boyfriend's dog, Suki. One night, we went out to a bar and brought home a pair of Danish girls. I took one of them to a bedroom, and when we finished having sex, I took off my soiled condom and tied it in a knot. I did this a lot. Sometimes after tying it, I'd twirl the rubber around and playfully whip the girl with it. I thought this was hilarious.

On this particular night, I remember flinging the condom across the room and then going into the living room to smoke a cigarette. When I did, I saw Suki run into the bedroom. Later, when I went to pick up the condom off the floor, it was gone. It didn't take long to put two and two together: Suki, a tiny, ten-pound Boston terrier, had scarfed down the rubber.

I was worried this condom might get tangled up in Suki's intestines and kill her, so for the next three days, I monitored her movement as much as possible. On the morning of the fourth day, I woke up and found it in a pile of her poop. It was in remarkably good condition, and I remember thinking, *If a dog can do it, I can do it.* In fact, I felt like I *owed* it to this poor dog to swallow a condom myself. I didn't really see the point in downing a rubber full of semen, but it was only a short mental hop from there to the idea of turning myself into a drug mule just for fun. The more I thought about it, the more it made sense: between my love for drugs and my love for video footage, it was the perfect stunt—swallow a condom full of weed in one country, fly to another, shit it out, smoke it, and film the whole thing.

It took until May 2003 before I finally made it happen. We were on tour in Norway, getting ready to fly to Sweden, and I was all jacked up on coke. I had a lot of weed and hash with me and decided now was the time to pull off "The Poo Rubber."

I jammed the weed into the condom without even breaking the buds off the stems, then put a piece of hash and a rolling paper in there, tied it up, and tried to swallow the whole thing. The problem was that it was *huge*. It got stuck in my throat and wouldn't come out. I kept swallowing and swallowing over and over but couldn't get the damn thing down. Then I tried puking it back up. So there I was, on my knees, finger down my throat, gagging, but all that was coming up was blood. I started to freak out. I thought I might choke to death. A couple of the other guys on the tour tried to convince me I needed to go to the hospital, but the mere suggestion brought out the bravado in me: "No, the tour must go on!"

We flew to Sweden and after about twelve hours, I was pretty sure the condom had made its way into my stomach, although my throat still hurt like hell. I did a series of interviews to promote the tour and never failed to mention that I'd just swallowed this condom full of pot. Soon, the story was in all the local newspapers. I even posted something about it on my Web site. For the next six days, we toured through Sweden. After the show in Stockholm, I got to the hotel, climbed on the toilet, and my ass exploded. I looked into the bowl and there was the poo rubber. I pulled it out, opened it with my teeth, and then spent all night smoking the weed and hash. Part of the appeal of the entire stunt was so that I could toke up, look into the camera, and say, "That's some good shit." It was a *long* way to go for that punch line.

The following morning, as I was walking out of the hotel, I was ambushed by undercover cops. They immediately began insisting, "You have drugs in your body."

I denied everything. They'd read the interviews in which I'd bragged about the stunt but I claimed I'd only been joking. When we got to the police station and the cops began searching my backpack, the very first thing they pulled out was a little ecstasy pill with a smiley face on it. *Oh, shit.* Meanwhile, back at the hotel, the cops had raided my room and found all the stems. I got the feeling I might be in Sweden for a while.

The thing is, the ecstasy and the stems were relatively minor possession offenses. The cops were convinced the real prize was still in my system, so they took me to the hospital to draw my blood and get me an X-ray. The drug laws in Sweden were such that if they found any cocaine in my blood, I could be charged with possession. Lucky for me, I'd been unable to get my hands on any coke since getting to Sweden a week earlier, and since coke generally stays in your system for only three days, my tests came up clean. When it was time for the X-ray, I was marched through the hospital hallways in handcuffs as the other patients and their families stared at me with a mixture of fascination and horror. I then was laid down on a cold slab underneath a giant X-ray machine.

I was actually pretty happy to be getting the X-ray. I figured it would show that I had no drugs in my body and then I'd be released. But the cops told me that the X-ray revealed an object in my intestines that was one centimeter long, half a centimeter wide, and very sharp. They thought it had PCP in it and told me they believed I was using it as an anesthetic for my painful stunts. I told them I had no idea what the object in my intestines was, which was true. They decided to lock me up. I spent the next five days in a jail cell, smoking cigarettes, eating junk food, reading an Anne Rice novel they'd given me, and shitting into plastic bags, which the cops would then pick through, looking for the drugs I'd already smoked.

At one point, I was hauled in front of a judge, who'd read the account of the entire incident on my Web site. I insisted to the judge that the whole thing was just a ruse. "I thought it would be funny if I told a joke that caused the Swedish taxpayers to pay the police to dig through my poo," I told him. After this brilliant legal argument, I was sent straight back to my cell.

We were allowed one hour outside each day on the roof of the jail. On my fifth day in lockup, I met a prisoner up there who was a heroin addict. At that point in my life, I had a lot of curiosity about heroin. I'd never done it but had this vague plan in the back of my head: If life ever got too awful to deal with anymore, I'd deliberately become a heroin addict. It seemed like a great way to commit suicide. Talking to this guy completely changed my mind. The way he talked about heroin, it didn't sound like the blissful fog I'd imagined. It was all degradation, desperation, and demoralization.

I remember asking him, "Can you ever have enough money to stay high on heroin for life?" He promised me that whatever I had, I'd blow it all on heroin and that killing myself would be next to impossible if I was doing it regularly. I'd have too high a tolerance to overdose. That really messed up my future plans to become a smack addict, and I'm glad it did. As bad as my drug habit got, I've never to this day tried heroin, and I'm unbelievably thankful for that junkie I met on the roof of that Stockholm prison who steered me clear of it.

Later that same day, I was taken back to the hospital for another X-ray and told that the object in my intestines had moved only three centimeters. This news convinced the cops that whatever it was, it wasn't coming out any time soon. They decided to charge me with possession of the ecstasy and marijuana stems that they'd found, and let me go after paying a fine of about $6,000. I still have no idea what that thing was in my intestines, or whether the cops were just bluffing.

Back in the U.S. my arrest had been big news—it was on CNN, *Dateline*, MTV News—which, for a guy who'd do just about anything for attention, seemed like a pretty fair reward for my detour into the Swedish justice system. Tremaine, however, was not amused. He was in the process of trying to get visas sorted out so Pontius and I could travel to South Africa to film the *Wildboyz* pilot. Let me tell you, when you're trying to get a visa to do a show about international travel, there aren't many things you can do to complicate the situation more than getting global coverage of your arrest and incarceration on international drug smuggling charges.

When I got out of jail, I met back up with Dunlap and the rest of the touring brigade, which at that time included Bam, Wee-Man, and Candy. As much as I was enjoying the lunatic life I was leading, when I was locked up I'd come to the realization that my relationship with cocaine was out of control. With booze, weed, and pills, I could get wasted, go to sleep at night, and wake up feeling relatively normal the next day. As soon as I touched coke, I was locked into multiple-day sleepless benders. Any semblance of normalcy was gone, and I couldn't stop myself from doing it. I'd look at my schedule and just hope that anything really important I had to do would land in between coke benders. As I sat in that cell, missing Candy and thinking about how much I loved her, I realized how shitty it was to let coke rule my life the way I did. I knew it would make Candy incredibly happy if I stopped doing it, so when she and I had a moment alone, I told her that I was quitting coke. Well, sort of. What I said was, "I'm not telling you I'm never doing cocaine again, but I am telling you that I don't feel like doing it now." It was the most noncommittal declaration of all time. I knew I had a problem and needed to stop, but I was reserving the right to change my mind about that at any time.

15

MY SON IS A SHITFUCK

As it turned out, my arrest in Sweden didn't prevent
me from getting that visa to go to South Africa, and
in June we flew down there to tape the *Wildboyz* pilot.
The basic idea for the show was that Pontius and I
would travel the world, interacting with wild animals
and indigenous people, and then our exploits would
all be presented in a mock-educational format.

When we got to South Africa, things got out of hand
almost immediately. Pontius and I were staying at a
five-star resort/lodge outside a town called Gansbaai
in this nice, rustic wooden cabin. It was on the ground
floor, alongside a similar cabin, with a third one sitting atop it. Each place had a bedroom, a living room,
and a little egg-shaped fireplace with a long metal
tube that served as a chimney jutting from the top of
it into the living room ceiling.

On our third or fourth night in South Africa, Pontius

and I were sitting around our cabin getting drunk along with this shark expert lady who we were working with down there. We'd been told if it got chilly at night to make a fire, so I loaded all the precut logs and the wax blocks that were sitting in a basket in the living room into the fireplace and then lit it. The fire was soon raging. The metal chimney tube got so hot that it was glowing bright orange and I was lighting cigarettes off it. All seemed fine until it wasn't.

Suddenly, flames burst out where the chimney tube entered the ceiling. There was a kettle on the stove in the kitchenette. I ran over, filled it with water, and made a feeble attempt to throw it on the fire but it was too little, too late. By the time I threw a second kettleful of water, the whole ceiling in the middle of the living room crashed down with flames pouring out of it. The fire had been raging above the ceiling long before we figured it out. We had no choice but to bail.

The people in the two cabins attached to ours were in real danger. It was the middle of the night and they were sound asleep. We ran around yelling, "Fire! Fire!" trying to rouse everyone. There was a honeymooning British couple in the cabin directly above ours and we had to climb up there, smash out their windows, and help get them out.

We were drunk, covered in soot, and bloody from busting out the windows when the fire trucks arrived. They couldn't do much. All three cabins burned to the ground. I thought for sure that *Wildboyz* was cooked. MTV would see that we were more trouble than we were worth, the production would be shut down, and we'd have to pay for all this damage.

TREMAINE: I was asleep and one of our production guys, Guch (pronounced "Gooch"), woke me up. He's like, "Jeff, wake up! There's a fire!" I jump up in my bed and Guch is a silhouette in front of this inferno glowing orange. I'm like, "Holy fucking shit!" I ran down there and it was a blazing mess. Once I found out everyone was safe I was super pissed because I thought for sure we're going home the next day and that we had blown our chance. I'm baffled to this day why that didn't happen. I don't think anyone at MTV ever heard another word about it.

That night, they moved Pontius and me to another cabin in the resort and nobody ever bothered us about it again. I'm not sure how, but it didn't cost us or the production a cent. We went on filming as planned. What's more, that honeymooning British couple were journalists. They later wrote a story about how the *Wildboyz* saved their lives. We'd gotten drunk and burned down part of a resort, but we were portrayed as heroes.

FOR PONTIUS and me, swimming with sharks had kind of become our thing, and we planned a climactic stunt for that pilot that would put our previous shark adventures to shame: we were going to swim with great whites and do so outside a protective shark cage. I couldn't think of anything that would make us bigger badasses. MTV approved this idea as long as we did it with a local guide named Andre "Sharkman" Hartman, who was *the* expert on great white sharks.

Unfortunately, the day before we were supposed to go out with him, he canceled on us. Apparently, some oil tycoons offered him an obscene amount of money to take them out the same day. We couldn't reschedule and MTV made it clear we couldn't swim outside the cage with the great whites unless he was supervising. We were crushed. Swimming inside a shark cage would be completely pointless.

Pontius and I dealt with this dilemma the way we normally did: we went to a bar and got drunk. There, we devised a plan. We may have to film from in the cage, but we made a secret pact to jump in the water on the other side of the boat and then swim to the cage before getting in. That way we'd have some time out of the cage with the sharks. A guy sitting next to us overheard the conversation and offered what sounded like some pretty informed advice.

"If a great white shark finds you swimming, he's going to be curious and take a bite out of you," he said. "He won't like the way you taste, so he's not going to eat you, but you'll bleed to death. But the great white can't see its own body, because its eyes are so close to its nose. If you jump off the boat on top of the shark or right next to him, you'll startle him and he'll bolt."

We continued talking to this guy, soaking up his wisdom, and then he introduced himself. It was Andre Hartman. It just so happened he was drinking in the same bar we were that night. As the evening wore on and the drinks flowed, we convinced him to cancel his date with the oil barons. The following morning, he took us out on his boat, and Pontius and I jumped in the water not three feet from a great white. The moral I took away from that story was that sometimes drinking away your problems in a bar is exactly the right way to solve them.

WHEN I got back to L.A., I moved out of my apartment with Schliz and into a place with Candy. We had about enough time to put down our bags before we left to go on the Lollapalooza tour, where they'd booked my traveling carnival of sins to headline the second stage for a stretch of shows. The tour went okay. It was my first time bunking on a rock-and-roll tour bus, which made staying drunk easier than ever before. I got arrested one day for public urination, and then a buddy and I hurled a bike rack through the plate-glass window of a hotel lobby later the same day after being informed that the hotel had no vacancies. I can't believe that I never got in trouble for that drunken tantrum.

MTV picked up *Wildboyz* and I spent much of the summer and early fall traveling for the first season. Our first trips were to Alaska,

Australia, New Zealand, and Florida, and we'd eventually hit every continent except Antarctica during the show's four-season run.

Once Candy moved out to California, things started to crumble between us. I felt like she'd gotten the fame bug and wanted to be a star herself. That in and of itself might not have been a problem, but I believed she started to see me as an embarrassment, as someone holding her back. I got the sense she felt she could do better than me. There's a distinct possibility I was just paranoid and that those ideas were as much a projection of my feeling like I wasn't good enough for Candy as they were anything else, but even if it was just my perception, it quickly poisoned the waters between us.

Although Candy's age hadn't initially bothered me, with time I began to feel like I was corrupting her. She was young and had her whole life in front of her. She needed to get away from me before I ruined it. I was already twenty-nine, but we both had a lot of growing to do and I was convinced we couldn't do it together. I tried to tell her all these things but did so without much in the way of grace or charm. It came from a good place but didn't really lead to one. She'd moved to California to be with me, and now I was saying I didn't want that anymore. I didn't handle the whole thing very well.

There was a lot of yelling and crying. Then I got belligerently drunk and destroyed a bunch of shit in our apartment. Along with my friend Tommy Caudill and his buddy Ty, I broke out windows, bashed in walls, and fucked up some appliances. I also posted a bunch of shit on the Internet about trying to kill the pope. The cops were eventually called to the apartment—for the destruction, not the pope threats—so Ty and I took off and went rampaging around Hollywood. We stopped and drank with a bunch of gay guys who were having a barbecue, then ended up in front of this titty bar called Crazy Girls.

There was a photo shoot going on outside the strip club and when they saw me, someone invited me over to be part of it. It was a pretty elaborate production, with big expensive lighting rigs and fancy cameras. Someone said something I didn't like—I can't remember what—and I just went on a tear. I destroyed their lighting equipment, knocked a camera out of some guy's hands and did an incredible amount of damage in a matter of seconds. I was out of my mind.

I then walked into the strip club and started talking to one of the dancers. Ty followed, but only to urge me to get the fuck out of there. Apparently, the guys in charge of the photo shoot were some gangster types and they were looking for me. We made a getaway out the back of the club, jumped over a fence, and ran. Next stop was a tattoo parlor on the Sunset Strip. Both Ty and I got "SHIT" and "FUCK" tattooed on our knuckles. To this day, I'm incredibly proud of the place I've carved out for myself in life that these tattoos haven't really held me back one bit. I can't imagine Ty has had it as easy. After that, we cruised over to the Rainbow Bar & Grill, which was one of my favorite hangouts back then.

Eventually, I came home that night, kicked a hole in my apartment door, passed out on the sofa, and pissed all over myself. The next morning, I told Candy that was it. We were through. Then I called a cab and went to the airport. I was still covered in piss and hadn't even bothered to grab a bag. I just had to get the fuck out of there.

I bought a ticket to Florida. For some reason, I felt like the only place I could go at that point was home. To Mom.

I left a huge mess behind me. We were immediately evicted from that apartment. Simonetti and a few of my other buddies moved all my furniture and belongings into a storage unit, but Candy was homeless, albeit temporarily. The gangsters whose photo shoot I trashed apparently spent the next few days looking for me around that apartment, but I was gone.

WHEN I got to Florida, it turned out Mom was in the hospital. I went straight from the airport to see her. Her condition had deteriorated so much that she had a "Do Not Resuscitate" order on her bed.

When I got there, I could tell right away she didn't have much fight left in her.

Growing up, I don't think I ever would've described my mom as a fighter, but for the five years after her aneurysm she was an absolute warrior. She had fought like hell to stay alive, but now she was exhausted. I didn't really know what to do, so I walked over to her bedside and said, "Hey Ma, check out my new tattoos," and raised my knuckles for her to see. She kind of squinted at them, struggling to make them out. "Shit . . . Fuck," she said, and giggled. She repeated the words a couple times slowly, then said, "My son is a shitfuck!" and laughed even louder. I was laughing, too, and crying at the same time.

Being able to make Mom laugh in that state made me feel better than anything had in a long time. When she laughed it seemed to make all the pain go away—hers and mine. I was never sure how much she understood about what my life had become—that I'd been on TV and in a number one movie. Sometimes I'd tell her these things and she'd stare back blankly. But other times, she'd make some sort of crack at my expense and prove that she was still in there. About a year earlier, I'd been in very preliminary talks with a publisher interested in publishing a book about my life. When I reported this news to Mom, she looked at me and responded, "And just who is going to write this masterpiece?" I loved it when she made fun of me like that. At that point, I'd do anything to make her happy.

PONTIUS AND I were scheduled to be presenters at the MTV Latin Video Music Awards in Miami a week or so after I'd gotten to Florida. MTV put us up at the Sagamore on South Beach the night before. Pontius hardly ever did coke and I hadn't touched the stuff in six months, but for some reason, he suggested getting some. It took me about half a second to be convinced of the wisdom of this idea.

"Absolutely," I told him. "I'll make a call."

It's really impossible for me to explain why after six months off coke, I so readily agreed to go right back to it. I hadn't even really missed it that much. I'd been busy working on *Wildboyz* and spending time with Candy, which made it pretty easy not to do coke. I felt like I was in much better physical and mental shape without it. But if logic applied to addiction, nobody would suffer from it. Once I got my hands on some coke that night, I just picked up right where I'd left off and became a full-blown cokehead again.

That night with Pontius in Miami was a total mess. It's probably easiest to explain *Hangover* style, starting at the end. I woke up the next day, with my right foot swollen up like a fleshy, purple and blue balloon. I'd broken a bone in my foot and dislocated my toe. Pontius woke up naked on the roof of an SUV and was taken by the cops to a mental hospital.

We'd done a bunch of coke and then split up from each other pretty early in the night. I'd busted my foot trying to do a back flip off a bar. I'd been so loaded that I carried on partying, walking from bar to bar with my pinky toe completely out of the socket and a broken metatarsal in my foot. When I eventually went to the hospital after the Latin VMAs, the X-ray was quite a sight: it showed my pinky toe just floating around on its own. They put a temporary cast on me, gave me some crutches, and sent me on my way. Days later, an orthopedic surgeon would give me an injection to dull the pain while he rammed the toe back into the socket.

PONTIUS: I don't remember getting up on the SUV. I know I was so out of it that I thought it was my bed. A guy we knew was walking to his condo and saw me sleeping on top of this SUV, naked, with my clothes folded beside me and my wallet and everything right there. He took everything and put it in his condo. I got woken up by the police and was very grumpy. According to the cops, I tried to start a fight with them and got pepper sprayed, which stopped me dead in my tracks. They took me to the psych ward of the hospital. Because I was naked, I put on some little gown but it fit only halfway around my waist, so my butt was hanging out. As I sobered up, I wanted to go back to my hotel but couldn't figure out the name of it. I was like, "Come on, I gotta get out of here. I've got to present at the Latin VMAs!" They eventually found where I was staying and dropped me off at the hotel in that little fuckin' gown.

Pontius and I actually presented at the VMAs—I had to be carried out onstage—and then I spent a couple more days hobbling around Miami on crutches before returning to Boca to see Mom. By this time, she'd moved out of the hospital and back home, but not because she was improving. There was simply nothing more the doctors could do for her.

We were given instructions to do what we could to make her comfortable. A hospice nurse came to the house and examined Mom. This nurse told us she was really impressed with the condition Mom was in. Considering she'd been immobile and suffering from bedsores and dozens of other ailments for years, Mom was really in good shape. It was clear, this nurse said, that somebody had taken incredible care of her.

I was both heartened and horrified by that observation. I'd thought Mom's life at that point couldn't be any worse, that she'd drawn the shortest fucking stick God had to offer. She'd been barely coherent for years and in constant pain. It seemed like a living hell. In my mind, in my experience, I couldn't factor in much room for worse. But here's this nurse whose entire job is seeing people on their deathbeds and she's saying that Mom is actually one of the *lucky* ones. In one sense, I felt really proud that Cindy and I (especially Cindy) had managed to do as well as we apparently had done with Mom. But I was equally terrified at the idea that "life" included this whole dark well of torturous existence even beyond what Mom had endured.

That knowledge that the end will come and it won't be pretty had always pervaded my thoughts. Since I was a teenager, I'd been gripped by the idea that the one thing we fear the most—death—is the only thing in life that we know we'll face. It all felt cosmically unfair. I already had an unreasonably negative outlook on life. The fact that Mom should be considered fortunate to be in the grisly condition she was in as she approached her final days only made any thoughts of the future all the more terrifying.

Mom died on November 7, 2003. Cindy was sitting next to her, holding her hand, when she took her last breath. I wanted no part of that. I was in the house but felt like Mom was too proud and wouldn't have wanted an audience for that moment. Cindy felt differently and wanted to be there, comforting her. I wasn't sure which one of us was right, but I guess our attitudes toward that final moment were a pretty good encapsulation of the way we'd dealt with Mom's aneurysm from the beginning.

The overwhelming emotion I felt afterward was relief. The end was not nearly as traumatic as the five years that preceded it. At least she was no longer suffering. In those final few days, we'd known it was coming; it was just a matter of when. I'm ashamed to say I spent a lot of that last week or so just trying to numb myself with drugs. I remember working through an entire bottle of GHB while spending one of those final days with Mom.

I've often thought about whether it would've been better—for Mom, for me, for Cindy—if Mom hadn't survived that aneurysm, if it had killed her five years earlier. Life became so physically painful for her, so filled with daily indignity and suffering, that maybe it would've been better not to have had to bear it. But she got to live long enough to see her children succeed in their chosen fields and to meet her granddaughter. And even if her quality of life was gravely compromised, the way she fought to maintain it right until the end makes me believe that she wanted those years. And more.

16

STEVE-O: INTERNATIONAL GOODWILL AMBASSADOR

From the start, *Wildboyz* was a slightly more professional operation than *Jackass* was in its early days, but no less risky. The fact that nobody ever got killed by a wild animal or condemned to a long stay in a foreign prison is nothing short of a freaking miracle. I truly believe we've had angels looking out for us, some sort of higher power that wanted us to keep doing what we were doing. I can think of no other way to explain how we got away with all the shit we did.

For starters, there was the drug smuggling. We were constantly toting weed with us from one country to the next. We had a few different methods. For the first trip to South Africa, we ground it up, compacted it, wrapped it in Saran Wrap, and then dropped it into a bottle of shampoo. That worked but wasn't ideal. We later learned it was possible to pack an eighth of weed down tightly into a tiny ball and place it in a natural crater in the soft, fleshy palate underneath your tongue and still talk normally. I also regularly put "The Poo Rubber" to practical use. From my painful experience in Sweden, I learned to pack the condoms much, much smaller. I'd typically swallow three or four poo rubbers before boarding an international flight. "Ass grass," is what we came to call it.

Most of the people in the *Wildboyz* crew who liked to smoke weed participated in this international drug smuggling operation. In fact, by the end of the show's run in 2005, we had a rule: you weren't allowed to smoke weed unless you were down for smuggling some. One guy would just walk through airports with it in his pocket. It's really unbelievable that none of us ever got caught.

Besides the animal stunts, everywhere we went for *Wildboyz* we always shot scenes with native tribes. Trip Taylor would generally ask that Chris and I be dressed up in the tribe's traditional garb and participate in their sacred rituals. As you can imagine, it often took a pretty delicate negotiation to get these tribes to agree to this—and in the case of the Seminoles in Florida and the Aborigines in Australia, there were definitely some tribe members who walked out—but Chris and I usually managed to win people over. We weren't trying to be demeaning or mean-spirited and that generally came across. You might think I'm kidding if I say that Chris and I were really goodwill ambassadors, but to the extent that two frequently drunken, goofball TV stars can be, we really were. To this day, I'm really proud of what we accomplished on that show.

Even though the travel for *Wildboyz* generally happened in increments of only a couple weeks at a time, it was intensely grueling. Tremaine kept everyone working their asses off. In retrospect, a lot of those trips we took—to Brazil, Argentina, Central America, India, Indonesia, Thailand, Kenya, Rwanda, and so on—kind of blend together. It's sometimes hard for me to differentiate one country from the next. I can't attribute that to how loaded I got all the time, either. We just did so much in so many places, and the pace and intensity of our work schedule was insane. At one point, in India and Indonesia, we filmed for twenty-nine days in a row. And they were twenty-nine *long* days.

Despite our hard work, we occasionally had to cut a few corners. I remember when Pontius and I were first on *The Tonight Show* to promote the *Wildboyz* Season One DVD, Jay Leno came backstage to chat with us before the show started. He brought up the stunt in our clip from our "South Africa" episode in which Pontius and I dressed up in a zebra costume and got chased down by two lions. In it, one lion eventually tears the head off the zebra costume and runs away with it.

"There's something fishy about that clip," Leno said to us. "For starters, that gravel. I've never heard of there being a gravel road on an African safari. Also, that lion must have worked with trainers. Because there's nothing in a lion's DNA that will make him go for that fake zebra's head."

Leno was sharp. That footage was actually filmed in California, not South Africa, and with captive lions from a company called Hollywood Animals. Although that's definitely cheating, there's nothing safe about having any kind of lion chase you down and pounce on something you're wearing on your head.

We didn't do that kind of thing too often, but there were some other occasions when we took liberties with the truth to make *Wildboyz* a better show. Any time you see Manny with us, if we're claiming to be anywhere other than the U.S., it's not true. Manny never traveled with us outside the country. So during one of our "India" episodes in Season Three, when he's in a raft with us right before a Bengal tiger jumps into the river and attacks our boat—that's another Hollywood Animal. When Manny sneaks up behind a male lion and grabs its tail in "Kenya"—that happened in California.

Sometimes, we tried to do a stunt the right way but it just didn't work out. In that same "Kenya" episode, Pontius and I lay down in a hammock that has flanks of meat hanging from it and hungry lions underneath it. We tried to do that in Kenya but didn't attract any animals, so we re-created it with Hollywood Animals in California. We had also brought that two-man zebra suit to South Africa and tried to get footage with a lion on safari, but our tour operator wouldn't let us get anywhere near a wild lion with it. It would've been great if we could've done all of those stunts with genuinely wild animals, but I don't think anyone can call us wimps for doing them the way we did.

In fact, I almost got mauled by a trained lion when we filmed a *Wildboyz* Nintendo DS commercial in California. At the time, I was sitting on the branch of a tree while three lions milled around on the ground beneath me. I was worried enough about the situation that I shouted, "What's to stop one of these lions from climbing up this tree and killing me?" The animal expert on the set confidently replied, "Don't worry. Lions don't climb trees." Apparently nobody told that to the three-hundred-pound lioness who proceeded to effortlessly scale the trunk and then get on top of me out on the branch. Looking back on it now, her pawing me was probably more a sign of affection than an attack, but at that moment, I really thought I was going out, Siegfried & Roy style. Based on the way everyone on the ground was freaking out, I don't think I was alone in that opinion. A ladder was quickly brought in and one of the animal handlers lured the lioness down with some chicken, but the whole episode was terrifying.

Overall, *Wildboyz* had a pretty profound effect on me. *Jackass* obviously changed my life forever, but the experience of doing *Wildboyz* changed the way I thought about my life. Prior to that, I always felt like the human race was calling the shots on Earth. We'd paved over the world and were this thriving, dominant presence on it. *Wildboyz* took me to all corners of the globe and completely changed that idea: humans aren't thriving on this planet; they're struggling and suffering. In the same way that trip to Nairobi with my family as a kid had opened my eyes to the existence of real poverty, my travels with *Wildboyz* taught me that far from being the exception, that poverty I saw in Nairobi is the norm.

I remember driving along a remote stretch of roadway in Kenya and seeing a man on the side of the road carrying a huge basket on his head. We were miles from the nearest settlement, and here was this guy just walking. He was likely oblivious to much that went on outside his own experience. TV, the Internet, drugs, celebrities, politics—what could these things possibly matter to this guy? At first, I felt sorry for him and all he was missing of the world, but the more I thought about it, the more I realized I should envy him. If he was missing out on anything, he likely didn't know about it. His life probably made sense to him. I don't think mine made any sense to me at all.

All these thoughts made me feel simultaneously guilty and grateful for what I had in this world. It also made me sad. As I saw the world in all its harshness—the scars of genocide in Rwanda, the crippling poverty everywhere—I began to feel that knowledge and wisdom were more of a curse than a gift. The more you knew and understood about the world, the more aware you were that it's a cruel and shitty place. Ignorance really is bliss.

It's probably putting too high-minded a spin on my drug addiction to say that these ideas fueled my relentless quest for oblivion, but at the very least I used them to justify it. The world was completely fucked and there was nothing I could do about it. This was a painful truth and a great reason to get as fucked up as I possibly could.

IT WASN'T only *Wildboyz* that kept me busy. When I flew home from those twenty-nine consecutive days of shooting in India and Indonesia in the spring of 2004, I landed at LAX and made a beeline for Dunlap and Berk's office. I spent three hours there drinking whiskey, then went straight back to LAX and flew out to Panama City (via Atlanta) to start a thirty-five-date tour that would take me through North America and Australia.

The tours seemed to be getting more ridiculous each time out. On our previous trek through Canada, our show in Montreal erupted into a full-scale riot. When the show let out, fans were smashing car windows, exposing themselves in the street, and hurling trash cans around until the riot police showed up, arrested a bunch of people, and forcibly dispersed the crowd. At another stop in Canada, it was below-freezing cold, and we got this big-breasted girl to take off her shirt and freeze her tits to a square metal pole outside. Eventually, I pissed all over her tits to defrost them off this pole. After this ritual humiliation, the girl still fucked me that night, freezer-burned tits and all.

> **DUNLAP:** It was just Mötley Crüe shit. At the peak of it, I didn't really care if we missed a show here or there, if something got canceled because Steve-O was in jail, because it was the controversy that sold the tour in the first place. Nobody was going there to see a guy perform a nice song and dance. They were going there to see hell break loose, and if the press told you, "Hey, your show just got canceled because this guy's in jail for smuggling drugs or he's on drugs or we can't find him," all that meant was more promoters were going to book shows.

Overall, I was starting to become less of a fun-loving idiot and more of an arrogant dickhead. On that flight from Atlanta to Panama City, Florida, the day I got home from Indonesia, I put my dickishness on full display and decided to light up a cigarette. My reasoning—if you could call it that—was that although flight attendants always announce that tampering with the restroom smoke detector is a federal offense, nobody ever says that smoking is. So I lit up and was promptly told by a male flight attendant to put the cigarette out. I made a point of putting it out on my wrist and calling him a "fucking faggot" to boot. Once he left, I lit up another one. He took that one away and I carried on being a belligerent douchebag. Then I lit up a third. When the plane landed in Panama City, airport police boarded it. I went into my rant about how smoking wasn't a federal offense so if they wanted to charge me with a misdemeanor, go right ahead. None of these cops were terribly bright and none seemed to know much about FAA regulations, so after detaining me briefly at the airport they let me go. I later got fined $25,000 by the FAA and was apparently banned from Delta Airlines. I say "apparently" because I was never given any formal notice of my ban, but a few years later I tried to get on a Delta flight and was told I was on their no-fly list. As far as I know, I still am.

The next show was in Jamaica, but after the smoking incident, flying from Panama City was out of the question. So Dunlap hired a car service to take me on a five-hour ride to Atlanta. I climbed into the car wearing no shirt or shoes, carrying only my backpack and accompanied by two random chicks. On the way to Atlanta, I had sex with both of them in the backseat. When I flew out of the Atlanta airport to Jamaica, the girls stayed in the car for the return trip to Panama City.

Around this time, the shows themselves were getting a little stale and we were no longer regularly playing to packed houses. I was also beginning to alienate my friends. After a disastrous show in Acapulco—I'd taken a bunch of Valium beforehand and the crowd was straight up booing me—I tried to lay the blame on Preston and Dave England. I became such an asshole about it that Preston and Dave quit the tour and went home. Dunlap hired this snake handler named David Weathers to replace them. Weathers would release a twelve-foot king cobra onstage and then kiss it on the head. It was an unbelievably awesome act but totally reckless. If Weathers had gotten bitten—and he'd been bitten by plenty of venomous snakes—who was going to corral that cobra and keep it from killing audience members? Me? Dunlap? Any of the rest of our wastoid crew? This wasn't some defanged or devenomized snake. It was the real thing and it could take down a fucking elephant. I frankly can't believe that clubs let us get away with that shit.

IN THE summer of 2004, I was in the back of a cab, riding through New York City, when my cell phone rang. It was Knoxville.

"Hey, I'm at Terry Richardson's studio," he told me. "He wants to do a bukkake shoot and we're just a few cocks short. You game?"

Bukkake, for the uninitiated, is when several dudes shoot their loads on one girl. Of course I was game.

Terry Richardson is a famous—or, perhaps, infamous—photographer known for his extremely risqué, sexually graphic photo shoots. I'd met him the year before when he shot press photos for the Lollapalooza tour. We'd hit it off pretty well.

When I arrived at his studio that afternoon, Knoxville immediately made it clear that he, personally, wanted no part of this photo shoot. When Terry explained the concept to me, I understood why. He wanted a photo of me pulling a girl's hair while I shot a load on her face and someone else pointed a gun at her head. Knoxville later told me he had no idea a gun would be involved. Regardless, the whole thing sounded fine to me.

The girl in question was a young-looking model—I was assured that she wasn't *too* young—and soon she went to work giving me a blow job. I had her hair in my hand but having someone holding a gun to her head was really throwing me off. As I've said, I'm quick on the draw, but something about a dude holding a gun was not particularly arousing. We devised a solution: once I reached the point of no return, so to speak, I'd call for the gun to be brought into the frame. So that's how I came to be yelling "Gun! Gun! Gun!" one beautiful summer afternoon in Manhattan as some dude brought a pistol to the head of a young model whose face I was about to cum on. I know: *classy.*

Later that same night I met a gorgeous Danish model named May Andersen. Knoxville knew her somehow and brought me along to her birthday party at the Gansevoort Hotel. He introduced us, we got fucked up together, and I spent that night with her in her hotel room.

May was only twenty-two but already a reasonably big deal in the modeling world. She'd been in Victoria's Secret catalogs and two *Sports Illustrated* swimsuit issues. We didn't really have a ton in common beyond the fact that we both liked to party—*hard*—but we ended up dating for the next six months or so. Looking back on it, I probably wasn't ready for a serious relationship at that point in my life. I mean, I don't know if the fact that just a few hours earlier I'd been getting my cock sucked by a complete stranger while someone held a gun to her head automatically meant that my relationship with May was doomed to fail, but it probably didn't help.

May had a good head on her shoulders. I am forever in her debt for the fact that she was the one who finally pushed me to ditch Dunlap and Berk. She met them and couldn't believe that they represented "my team." By this time, my problems with Dunlap and Berk had multiplied, but the most pressing was the fact that they'd basically stopped paying me. They kept claiming that they were "cash-poor" but essentially they'd spent *my* money on trying to expand *their* business. As Berk put it in an e-mail to my dad around this time, "I admit there have been cash-flow issues—even some poor choices in money management and allocation of funds. Steve is behind [in getting paid]." That, in my opinion, is putting it very mildly.

May set up some meetings for me with people she knew at the William Morris Agency that resulted in my finally getting an agent. I told Dunlap and Berk that we were officially severing ties, though unfortunately we stayed entangled for some time after that. Unsurprisingly, my relationship with them was finally terminated for good with a lawsuit, the details of which I will spare you.

DUNLAP: I'll say this: When this all happened, we were all pretty young and all very ambitious. It all went down under a lot of drugs and alcohol and after years of that and all the traveling, people just started having different opinions. The life insurance policy meant nothing to me. It never did. The last thing I'd even think about is to wish Steve would die for a life insurance policy. To be honest, it was probably a really bad judgment to go down that path. But shit, I was twenty-three years old and going at it as best I could. I'm proud that Steve-O and I were able to launch a tour and make it successful. There was nobody on TV then who had a tour. Since then, every person who's got a reality show does appearances in every nightclub all over the world, but before that it was kind of a new concept. The fact that Steve-O had this circus background and a real Mötley Crüe attitude made it all happen.

Now that I've got a few years of distance on it, I have somewhat mixed feelings about Dunlap and Berk. They were undeniably greedy, but the fact of the matter is my career probably wouldn't have gone the places it did without them. *For better or worse.* What Dunlap and I did together really was amazing, and the fact that we pulled it off without more lawsuits, felonies, hospital visits, and other equally bad shit happening is even more amazing. In his own way, Dunlap always had integrity: he was completely candid about what he called his own extreme sport, Aggressive Moneymaking. I respect him for that and always did.

For a while, Dunlap and Berk were also some of my closest friends. In the same way that a band grows unreasonably close when they're on tour together, I became very tight with those guys—particularly Dunlap—over the wild experiences we shared. It's too bad things went the way they did between us, but I can honestly say that I no longer get worked up over it. I'm sure we've all grown up a whole lot since then, and I wish those guys nothing but the best.

HOOKERS, TRANNIES, AND MAKOS, OH MY!

Wildboyz got good ratings, but after two seasons, we were bumped over to MTV2. The network execs sold the move to us in as positive a fashion as possible, telling us they were trying to relaunch MTV2 and wanted *Wildboyz* to be the network's flagship show. That may have even been true but mostly it felt like a demotion.

Despite that, *Wildboyz* probably could've kept going after Season Four. It just didn't seem like there was a point. Over time it had essentially evolved back into *Jackass*. During our final trip to Russia there were no stunts that wouldn't have fit in just as easily on *Jackass*. Knoxville came along on that trip too, which contributed even more to that vibe.

Not that it wasn't a great trip. We got horsewhipped by Cossacks, attacked by police dogs, and floated around in a zero-gravity airplane at a cosmonaut training center. I also did a flip and a half from a handstand off a ten-meter diving platform, landing on my face, and rode a MiG fighter jet to the edge of the Earth's atmosphere. At one point, we hired a bunch of Russian hookers to film an orgy scene with us while we were dressed in these big, furry polar bear costumes. (The hookers wore just the polar bear heads.) I actually had sex with this Russian prostitute *on camera* while dressed as a polar bear. Tremaine insists that he used his own money for the hookers, not MTV's. The idea behind the whole thing was to submit our all-time most ridiculously unacceptable footage to MTV's standards and practices department for a laugh, which we did. You won't be surprised to know that the polar bear porn never made it to air.

We were all going for it in a serious way in Russia, but Knoxville in particular was really throwing his body around in a fashion he hadn't done since the movie. He volunteered to be shot with rubber bullets, wrestled a beefy Russian woman, and was beaten up by antiterrorism commandos. After Tremaine saw all that, he pulled Knoxville aside and said, "Look, if you still have this in you, let's not waste our time shooting this for MTV2." That's when talk about doing a second *Jackass* movie got serious.

It's a point of pride for me that *Wildboyz* may well have been the most homoerotic show in the history of basic cable television. Pontius and I run around through much of the series wearing little more than thongs (and sometimes not even that), frequently dress up in unflattering women's clothing, and are inappropriately affectionate with each other all the time. As the series went on, it seemed almost every single segment had us joking about jerking each other off, having sex with dudes, or something along those lines.

This kind of humor had its place in *Jackass* from the beginning. The movies certainly have more full-frontal male nudity than almost any R-rated film you'll see. I think everyone involved with *Jackass* would agree that all the homoeroticism was intended to stir shit up. There was always something funny about straight guys pretending to be gay—

especially because we knew how uneasy that made a lot of viewers. We were all pretty comfortable with our sexuality, but our audience was heavy on teenage and twenty-something-year-old dudes, many of whom were openly homophobic. To me, all the guy-on-guy action in *Jackass* and *Wildboyz* was a noble attempt at combating homophobia.

It was in Russia that I brought all this swirling homoeroticism to what I considered its natural conclusion. We'd been drinking vodka all day, traveling on a bus. I'd finally fired Dunlap and Berk and was excited to shoot stuff on my own for my brand-new company, Ballbag, Inc. I wanted some shocking footage to contribute to this venture, and with my brain swimming in vodka, a plan was hatched. Pontius got naked and I addressed the camera.

"Let's face it: all *Wildboyz* has been is an agonizing wait to see this happen." Then I lifted Pontius's wiener with my fingers and planted a kiss right on the head of his dick. "So there it is," I continued, looking at the camera. "Now you've seen it, so now it's over."

PONTIUS: It's a fucked-up situation because you don't want your dick to look small when some dude is kissing it, but if your dick looks too good it'll look like you're enjoying it. It's such a catch-22. The funny thing is, during that time Steve was having this total struggle about whether he was being too gay. He would be really into doing that kind of humor and then have these breakdowns against doing gay stuff. In India, we were at this Kama Sutra temple and there was this instructor telling us to go through all the positions. One of us would have to be bent over or holding the other one up in the air, and Steve-O would not participate. The week before, a couple of his friends gave him a bunch of shit like, "Why don't you get back to doing stunts instead of running around being a faggot?" That bummed him out. Maybe that's what led him to these extremes. I think he was kind of rebelling against something inside of him by doing that dick kiss. It's all about, "What don't I want

to do?" With all the gay stuff on *Jackass* and *Wildboyz*, it wasn't
the idea ever to shock people, but just to kind of push our own
limits of humor. It was a frontier of humor that hadn't been
done enough really. My feeling was, if the world's not ready for
it, that's good.

The footage of the dick kiss has never been released, but I made a
point of telling a magazine interviewer about it, and afterward the story
zipped around the Internet pretty quickly. On a personal level, I've
never felt like I was anything other than heterosexual, though it's worth
mentioning that a couple years earlier, I'd had an experience that I kept
to myself for months—and I was never the type to be able to keep a
secret.

Around 2003, I was drunk in a club and met what I initially thought
was a hot chick. A friend told me she was actually a hermaphrodite
who'd had the male bits surgically removed. I didn't let that stop her
from giving me a blowjob. I later found out that the hermaphrodite
story wasn't even true. She was actually a post-op transsexual. Even if
I'd known that then, I very well may have gone through with it anyway.
For starters, I was hammered, but I also recall feeling like this person
seemed pretty troubled. I wanted her to feel worthy of affection. Yes,
what I'm trying to say here is that letting a dude suck my dick was an
act of selfless benevolence and generosity on my part. *So there.* Plus,
I've had sex with plenty of chicks that looked way more like dudes than
that dude did, so what's the big deal?

FILMING FOR *Jackass: Number Two* began in early 2006. Before we even started, I sent Tremaine, Knoxville, and Spike an e-mail
promising not to touch cocaine for the duration of the shooting. As bad
as my coke habit had been on the first film, it had only gotten worse
since then. After six months off the stuff in 2003, I'd returned to it with

a fury. I knew that nobody would want to work with me coked up all the time and I recognized that I really couldn't keep living like this anyway, so I made that promise on my own initiative: no coke. And I stuck to it.

It didn't turn out the way I anticipated though. As hard as it is to believe, my behavior was worse without coke than it had been with it. Not snorting coke didn't mean I was going to clean up, it just meant that I filled the void with other substances—and more of them. Booze and pills—mostly Xanax and Valium, but occasionally Adderall too (which actually had pretty similar effects to cocaine)—became a more central part of my life. I found that for some reason, without the coke, it didn't take nearly as much alcohol for me to get completely out of control. I also upped my intake of nitrous considerably. There were stretches when I'd sit around my apartment all day and night, just chain-huffing nitrous.

It's probably wrong to blame my behavior while filming the second movie on this new regimen of booze, pills, and nitrous, but I'm sure it contributed to it. Instead of being an annoying coked-up lunatic who wouldn't shut the fuck up for days on end, I became a much meaner drunk and self-absorbed asshole. I'd regularly throw temper tantrums over the smallest perceived slights. If I felt like someone wasn't affording me the respect I deserved, I'd lash out, curse people out, sometimes even spit on them. I'd bring chicks back to my hotel room and before even trying to fuck them, if they did the slightest thing to annoy me, I'd lose my shit. I'd hurl stuff around the room and scream at them to get the fuck out and leave me alone. The joke around the set was that if you want to get laid, just hang out outside Steve-O's hotel room, because I was regularly throwing violent tantrums and kicking groupies out of there in the middle of the night.

ONE OF the first stunts I did for the second movie was "The Butt Chug." The stunt had a long history. We'd actually filmed a version of it for the first movie. The whole idea came about because I used to regularly fill straws with beer and then release them into my nose to get a laugh. I could even drink from a beer bottle with my nostril. So I wrote a skit for the first film called "The Nostril Beer Bong." We attached smaller hoses to a beer bong and I funneled a beer through my nose. It all worked fine—I actually couldn't believe how fast I pounded an entire beer through my nose—but it just didn't get a big reaction from the other guys. Afterward, Knoxville said, "Dude, that sucked. Stick it in your butt."

I shook my head. I'd already refused to stick a toy car up my butt for a stunt earlier in the filming and this seemed to fall into a similar category. "We've established that I don't stick stuff up my butt," I said. "And it probably wouldn't work anyway."

That was the wrong response. Had I just left it at, "I don't stick stuff up my butt," I would've been fine, but questioning whether it was possible struck right to the heart of the *Jackass* mission statement. Spike Jonze always says that on *Jackass* we're not really entertainers, we're scientists, constantly trying to answer the question, "What would happen if . . . ?" Once I said the butt chug probably wouldn't work, everyone had to know if I was right.

So they quickly modified the beer bong and I lay down on the ground, pulled down my pants, and stuck it up my ass. Then a beer was poured in and—wouldn't you know it—it *was* possible. I found a rhythm where I'd kick my legs a little and the level of beer in the funnel went down. My butt was actually chugging a beer. The only problem was the footage was shot in a way that was entirely too graphic for the movie, even by our standards, so it never even got edited. We reshot it for the second film, taking more care with camera angles so it wouldn't look quite so much like gay porn. Afterward, Bam took a toilet plunger to my ass to suck the beer back out. What you don't see is that off-camera they'd actually poured beer into the plunger so it would look like it was pouring out of my ass. This was notable because it was one of the very rare times we cheated filming *Jackass*. That was hardly cheating though, because all of the beer in that funnel legitimately made it up my ass, enema-style, but what came back out did so back in the bathroom at the hotel, without the plunger.

Early on in the filming I sustained a pretty gnarly back injury that kept me from participating very much in the stunts and sketches. At a certain point, I recognized this was happening and began to get a little desperate to get some good footage. Which I guess is a good way of explaining how I ended up attached to the end of a fishing line with a hook through my cheek in shark-infested waters in the Gulf of Mexico. Twice.

The first time we did it, they hired a professional body piercer to come out on the boat and pierce my cheek with this big hook. That hurt like hell. Unlike most of my previous shark encounters, I wasn't allowed to have Manny right next to me, because I needed to be in the shot all alone, which made the whole ordeal much scarier. But when Tremaine watched the raw footage later that night, he wasn't happy with it. There weren't that many sharks and this random body piercer just looked out of place. He wanted to do it again with Pontius ramming that hook through my face instead. I felt like I'd missed out on so much filming that I couldn't afford to say no.

So we went back out. The face piercing part hurt unbelievably badly, but at the same time it always feels great to know that I'm getting gnarly footage. Very shortly after Manny started hacking up bloody fish in the water, there were plenty of sharks on the scene. You can tell in the film that I'm completely terrified. I was at the surface, flapping around like a dumbass, and Manny was in the water with me, keeping watch from a distance. After a minute or so, I heard Manny yell, "Steve-O! Watch out!"

I knew that was very bad news. Manny is generally perfectly comfortable surrounded by sharks, so if he senses danger something is *really* wrong. He'd spotted a large mako going for my foot. Hearing Manny yell made me jerk around toward him and in doing so, I kicked the mako in the head and it swam away. Then I got the fuck out of the water.

Kicking that shark in the head was an incredible stroke of luck. If I hadn't, I'm quite sure he would've chomped on me, and makos are no joke. It's fairly likely there would've been nothing left of my foot. At the time, we were in the middle of the Gulf of Mexico, an hour and a half from shore. What's more, this was about nine months after Hurricane Katrina, and even once we got to shore, I think the medical facilities were still pretty wrecked. But the footage was awesome.

That whole trip to Louisiana was crazy. We stayed for a while in New Orleans. The place was still a shambles from the hurricane and its aftermath. That was the only time we ever had security assigned to us. Crime was terrible down there, so we weren't supposed to go anywhere without our security. For me back then, having a security detail was an invitation to more trouble. I'd become a belligerent jerk, but the one thing that kept my behavior remotely in check was fear of getting my ass kicked. With security, that fear went out the window.

One night, Knoxville and I were drinking in the lobby bar and this guy was harassing Knoxville a little. Nothing terrible, just saying things like, "Hey, Knoxville, why don't you buy me a drink? You're rich! You can afford it! Buy me a fucking drink!"

"I did," Knoxville responded. "I got you a White Russian, but I might've cummed in it."

The whole situation had nothing to do with me and probably would've fizzled out, but I jumped up, got between this guy and Knoxville, and shoved him across the bar into the arms of our security guy, who hauled him away. I never would've escalated this situation if I didn't know our hired armed muscle was sitting at the end of the bar waiting to clean up my mess.

As it happened though, this guy I shoved wasn't alone. He was part of a group of dudes who were looking to cause trouble. Later the same night, Tremaine and Bam ditched their security detail and went to another bar. The guy I'd shoved was with his friends now and started getting into it with Bam and Tremaine. Things got testy in the bar, and then when Tremaine and Bam went to leave at the end of the night, one of these guys nailed Tremaine in the forehead with a D-shaped bicycle lock. It took fifteen stitches to close up the gash. I wasn't even there, but my actions clearly antagonized a group of guys who later in the evening busted our director in the head with a bike lock. That sucked, but fortunately Tremaine didn't get pissed at me. In fact, I seem to recall him being most angry at the doctors for not letting him try to do the stitches himself.

Filming for the second movie included a full cast trip to India that, in retrospect, was probably a giant waste of money. Only two sketches from that whole trip made the movie. One was Preston chasing Wee-Man through the streets, which was funny, though not a new joke by a long shot. The other was the leech I had put on my eyeball, which really could've been done anywhere. That whole stunt was another example of my feeling desperate to get some usable material into the film. The medic on the set was telling us not to do it, but I didn't want to hear it.

"Tell that medic that I happen to be very light on footage," I said. "And I have another eyeball."

Prying my eyelid open for nearly a minute to do the stunt actually hurt more than having the leech attached to my eyeball. Knoxville wanted me to keep it on for longer, but I couldn't really take it much more. People always seem to think because of the pain I've put my body through over the years that I must have a really high tolerance for it. In fact, the opposite may be true. I'm a total pussy when it comes to pain. In fact, most of us *Jackass* guys are. That's what makes the stunts worth watching. It would be far less entertaining to see a bunch of guys who could do all this shit without flinching. I think it's the very fact that we're no tougher or stronger than anyone in the audience that makes our stuff compelling. We're just stupid enough to do it.

TOWARD THE tail end of the filming for *Jackass: Number Two*, I was catching a lot of shit from Dad about my lifestyle. He was genuinely worried about my health and I was hearing about it constantly. In order to get him off my back, I agreed to get an extremely comprehensive medical exam from a doctor over at UCLA.

I went in, they ran a battery of tests, drew lots of blood, the whole deal. I was pretty nervous about all these tests. After that life insurance exam years earlier, I'd vowed to never have unprotected sex again. I'd gotten better about it but didn't have a perfect batting average. I didn't get any less nervous when I got a call from the doctor a few weeks after the exam telling me I needed to come in to get the results. *If everything was fine, wouldn't he just tell me over the phone?*

When I returned to the doctor's office, I had one big question.

"Doc, how's my wiener?"

"Your wiener is fine," he told me.

"Really? No STDs?"

"Nope. You're clean."

I was so relieved that I barely heard what he said next.

"But there's a problem with your heart."

"What?"

"You have cardiomyopathy," he told me.

I shrugged. "Well, I'd rather have a fucked-up heart than a fucked-up wiener."

"No, you don't understand," the doctor continued. "You have the heart of a ninety-year-old man. At this rate, there's no chance that you're going to live to be forty." He told me I had to stop drinking immediately. All the alcohol had made my heart enlarged. I walked out of that doctor's office stunned. I'd just been issued a death sentence.

That night I was scheduled to be a guest host on *Loveline* with Dr. Drew. I announced the news of my impending demise over the airwaves. The following day I went to LAX and bought myself a first-class ticket to London. I never paid to fly first class but figured since I was dying, what the hell. My entire purpose for flying to England was because I had a hankering for pickled onion flavor Monster-Munch, this corn snack you can only get over there. I loved that shit so much, and since I couldn't drink anymore I wanted to treat myself. I spent a few days in England hanging out with my friend Brad, who was a fan I'd met through my online message board. Brad has all these tattoos of me on him and I added to them by tattooing my own autograph on him. Then I went to Amsterdam and smoked a lot of weed. It was my little "Steve-O's Dying" tour.

I got back to the U.S. and Dad figured I needed a second opinion, so he arranged an appointment with a heart specialist in Florida. It had been a few weeks since the original diagnosis, and I'd already started drinking again. I mean, if I was going to die anyway, what's the difference? This doctor ran a bunch of tests and then commuted my death sentence. Apparently my heart was only ever so slightly enlarged, hardly anything out of the ordinary and certainly nothing to make a big deal about. I was relieved, though perhaps not as much as I should've been. I guess a part of me never believed I'd live to see forty anyway.

18

PAPARAZZI STUNTMAN

From my very first taste of fame, I got off on it. It not only fed the need for attention I'd had since, well, birth, but also I loved the perks. Getting special treatment in a store or a restaurant, having hot chicks want to sleep with me—there was nothing about these things that wasn't awesome, as far as I was concerned.

Being a celebrity also put me in the orbit of other celebrities. I'd see them at parties, events, clubs, wherever, and the fact that I had my own measure of fame meant that they generally wouldn't recoil from me or look at me like something they'd scraped off their shoes. Fame was like being a member of an exclusive club: other members were honor-bound to acknowledge you.

Back when I'd gotten out of jail on those charges stemming from the show in Louisiana, I was sitting around my apartment bumming out on the fact that

I couldn't do any drugs. On a whim, I went to Tommy Lee's Web site and left him a message telling him all the shit that I'd gotten myself into and how I was a huge fan. Now, I didn't know Tommy at the time (unless you include my starry-eyed backstage meeting with him when I was thirteen), and that guy must get hundreds of e-mails from random fans through his Web site. But the dude returned my e-mail, saying: "Tommy Lee here. Dude, you're in almost as much trouble as I've been!" After that, we became buddies.

In November 2004, I showed up unannounced, video camera in tow, to a book signing Tommy was doing at Tower Records and made a bit of a scene. We pounded a bunch of drinks together and then went to the set of *Jimmy Kimmel Live!*, where Tommy was supposed to promote his book. I kept the camera running the whole time and wound up destroying some furniture in his dressing room to make the footage more interesting.

A couple weeks later, I was at Disney World with May, Cindy, and my niece, Cassie, when I got an e-mail from Tommy telling me I needed to call him urgently. He had big news.

"Dude, I've been rehearsing with Mötley Crüe for the past week," he told me. "We're getting back together. We're going to tour." This was huge. The original band members hadn't played together since the 1990s. "We're having a big press conference and show to announce the tour," he continued. "I want you to get onstage and introduce us."

As bummed as I had been about Nikki Sixx's nonappearance in the first *Jackass* movie, this would make up for it and then some. For years, Mötley Crüe had been my spiritual guides, and now they actually wanted me to play a small part in their own story. When I got onstage a few weeks later to do my part, I did my lightbulb trick, slicing my tongue and bleeding all over the place. Then I baited one of the Crüe's longtime rivals.

"Gene Simmons is a pussy!" I yelled to the audience. "Real men use real blood." Needless to say, I filmed the whole thing.

Those encounters were two of the first things I'd filmed on my own in the post–Nick Dunlap era, and they launched the idea for what I'd hoped would be my next DVD, *Paparazzi Stuntman*. The idea was simple enough: I'd just cruise around with my video camera and film myself doing fucked-up shit with, to, or near other celebrities.

I'd always gotten a little thrill from hanging out with famous people. About a year after moving to California, I met Val Kilmer through his personal assistant, who was a friend of mine. On the surface, Val and I didn't seem to have much in common, but we actually got along great. We partied some together and I think he got a real kick out of me.

A few months after I'd met Val, I actually forced my way into one of his movies. I was touring through New Mexico, and he was in Albuquerque filming this real stinker of a film called *Blind Horizon*. I called him on his cell phone and said, "Val, I'm in Albuquerque when you're filming. I'm gonna be in your fuckin' movie. Tell me where the set is." Then I just showed up.

Amazingly, they actually wrote me into the movie's final scene. If you have the misfortune of ever catching it on TV and make it to the end, you'll see me. I think it probably says something about how little they thought of this film while they were making it that they just threw me into it at the last minute.

I'd been kind of a dick about the whole thing but Val took it all in stride. Afterward, he invited me back to his ranch in New Mexico, where my old buddy Ryan Simonetti met up with us. I'd grown a little goatee at that point and Simonetti blew a fireball off it in Val's living room.

When I think about it, what I enjoyed about meeting other famous people had less to do with them than it did me. Sure, it was cool to spend time with someone I admired, but, more important, I discovered hanging out with another celebrity is a surefire way of getting more attention for myself. *Paparazzi Stuntman* would give me an excuse not only to force my way into the lives of the rich and famous, but also to make myself the center of attention while I was there.

I FIRST met Paris Hilton at the premiere for *Wonderland*, in which Val starred and she had a small part. At the time, I was only vaguely aware of who she was and we didn't really become instant friends or anything. But for New Year's Eve 2004, she had this big party on South Beach that I went to with May. I had a good laugh with Paris that night. (I also partied with Kid Rock until 2 p.m. the following day, but that's another story.) After seeing her around town a few more times, Paris and I eventually became friendly enough that she invited me to a small birthday party she was having in early 2006 at a restaurant in L.A. called the Spanish Kitchen. The guest list was limited to family and close friends. My first thought was, *Oh my god, this is great! What am I going to film?*

I knew there was going to be a ton of paparazzi lurking outside the restaurant. After dinner, I told Paris, "Okay, it's time for your present." While she watched from inside the restaurant, I walked outside, right in front of the cameras, with a gift-wrapped six-pack of Budweiser cans. After I unwrapped it, I began smashing the cans on my head and spraying beer at the paparazzi. Then I yelled, "Can't a lady en-fuckin'-joy her birthday without you guys harassing her?" That was really rich considering I had Simonetti there filming the whole thing for *Paparazzi Stuntman*.

It's safe to say that Paris enjoyed that stunt because the following day she invited me to go to her much bigger birthday party at a club in Vegas. At the time, she was dating Stavros Niarchos, who was heir to a Greek shipping fortune but only twenty years old. Because of all the attention this party was going to get, he couldn't go (he was underage), so Paris brought me on a private jet with her to Vegas instead. It wasn't a date or anything, but she flew me out there and put me up in a hotel room. I had a great time. I remember really offending her mom at one point when I told her I was going back to my room to jack off.

People give Paris a lot of shit, and for a while, everything she did was dissected and criticized in the press, but I have to say I think she's pretty cool. She always had fun and never really gave too much of a shit about all the bullshit surrounding her. On the way back from that trip to Vegas, I showed her and her sister some of the X-rated QuickTime videos I'd recorded with various girls over the years. Given Paris's own history with amateur porn, I suppose it could've been a really awkward moment (not that I'd ever had a history of avoiding those), but she just thought my little videos were hilarious.

I hung out a fair bit with Paris over the years, though there was never anything even remotely romantic going on. I think the fact that I was always "on," and constantly willing to do some crazy stunt for a laugh endeared me to her and her friends. I was a constant source of entertainment, not unlike a court jester.

I later abused my court jester role by going on *Jimmy Kimmel Live!* after Paris and Stavros had been in a fender-bender and telling the world that I'd given Paris a nitrous balloon thirty minutes before the accident. The nitrous had nothing to do with the accident—Paris wasn't even driving—but it was just my way of inserting myself into a story that had nothing to do with me in order to get some cheap publicity. Paris had to have been pissed, but to her credit, she didn't seem to hold it against me. I think she accepted me for who I was—a reckless fame whore who simply couldn't keep his mouth shut.

In 2006, before we started shooting *Jackass: Number Two*, I met Nicole Richie and we hung out a few times. Everywhere she went, she was chased and swarmed by paparazzi. I had never experienced anything like that. Having all these people frantically scrambling around, taking photos of us, felt like the culmination of what I'd been working toward for much of my life. Here I was, the world's biggest attention hog, finally getting all the attention in the world. I remember the first time I walked into the *Jackass: Number Two* production offices, I was brazenly fanning myself with a stack of tabloid magazines, all of which featured photos of me with Nicole. The whole thing made me feel powerful and important, and I wasted no time in handling the whole situation like a complete asshole.

Nicole and I were not a romantic item. She told me in no uncertain terms that she'd just broken off an engagement and wasn't even considering dating anyone. I think she just thought I was funny and figured it would be fun to be friends. The tabloid media were dying to report that we were dating, and whenever I was asked about it, I made a point never to deny it. Truthfully, the way I handled that was beyond inappropriate. Nicole was never anything but sweet and nice to me and she didn't deserve that in return. But I was desperate for attention, and if that meant tossing my friendship with Nicole to the media wolf pack, so be it. The last message I got from her was that she didn't want to hear from me again, and I agonized over whether mentioning this here— even as something I'm extremely sorry about—was the right thing to do. I hope I made the right decision.

AS THE *Jackass: Number Two* premiere approached in the fall of 2006, I found myself in a spiritual panic. I knew the movie would do well and I wasn't really that upset that I wasn't featured in more sketches. What was driving me mad was that I couldn't see beyond the movie. My future was completely unclear.

Despite all that went down with Dunlap and Berk, they did keep me busy. My schedule was always filled with tour dates and DVD releases. After I fired them, I still did appearances from time to time and got paid far more for far less work, but the long tours pretty much ceased. I was working on that *Paparazzi Stuntman* DVD but really had no grand plan with regard to how or when I'd release it. *Wildboyz* was finished, and the stuff we'd done for *Jackass: Number Two* seemed so outrageous that I couldn't imagine us ever trying to do another one. There was simply no topping what we'd done. I'd resigned myself to the idea that there weren't going to be any more *Jackass* movies. In fact, I felt sure that there weren't going to be any more movies for me at all.

For a long time in my career, each new project had been bigger than the last. Everything had grown and grown, and now it felt like everything I'd been working toward—the fame, the career—was peaking. I'd never be this big again. I'd never be this famous again. Now it was just going to be a sad downhill slide toward obscurity and irrelevance. I wasn't an actor like Knoxville or a pro skateboarder like Bam. I was just a guy with few marketable skills other than a willingness to do anything for attention.

In the days and weeks before the premiere, I was either out getting wasted and trying to drum up attention from the paparazzi, or I was home at my West Hollywood apartment huffing case after case of nitrous cartridges. Each case held six hundred cartridges and it'd take me only a day or two to get through one. Those semiconscious dream states that had always been the goal of my nitrous use began to become indistinguishable from reality. I started to hear voices and experience hallucinations that I was sure were real. It got to the point that I would watch people walk through my apartment who were never actually there.

I've often said that showing up at that *Jackass: Number Two* premiere felt like arriving at my own funeral. It really did. Sure, I knew logically that I'd be able to continue working, but I believed that none of the work would ever be as significant or impressive as this, which made the rest of my life seem utterly depressing, even pointless.

That night, we had a pre-party at the Roosevelt Hotel. I got in a limo with my dad, my sister, my niece, Dr. Drew, and Ron Jeremy—I know, random crew—for a very short ride to the theater. When we got there, I immediately pulled out my dick and started pissing on the red carpet. Cassie, who was all of four years old at the time, was standing right next to me. Dad was furious.

I wish I could say that pissing on that red carpet was just the act of a man so loaded he didn't even realize what he was doing. I was loaded all right, but that little stunt wasn't about booze, it was about desperation. I was mad at that red carpet and everything it represented. I was mad that it would never be there for me again. I was mad that I had nothing more to offer it. I knew this was my final hurrah. That piss was a farewell and a "fuck you" to the red carpet, as well as a last-ditch effort at generating enough publicity to maybe earn myself one more trip back down it.

THAT PREMIERE was an emotional watershed for me, but on the surface not much about my life changed in its aftermath. The film was a huge hit, but I continued living the life of drug-addled attention whore, always eager and willing to drop the names of more famous friends in an effort to keep my own in circulation.

One such name was Lindsay Lohan. May introduced me to Lindsay in 2004, and after partying with her once in 2006, we hung out together every once in a while. Although she had a definite sense of entitlement, Lindsay was fun to party with and I think she found all my antics at least mildly amusing.

Around this time, so much as whispering Lindsay's name in the presence of any sort of recording device more or less guaranteed a story would be all over the Internet within hours, if not minutes. So when the video of that drunken rich dude, Brandon Davis, calling Lindsay a "firecrotch" went viral, I stuck my nose into the story by coming to her defense to TMZ.com. It may have looked noble, but my motivation was not. I just wanted a little of the spotlight deflected my way. In fact, I actually invited the TMZ cameraman to come interview me in my own apartment. I have to be the only person in the world who has ever done that.

If there was any doubt as to my bad intentions, I eventually went on *Stern* and reported that Lindsay had stolen a bag of coke from me. Again, this just enabled me to grab a small part in the bigger ongoing story of Lindsay's drug use, which the tabloids couldn't get enough of. There was another story that surfaced around that time about Lindsay borrowing money from me. It was completely false, as was the one about Brad Pitt getting caught smoking a joint with me. It says a lot about where my head was at that I was completely stoked about both of those stories: I figured if the tabloids were lying about me then I must be a really big deal.

Even without the tabloid press, I was constantly trying to take advantage of my famous friends and associates with this *Paparazzi Stuntman* video. Lindsay, in particular, was a pretty unwilling participant. She was over at my apartment getting loaded one day when I suddenly sprang the camera on her. I probably never would've gotten her to sign a release form allowing me to use the footage if she hadn't left her wallet above the toilet in my bathroom. When I found it a few months later, I texted her about it and she asked me to bring it to her. She was in Wonderland rehab at that point so I met her on the driveway of the place, and asked her to sign the release form. I never presented it as a one-for-one deal, but it felt like a shady exchange: you sign my release form; I give you back your wallet.

Getting those release forms signed was sometimes more of a stunt than whatever I'd filmed. I got Paris to sign one in the living room of her house. Once her handlers realized what had happened, they mobbed me and demanded I give it back to them. I told them, "Fuck no," and got the hell out of there.

I collected all sorts of great footage for *Paparazzi Stuntman*. There were bits with Paris, Linsday, 50 Cent, Ron Jeremy, Tommy Lee, Nikki Sixx, Method Man, Michael Clarke Duncan, Mario Lopez, Carson Daly, Dr. Drew, Knoxville, Bam, Wee-Man, and a bunch of other people, but ultimately the thing never came out. My best explanation as to why is that I was simply too fucked up to deal with it and no one else I was working with was able or willing to pick up the slack. It's still possible that *Paparazzi Stuntman* may someday see the light of day. Part of me thinks that maybe that stuff is better left unseen, as a chapter of my life I've since moved past. But another part of me thinks it's an incredible project that I'd love to put out. It remains to be seen which part of me wins this argument.

MY EAGERNESS to say and do outrageous things made me pretty popular with people who booked talk shows. I appeared on *Howard Stern* more times than I can count, and was also a frequent guest on *Jimmy Kimmel Live!*, *The Tonight Show with Jay Leno*, and *Last Call with Carson Daly*. There was always pressure to do something memorable whenever I showed up at these places, and it was rarely a problem for me to rise to the occasion. When the producers of *Too Late with Adam Corolla* wanted me to do something crazy, they actually went for my suggestion of getting completely drunk and then trying to blow a high score on a Breathalyzer. As it turned out, I got so shitfaced that I blacked out an hour before the taping. Apparently, there was an epic battle between the producers over whether my interview would even happen. When it did, I attempted to wrestle Corolla to the floor on the air and cut my leg smashing a glass table with it. I have no memory of any of that. I also used to go booze it up or huff nitrous regularly on Tom Green's web TV show.

All told though, the talk show I probably spent the most time on was *Loveline* with Dr. Drew. I'd first appeared on it to promote the first *Jackass* film, and then after Corolla left the show, I became one of a few regular guest hosts for a while. I can't say exactly what Dr. Drew saw in me, but we seemed to have pretty good chemistry and quickly became friends.

For a while, I was holding out hope that KROQ might choose me as a permanent co-host for the show, but ultimately I sabotaged whatever chance I had of that happening at the 2005 KROQ "Almost Acoustic Christmas" concert. I showed up with this gnarly meth addict/gangbanger I'd met back in Albuquerque who went by the name

Dreamer. Dreamer was a scary-looking dude with a huge gang tattoo on his neck, and he and I had been up for three days doing drugs together. Dr. Drew interviewed me and I was in such a shocking state that any thoughts the KROQ executives might've had of getting into business with me flew right out the window. Then I got up onstage and announced to the thousands of people in the crowd that I was going to be the new host of *Loveline*.

> **DR. DREW PINSKY** (addiction medicine specialist, host of *Celebrity Rehab with Dr. Drew*): In and around that scene there're a lot of people who are using, so to see people loaded was not uncommon, but Steve-O is kind of a force to reckon with. When he decides something is going to happen, it's going to happen. I didn't realize what he intended to do when we got out there onstage together. The way he announced it, it was sort of rambling and nonsensical—something about how he was going to take over the world of radio and whatever. I'm not sure the audience knew what they were hearing. The program director pulled me aside and said, "What does that mean? What is he talking about?"

Obviously, Dr. Drew's entire specialty is dealing with drug addicts, often celebrity drug addicts, but at least initially he was nonjudgmental about my drug use. One night after I appeared on his show, Drew was giving me a ride home when I realized I'd left my weed back at the studio. He actually gave me a ride back there so I could go pick it up. *That's* nonjudgmental.

> **DR. DREW:** We had multiple conversations about his drug and alcohol use, and early on his message to me was, "Stay out of it." Which I did. I don't push too hard if a person isn't ready. To do that is a waste of time. I just keep planting the seed and trying to turn them on to the idea of treatment. But with

Steve-O, I was pretty helpless. There was not much I could do except keep hanging around, being his friend. As time went on, I got increasingly concerned, not only about the kinds of stunts he was getting into, but the behaviors were getting more problematic. When that doctor overstated the heart condition he had as alcoholic cardiomyopathy and that still didn't stop his alcohol and drug use, I became more alarmed.

I guess Dr. Drew's first real attempt to actually do something about my drug problem came in 2007 when he asked me if I was interested in being on the very first *Celebrity Rehab* show he was putting together for VH1. I told him, "I have too much respect for the recovery process to make a mockery of it on television," which was a pretty harsh—although, in retrospect, remarkably spot-on (in my opinion)—criticism of the show. At the time though, that was just an excuse. The bottom line was I wasn't ready to get sober.

AS WILDBOYZ was winding down, I'd been in talks with Bunim/Murray Productions about developing a new show for me. Bunim/Murray were the people behind *The Real World*, *Road Rules*, and Paris and Nicole's reality show, *The Simple Life*, so I was pretty excited to work with them. But for a long time, this collaboration just produced a lot of false starts.

First, there was an idea they came up with for a reality show starring me and Clay Aiken. We'd be roommates in some bumfuck state and be in charge of organizing a state fair. That one never really got off the ground because, in a not-so-surprising twist, Clay Aiken turned it down.

Then there was an idea for a show called *Camp Steve-O*, in which I'd be the director of a summer camp for kids. We actually made a little three-minute reel for that in Cindy's backyard featuring me interacting with kids from her neighborhood. We shopped this three-minute reel around to a few places, but the consensus we got back was that the show would have to focus a lot on the kids and—to put it bluntly—nobody gave a shit about kids.

Someone had the idea of shifting the concept a little and making the camp someplace that kids would send their parents in order to make them cooler. That pitch showed enough promise that we got a budget from MTV to shoot a pilot. I thought the pilot worked but MTV disagreed and didn't order the show. I was frustrated and disappointed, but this was early 2006, when we were filming *Jackass: Number Two*, so I figured I had bigger fish to fry anyway.

Bunim/Murray wasn't going to let the concept die. They decided the real problem with the *Camp Steve-O* pilot was that we were stuck in one place. And why did I have to be helping parents? Couldn't it be anybody? Why not have me travel around helping people who just wanted to be cooler? What if I roamed around in a van helping to "de-wussify" America?

The van soon became an ambulance and the show became *Dr. Steve-O*. We shot the pilot in August 2006, but for reasons that I either don't remember or were never clear to me, it took a long time before anything happened with it. When *Jackass: Number Two* premiered that fall, *Dr. Steve-O* was looking very iffy at best, which only contributed to my feeling that the walls were coming down all around me. In fact, it wasn't until August 2007 that the USA Network ordered the show and we started filming, by which time I was such an unholy wreck that the thing was bound to fail.

19

OKAY, WHO WANTS TO HEAR ME RAP?

I made a rap album. You've almost certainly never heard it—it was never actually released—and you're quite fortunate that you haven't, but as with so many terrible ideas, the story behind how it came to be is ultimately a lot more entertaining than the album itself.

It all started onstage with Ol' Dirty Bastard during the summer of 2004. We'd both gotten booked to perform at the same event—I think it was a rave—and I was intent on meeting him. I didn't know much about rap beyond what your average suburban white dude knows about guys like Snoop, Dr. Dre, 50 Cent, and Tupac. I was a casual fan. It was actually Dunlap who really loved rap, mostly for its emphasis on getting paid, and educated me about it. I got a kick out of the outrageousness of it all, especially that so much of it seemed to revolve around guys bragging about doing drugs, banging chicks, and fucking people up.

Ol' Dirty Bastard was a founding member of the Wu-Tang Clan, one of East Coast rap's most enduring groups, but arguably what made him famous was the fact that he was a drug addict in questionable mental health who couldn't seem to go a week without getting himself arrested. His rhymes were graphic and often nonsensical, and his entire public persona just screamed, "I don't give a fuck." He was either a lunatic or a genius. Maybe both.

When I walked into the room where he was booked to appear, he was already onstage performing. Well "performing" might not be the right word: As I walked toward the stage I saw ODB standing in front of the audience with his pants down, his dick hanging out, smoking PCP and passing it to people in the crowd. I couldn't fucking believe it. I thought this was the greatest shit I'd ever seen in my whole life.

Someone onstage spotted me and invited me up. I hopped up with my camera in hand and took two short QuickTime videos while I was onstage. In the first, ODB is barely holding it together. He's rapping but hunched over, barely upright, and clearly out of it. In the second video, which was shot only about five minutes after the first, he's sitting on the drum riser, holding the mic in one hand, the PCP in the other, completely passed out. It may have been right then that I first began to wonder if there was a place for me in hip-hop. After all, I could pull my dick out, smoke PCP, and pass out onstage. That sounded right up my alley.

As it turned out, the day after my rendezvous with ODB, I was scheduled to record an intro for a mixtape with DJ Whoo Kid. Whoo Kid was the main DJ/producer for 50 Cent and his G-Unit crew. He'd come up with the concept of doing a "Wildboyz" mixtape, so he called to see if I'd lend my voice to it. It had nothing to do with our TV show—it was just going to feature a bunch of tracks by 50, the Game, Young Buck, and a bunch of the other G-Unit rappers—but it seemed like fun.

When I met Whoo Kid at the studio, we lit up some joints and then he and some of the other guys there draped a few hundred thousand dollars' worth of 50 Cent's jewelry on me to help get me in the spirit of things. When the engineer hit RECORD, the first words out of my mouth were, "I don't have a racist bone in my body, but I like to consider myself a *nigger.*"

I was still working with Dunlap at that point and he was in the control room on the other side of the studio window. Dunlap doesn't scare easily—he's pretty unflappable. But when he heard the "N" word come out of my mouth, I watched all the color drain from his face. He suddenly looked panicked in a way I'd never seen him before.

As stupid as it may sound, I didn't mean any offense by what I said. In fact, it was coming from a good place. I just felt like if people of all colors could be considered "niggers," that would render the word powerless. It was nothing I'd really planned on saying. I've just always had a tendency to blurt out whatever was on my mind. I'm sure my judgment was at least mildly impaired by all the drugs and booze I'd been piling into my body, but really, I felt like I was doing my part to ease racial tension. Whoo Kid, for his part, didn't seem the least bit offended.

DJ WHOO KID (G-Unit DJ/producer): Everybody in the studio was dying because he's Steve-O. He doesn't look like he has a racist bone in his body. I put that on my video and people just looked at it and laughed. There was no, "Fuck Steve-O!" It wasn't like when that comedian said the "N" word. It was no comparison to that. He was really trying to be knee-deep into this thing called hip-hop. It was a weird concept but I think he wanted to be a nigga, N-I-G-G-A, the way we say it. He wanted to hang with us.

Once Whoo Kid realized I was willing to say basically anything into the microphone if I thought it might get a laugh or just a reaction out of people, he was all the more stoked. I talked shit about the rappers G-Unit was beefing with at that moment—Ja Rule, Joe Budden—and made a bunch of ridiculous idle threats toward them. I guess I felt like since I was obviously just some goofy white dude, no one would give a shit what I said. And for the most part, I was right.

Incidentally, that wasn't the only time I threw around the "N" word. In the coming years, it was always a good gauge of how hammered I was: if I started calling myself "a nigger" and threatening to kill the president, those were the two telltale signs that I was obliterated. There is at least one pretty widely seen YouTube clip of me expounding on my philosophy about the "N" word. I even once explained it to Mike Tyson, during an hours-long, coke-fueled conversation in the bathroom at some party in 2005. I suppose it ranks among the most dangerous stunts I've ever pulled—running off at the mouth about how I was a "white nigger" while locked in a bathroom with a coked-up Mike Tyson. I remember his response: "A nigger is anyone who uses that word." But he didn't get mad. In fact, we got along great, rambling on at each other for hours. It was a pretty weird scene I guess, but before we finally left the bathroom, he told me, "You know, Steve-O, everyone has got you wrong. You're a really smart guy." I was flattered.

After that initial studio session with Whoo Kid, we'd kept in touch and I'd really started getting engrossed in hip-hop. The following summer, I was hanging out at the Rainbow Bar & Grill on the Sunset Strip when someone mentioned that another G-Unit rapper, Tony Yayo, was shooting a music video the next day. I bragged, "I'm totally down with G-Unit," and talked someone into giving me a ride over to the set. When I got there, I heard that 50 Cent was there but was off getting tattooed. That sparked an idea for the *Paparazzi Stuntman* DVD: I'd get 50 to tattoo "G-Unit" on me.

Unfortunately, 50 left before I could track him down. I weaseled myself an invitation back to the hotel where the entire G-Unit crew was staying with the hopes of meeting 50 there, but when we got there he wasn't around. Whoo Kid suggested I hop on his tour bus and follow their entourage to Vegas for the next stop of what was called the Anger Management Tour.

The bus driver told me that there was no smoking allowed on the bus, so I lit a cigarette and hung my body out the window as we barreled down the highway. The driver saw me in his rearview mirror and pulled over. He was fucking pissed.

"Dude, I wasn't smoking on the bus," I pleaded. "I was three-quarters of the way out the window."

This bus driver was an older black man and he wasn't having any of my bullshit. "You think I need a fucking half-naked white boy hanging out my window on a fucking *rap* tour? Are you crazy?"

He had a point. All the buses in the caravan had pulled over at the side of the highway by this time. This driver wanted nothing more to do with me, so I was switched over to Young Buck's bus. I remember thinking as I climbed on there, "Oh man, that's one strike. I don't want to blow it with these guys. I'd better be careful." So I took a whole bunch of Valium and Xanax to ensure I'd pass out and not cause any more trouble. Very shortly thereafter, I was out cold on the bus floor with my mouth wide open. I was later told that Young Buck and a few others took the opportunity to fill my mouth with ketchup and mustard from these huge squeeze bottles. Apparently, I never even woke up, but at one point I swallowed down all the condiments and let out a loud, "Ha!" After that, they didn't fuck with me anymore.

When I finally awoke at the Palms Hotel in Vegas, I once again displayed my propensity for running off at the mouth in incredibly stupid—and borderline dangerous—ways. At the time, Young Buck was enmeshed in a court case over an incident at the Vibe Awards in December 2004. Someone had punched Dr. Dre and Young Buck was accused of stabbing that someone during an altercation that followed. There had been pretty compelling video evidence of this incident but Buck denied any wrongdoing. He'd been indicted only a month earlier and was out on bail. As soon as I spoke to him, I made a point of bringing it up.

"Yo, Buck, dude, if somebody smacked Dre when I was around, I'd stab that bitch too," I said. "Anyway, I saw that video footage. *Totally* inconclusive." I can only imagine what Buck thought of this bonkers-ass white kid spouting off about all this shit he knew nothing about.

As everyone checked into their rooms, I remained outside the front entrance to the hotel. Someone in the G-Unit entourage tapped me on the shoulder and motioned for me to follow him. We'd been traveling in these big-ass tour buses with huge gaudy murals depicting the artists on the side. But this guy led me to a completely nondescript RV and showed me in. It was 50 Cent's RV. 50 gave me a big hug and I immediately pulled out my video camera and filmed him recording the outgoing message for my voice mail. We hung out for a little while and despite the fact that he doesn't drink or do any drugs, he was completely cool with me.

At the concert that night, Young Buck brought me onstage during the "smoke break" portion of their set. He and some of the other rappers blazed up huge blunts onstage and shared them with me. I got a real kick out of the fact that I was smoking weed *onstage* with the G-Unit. As far as I was concerned, I was one of them.

Following the show, Eminem, who was headlining the tour, "hosted" an after-party for which he didn't actually show up. I went to the party with Kid Rock. When I'd first hung out with Kid Rock, I made some snide comment to him about how I was really impressed that he'd overcome having the same haircut as Vanilla Ice and gone on to have a successful career. The fact is though, the dude is incredibly talented—he can play just about any instrument in any style—and a really great guy to boot. That night, he jumped on the turntables at this after-party and then busted a bunch of freestyle rhymes. I was beyond impressed.

Whoo Kid gave me a key to his suite so I could crash on the sofa for the night, though I never actually ended up sleeping. I stayed up all night snorting line after line of coke. Whoo Kid got up the next morning and seemed pretty creeped out to find me still awake, still doing blow. The buses were leaving in a few minutes for Arizona, the next stop on the tour, so I grabbed my stuff and followed Whoo Kid out to the parking lot.

Once we got outside, I learned that 50 hadn't come out yet, so I scrambled to get prepared to film something with him for *Paparazzi Stuntman*. There was a huge double flight of cement stairs at the side of the casino, and I'd been thinking about tumbling down stairs on a bell-hop's cart for ages. Now I had an opportunity to get 50 to push me. I got some of the other guys to help me carry the cart to the top of the stairs. When 50 came out, I asked if he thought I'd be able to make it down both flights of stairs in the cart. He said he was down to help me try.

I loaded myself into the cart and he shoved me down the stairs. It was a pretty violent maneuver, and the cart ended up crashing about halfway down the first flight.

"One more try!" I yelled. 50 came running down to help me drag the cart back up the stairs. The second time down, I got all tangled up on the banister and the cart landed on top of me. It looked horrible, but I somehow escaped serious injury.

"One more try!" I yelled again. So again 50 and I lug the cart back up to the top of the staircase. This time, when he shoves me off, I actually go flying out of the cart on the way down and land hard on the concrete at the top of the second flight of steps. It hurt like hell, but I popped up and yelled, "G-Unit!" which was my way of saying, "Okay, I'm done." 50 was cracking up.

I'd planned on following the tour to Arizona, but decided, for once, to quit while I was ahead. I knew I had unbelievable footage and didn't want to take the chance that anything would happen to it. So I bid everyone a fond farewell and watched the buses pull out.

WHOO KID: The G-Unit, they loved Steve. They always thought of him as the cool white homeboy from *Jackass*. He was part of the crew. He would wear the same clothes for a week. Young Buck was a dirty guy too and when Young Buck is telling you that you need to change your fuckin' oufit, you're fuckin' dirty. Eventually, me and Steve-O became tight. I booked him for a party in Arizona once. I told the promoter the only way Steve-O is going to get there is if I personally fly to L.A., go to his house, get him out of bed, throw him in a private jet, and take him to Arizona. I called Steve-O and said, "I'm coming to pick you up." I went to pick his ass up and he was already fucked up. When we got on the plane he just starting doing nitrous and getting even more fucked up. He started hugging me, talking about love and all this stupid shit, hugging the promoter. Then he gets up, charges toward the pilot, and starts hugging the pilot while the pilot is flying the plane! The whole plane veered a little. The pilot is like, "What are you doing?" Me and the promoter grabbed him and held him in his seat for the rest of the flight. Once we landed, he kind of rolled out of the plane onto the tarmac, which was like 130 degrees. He's just sizzling on the tarmac for ten minutes. Fast-forward to the club, first thing he does is climb the stairs on his hands, get to the top, and start blowing fireballs. The side of the club catches fire, and everybody starts running. The promoter and the security guard threw water on the fire and kicked his ass out of the club. That was one of the normal days.

IN 2005, Preston Lacy had a roommate named Sam Maccarone. Maccarone was an aspiring director who'd made some short films and music videos. I really liked him. Whereas most of the *Jackass* guys never really tried to keep up with me in the partying department, Maccarone did. I was probably a worse influence on him than he was on me, but either way, we were absolutely toxic together.

Maccarone and Preston had begun writing and filming a bunch of sketches that were spoofs of TV shows and commercials. We came up with this idea for Trojan High Risk Condoms that I ended up filming with them on the roof of my apartment building. Eventually, they got some money and backing from National Lampoon to turn these skits into a full feature film called *TV: The Movie*.

From the start, the whole project was a mess. According to imdb .com, the film had a budget of $2.5 million. A great deal of that money was stolen by someone involved in the production. I'd guess the next largest chunk got spent on cocaine. The stuff I filmed for it didn't take a whole lot of my time, but it's worth mentioning here because that film was responsible for the first rap song I ever recorded.

It was for a skit called "Pads" that was intended as a parody of MTV's *Cribs*. In it, I played a washed-up celebrity with a drug problem named Steve-O who is trying to relaunch his career by putting out a rap album. I know—it was a *real* stretch. The skit was filmed in my apartment. I stumbled around amid piles of spent nitrous cartridges, empty beer cans, and dirty bongs, and gave a "tour" of the place, taking time out to do drugs and piss on the kitchen floor. The line between fiction and reality was thin and blurry. To tie in with the skit, we decided I'd record an actual rap song. I spent very little time writing it, and the result was a deliberately horrible song called "Hard as a Rock."

Around this time, I had a pitch meeting with Comedy Central about the *Camp Steve-O* idea we'd been working on. I played "Hard as a Rock" through some iPod speakers just to break the ice. At the end of the meeting, the bigwig from Comedy Central turned to me and said, "I'm going to level with you: I couldn't care less about your TV show idea but that rap song is fucking hysterical." He wanted me to make a whole album to put out on Comedy Central Records.

My lawyer at the time, a guy named Vernon Brown, had major connections to the rap world—he'd represented the Notorious B.I.G., among others. When he heard Comedy Central was interested in putting out an album with me, he upped the ante. He set up a meeting with Universal Records, who eventually agreed to give me $200,000 to make this album. All of a sudden, I was turning the joke at the premise of that *TV: The Movie* sketch—a drug-ravaged has-been remaking himself as a rapper—into a reality. It seemed to make perfect sense: to me, rap was all about sex, drugs, and acting like a lunatic. So was I.

Looking back on it, my first clue that the hip-hop community might not fully embrace me came at the Rock the Bells show during the summer of 2006. I'd met B-Real of Cypress Hill while hanging out at the Rainbow and we'd become friendly. He was performing at the show, so I rolled in with him and his crew. The Wu-Tang Clan were also scheduled to perform that night but without ODB, who'd died of a drug overdose just a few months after I'd shared the stage with him. They planned to do a little onstage homage to ODB and I figured, naturally, I should be a part of that. So when I saw his Wu-Tang mates Method Man and RZA backstage before the show giving an interview, I barged into it and announced my plan to get buck naked onstage and do a "double-back back flip"—that was where I whipped my dick and balls back and forth, catching them behind my legs before doing a back flip while still in the "mangina" position. *That* would be my ODB tribute. Method Man, who had appeared on *Wildboyz* and become, if not a friend, then at least a close acquaintance, laughed. But after the interview, he came up to me and warned me not to do it.

"The rest of the guys aren't going to think that's cool," he said. "They're going to kick your ass."

I was wasted as usual and undeterred.

"Let them kick my ass! That's what ODB would want!"

Regardless of what Method Man thought about the idea, when the Wu-Tang began their little ODB tribute, he brought me onstage and introduced me to ODB's mom, then seemed to leave it up to me what to do. I stripped down, did my double-back back flip, got my clothes back on, and then gave ODB's mom a hug. Most of the Wu-Tang seemed fine with the stunt, and some of them were definitely laughing, but I guess Raekwon was not. A couple songs later, I was still standing on the stage when he grabbed me by the neck and dragged me front and center.

"I don't fuckin' appreciate what you did!" he yelled. "That's no fucking way to show respect for ODB. He's not around to protect himself from your faggotry. You're going to apologize right now or I'm going to pound your face in. I'll go to jail! I don't give a fuck!"

It was a pretty impressive display of gangsterism. I was both frightened and embarrassed.

"I didn't mean any disrespect," I said meekly. His grip around my neck tightened and I realized quickly that he was not interested in getting into a debate about the respectfulness of my gesture. "I'm sorry! I'm sorry!" I squealed.

He released me and as I walked offstage, someone came up and said, "You gotta get out of here. It's not safe for you to stay." So I left.

WHOO KID had signed on as the executive producer of my album, but to his credit, he clearly didn't want to waste his time actually working on it. He passed me off on this guy—let's call him Jersey Joe. Joe was a white kid from New Jersey who seemed to be trying to ingratiate himself with the G-Unit. He was supposed to help get this album together. What he actually did was keep me hostage at his house in New Jersey for a few months, feed me PCP, and occasionally take me into New York City for a recording session. To be fair, I was a complete mess at the time, but Joe was a shady, shady dude. He struck up a dialogue with my dad and my sister, and fed them a line of bullshit to try to further his own goals.

TED: Joe presented himself as someone who was integral in the rap scene, well connected with celebrities and starting a business of babysitting intoxicated celebrities. At one point, he arranged to bring Steve to Florida for rehab. They forcibly got him on an airplane but for some reason they didn't get a direct flight to Miami. They changed planes in New York and Steve escaped. Steve was on the loose running around Manhattan on his own.

CINDY: At a time when it was so hard to get in touch with Steve or get through to him, Joe seemed like the answer. He was going to help us out, hook us up, babysit Steve, keep him out of trouble, and report back. He would say, "Steve dusted last night in this sketchy part of town with these guys and it was really bad, but now we've got him." Or "Steve was at a restaurant and this waitress was trying to give him three grams of coke, and he was pulling out his wallet to make a deal but I said no." He was telling us all the ways he was stopping Steve from doing drugs. We were just desperate for a babysitter/guardian angel and he was telling us what we wanted to hear. But we were completely duped. At another point, he called me impersonating Whoo Kid and threatened to abandon the album unless Steve did exactly what he wanted.

WHOO KID: Joe's a scam artist. He would use my name to get free products, free clothes. He even booked 50 Cent for New Year's Eve as me. He's the reason Steve-O and me had some kind of falling out, because he would call Steve-O and act like he's me. I don't know what exactly happened but this idiot called Steve's sister looking for him, acting like me. He cursed her out, like "Fuck you, you slut, give me fuckin' Steve-O!" Even to this day, when me and Steve get on the phone I give him a code so he knows he's talking to me instead of Jersey Joe.

Not only were Jersey Joe's stories about keeping me away from drugs or bringing me to rehab complete fictions, he was actually supplying me with drugs on a steady basis.

I wound up getting a lot of bona fide professionals to dirty their hands on my album: I recorded tracks with B-Real, old-school legend Kool G Rap, G-Unit affiliates M.O.P., and hit producers like Apex and Red Spyda. Ultimately though, having actual talents on the album really undermined anything that was funny about it. I was blown out for pretty much all the sessions too. One night when I was recording with Fame from M.O.P., I was in and out of a PCP blackout during which my $20,000 Rolex disappeared. The sad truth is that I was so out of it that I don't know if it was stolen, if I left it somewhere, or if I handed it to someone. But it's gone.

The project was always meant to be a comedy album, but once Universal got involved, I lost sight of the joke. I knew I couldn't rap and never pretended I could, but I did go around trying to live the life of a gangsta rapper, or at least my ridiculously over-the-top, self-aggrandizing vision of what I thought a gangsta rapper was. I started collecting air rifles that I'd keep around the apartment and wield as if they were real guns. I talked up my burgeoning rap career to anyone who'd listen and many who wouldn't—including the *Jackass* guys, who mostly hated everything about the idea. My song list included titles such as "Down with STDs," "Snitchin' Iz Bitchin'," "Paparazzi Beatin'," "I Got Guns," and "Crack Cocaine (Feels So Good)." I even made a video for a song called "Poke the Puss" where I rapped in a club, surrounded by expensive booze, slutty-looking girls, and Kool G Rap. Beavis and Butt-Head came out of retirement to trash it.

Even now, I can look back on that project and see how the whole thing could've been a performance art send-up of gangsta rap in all its ridiculousness. In fact, when Joaquin Phoenix did that mockumentary, *I'm Still Here*, about his transformation into a rapper, part of me thought, "Shit, he stole my idea." But the bottom line was I was so blown out on drugs that I'd lost the plot completely. Any marginally good idea buried at the bottom of that shit heap was always going to be obscured by my all-consuming interest in getting obliterated and desperately trying to maintain my celebrity. My rap album became an excuse to live like a maniac and gave me a reason to go on talk shows and act like a maniac. When I wasn't on someone else's show or jumping in front of some paparazzo's camera, I was filming practically every sordid development in this saga myself and posting the video to my Web site and Myspace page.

Amazingly, I held on to the project for a long, long time. The business end of it became a complete debacle, with producers and artists clamoring to get paid and Vernon Brown swimming in a legal and accounting nightmare. I certainly didn't help things by being unbelievably difficult to deal with and talking shit about Universal Records at every turn. I made life so miserable for my poor A&R guy that after I got sober and tried to make amends with him, he wouldn't even call me back. I can't really blame him.

In 2008, Universal finally dropped me, something that bummed me out at the time, but for which, in retrospect, I'm eternally grateful.

Walking down a flight of stairs on my hands with a skateboard balanced on my feet on the cover of *Big Brother*. Miami, 1999.

The stunt I put together for what would turn out to be the *Jackass* pilot. The whole point was to tip myself over after Ryan Simonetti ollied off the house and over my head. Simonetti made the jump through a fireball with his eyes closed, and I was the one who chose to wear a helmet. December, 1999.

GBROTHER

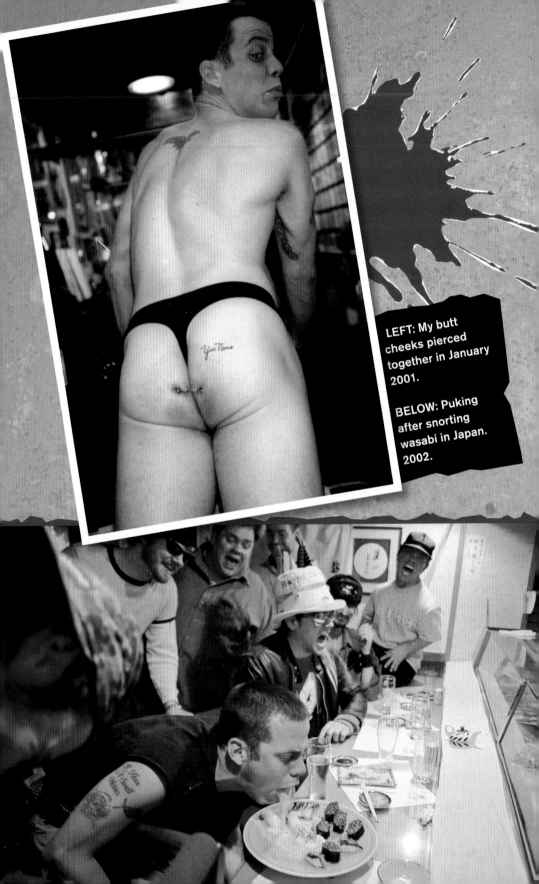

LEFT: My butt cheeks pierced together in January 2001.

BELOW: Puking after snorting wasabi in Japan. 2002.

Made up as a ninety-year-old for the final scene of the first *Jackass* movie. The makeup remover that was used to detach the prosthetics caused my cheetah-print bikini to expand, and ruined it. 2002.

ABOVE: Chugging tequila onstage at Lollapalooza. 2003.

RIGHT: Covered in blood after the show, as usual, on the tour bus. 2003.

Pontius, after we got drunk and accidentally burned down three cabins at an upscale safari resort in South Africa. 2003.

The *Wildboyz*, bareback in Costa Rica. 2003.

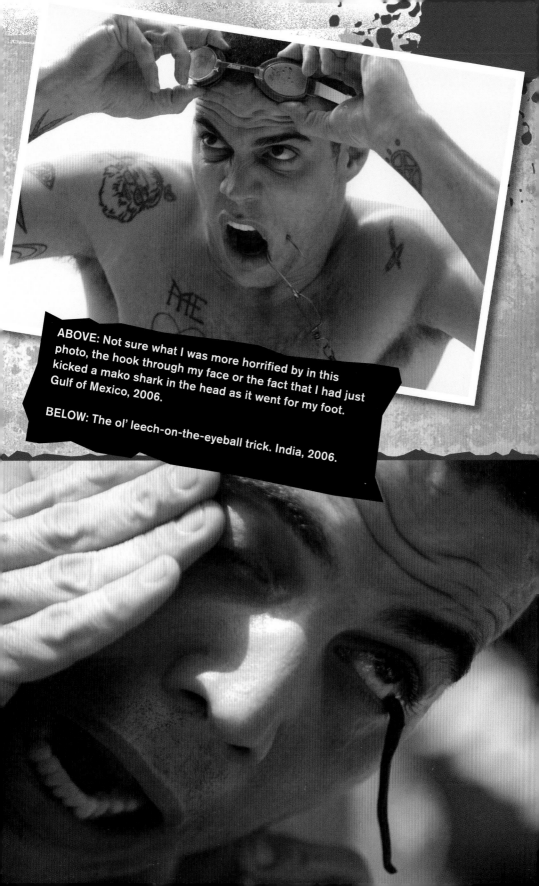

ABOVE: Not sure what I was more horrified by in this photo, the hook through my face or the fact that I had just kicked a mako shark in the head as it went for my foot. Gulf of Mexico, 2006.

BELOW: The ol' leech-on-the-eyeball trick. India, 2006.

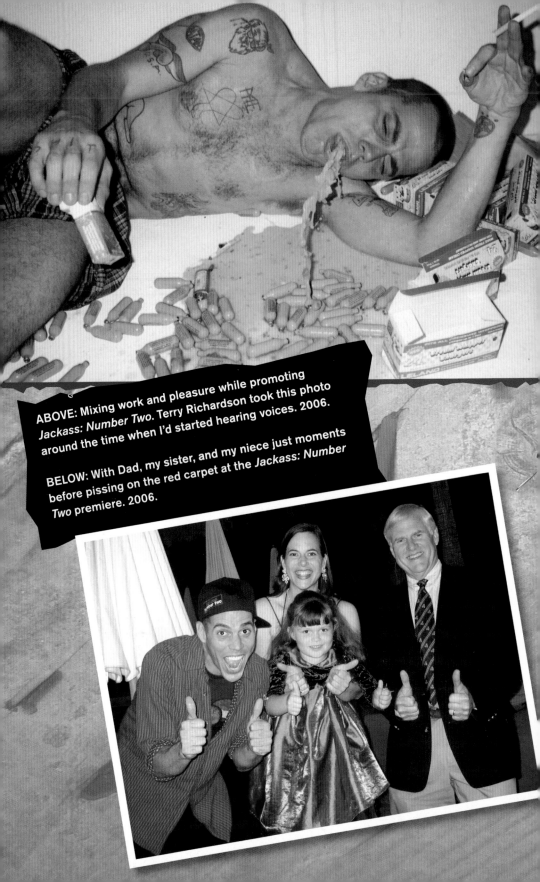

ABOVE: Mixing work and pleasure while promoting *Jackass: Number Two.* Terry Richardson took this photo around the time when I'd started hearing voices. 2006.

BELOW: With Dad, my sister, and my niece just moments before pissing on the red carpet at the *Jackass: Number Two* premiere. 2006.

ABOVE: Compared to the early days of *Jackass* and *Wildboyz*, the production crew was insanely large on *Jackass 3D*. To look at this scene, it's hard to imagine that I'd end up hospitalized with burns, huh? 2010.

BELOW: With the exception of these photos, "BB Gun Nipple-Piercing" has never been seen anywhere. The BB is still in there, and you're more than welcome to feel it. Just ask. 2010.

(After)

ABOVE: The opening scene of *Jackass 3D*. Not sure if the idea to give me angel wings had anything to do with it, but I was definitely a lot easier to work with on *Jackass 3D* than I'd been in the past. 2010.

RIGHT: Doing stand-up on my comedy club tour. 2011.

20

DEMONS AND ANGELS

Even with all the narcotics I've pumped into my body, I'm generally pretty great at recalling names, dates, and details of the events of my life. So it probably says something significant that the period covered in these next few chapters—starting around late 2006—is a little fuzzier in my memory bank. I still remember most of my outlandish acts of dickishness with clarity, but exactly where and when they occurred is less clear. Hence the increasingly frequent quotes from those unfortunate enough to have witnessed it all firsthand.

I've yet to mention my ex-fiancée, Brittany, but any discussion of me at my worst must include her. First off, I'm not entirely serious when I call her my ex-fiancée. Yes, I did ask her to marry me, and yes, she briefly consented, but I was such a mess that I don't think she ever really took it very seriously. I took it seriously at the time but only *because* I was such a mess. I'm getting ahead of myself though.

I met Brittany at a club in Vegas in the fall of 2006. If my relationship with May seemed doomed because of the shenanigans I'd been getting up to with Terry Richardson just a few hours before we met, the hours before I met Brittany were also quite telling.

I remember it was the night before *Jackass/Wildboyz* producer Trip Taylor's wedding, but I can't recall why exactly I was going to Vegas or why someone was flying me there on a private jet with Brooke Shields. But there we were—Brooke and I—chatting away for the whole flight like long-lost friends.

Once I got to Vegas, I went to a big party at this club called Tao. The gimmick was that bathtubs were set up all around this club and each bathtub had a bikini-clad model in it. I was sitting at a table with Paris Hilton and her personal photographer. This photographer suggested taking some pictures of me in one of the bathtubs with a couple of the models. I agreed, walked over to an empty tub, stripped myself naked, and started pissing in it. As with my red carpet urination from just a couple weeks earlier, this was not purely the work of a man too drunk to function. Sadly, there was once again actual thought behind my misbehavior.

My feeling at the time was that making these models sit around in bathtubs was demeaning. By pissing in the tub, I was not only making that statement but also ensuring no chick would have to sit in it again. I thought I was a hell of a guy—I was getting these chicks off work early! Amazingly, everyone else—particularly the club's bouncers—seemed to miss this deeper message. They just saw a drunken asshole pissing in a bathtub in the middle of a ritzy party and threw my ass out.

So I went to another club, which is where I met Brittany. She was gorgeous—twenty years old, long blond hair, ridiculous body. She worked as a swimsuit model and lived in Florida but was in Vegas that night with two friends. We all hung out together in their hotel room that night, and after I went back to California, Brittany and I kept in touch. At first, I'd just see her sporadically, either when I was back in Florida visiting family or when she came out to California for a modeling gig. Eventually, she started traveling a bit with me, and then, by the second half of 2007, things got serious—or seriously fucked up is probably more accurate.

One reason Brittany and I didn't immediately jump into a full-on relationship is because back then I started spending a lot of time with Kat Von D. I'd met Kat at the Rainbow but we were little more than acquaintances for a while. She was already pretty well known as a tattoo artist and a star of the TLC reality show *Miami Ink*.

In mid-2006, I was hanging out with Kat in Miami and we got to talking about how neither of us ever wanted to have kids. I wanted a tattoo to memorialize this conversation. Originally, I was going to get a picture of a cute little baby with a circle around it and a slash through it—y'know, "No Babies." Somehow, "No Babies" morphed into "Fuck Babies," which morphed into my getting a tattoo on my arm of a guy literally fucking a baby.

I've regretted plenty of my tattoos but none were so immediately *wrong* as that one. I could tell from the minute I stepped out of that tattoo parlor in Miami onto the street that I'd stepped over a line. Anyone who saw the tattoo was rightfully appalled. Kat eventually changed it to make it less offensive by turning the baby into an ostrich. It's amazing to think that a tattoo of a man fucking an ostrich could make anyone's body art *less* objectionable, but in my case it did.

Kat's relationship with me was really more motherly than a girlfriend-boyfriend kind of thing. Initially we partied a bit together, but when she recognized that I was rapidly going off the deep end, she actively tried to get me *not* to party. Kat's intentions were totally noble: she really wanted to help me clean up. I didn't want any help though, so I lashed out at her more than a few times in ways I'm ashamed of now. As she gradually withdrew from me out of justifiable disgust, I only lashed out harder. Sometimes that just meant nasty e-mails or texts, but the worst by far was when I posted a bunch of crap on my Myspace blog accusing her of cheating on her husband with a bunch of people and being anti-Semitic. It was all just scurrilous rumors that I was airing as if they were facts. They weren't. Even for me, that was a new low and one that still makes me feel fucking awful every time I think about it.

AROUND THIS time, I was still living in the same building in West Hollywood that I'd moved into with Schliz all those years ago. In 2004, I'd convinced Simonetti to leave New Mexico and move out to California to become my Ballbag Inc. editor/co-producer. He moved into the apartment with Schliz and I rented out a separate apartment in the same building for myself. Their pad became the "Ballbag Inc. Headquarters": Simonetti had all his computer stuff in there and we filled the living room with homemade skate ramps. Later, we knocked down the walls in that apartment to fill the whole place with ramps, and I rented a third apartment to serve as the Ballbag office. By that point, Schliz had moved out and J. P. Blackmon, our "shady prop guy" from *Jackass*, had moved in with Simonetti.

In 2007, I rented out a fourth apartment in that building for my personal assistant, Jen Moore. I'd first gotten to know Jen just after *Jackass* premiered. Within a couple of weeks of the first show airing on MTV in 2000, I was trolling the Internet to get a sense of whether I was famous yet or not. I found just one *Jackass* fan site and was disappointed to discover that it had virtually no information about me on it. So I clicked the "contact" icon, and fired off an e-mail offering to provide info about myself. Jen was the webmaster, and at first she couldn't believe it was really me e-mailing her. I quickly convinced her and we became instant friends. Knoxville let her fan site become the official Johnny Knoxville Web site and she set up an official Steve-O Web site for me as well. Around 2005, I got in the habit of forwarding her every e-mail that came in or went out of my account, and began referring to her as my "webmaster, confidant, and archivist." In 2007, I hired her to be my personal assistant. I probably didn't need a PA, but I had grown so irrational, unreliable, and unpredictable, I did need someone to help clean up all my messes and reschedule all the flights I was constantly missing. In reality, she was something closer to a baby-sitter.

The pledge I'd made to swear off cocaine for *Number Two* lasted over a year, until January 2007. But once I picked it back up, my habit was even worse that it had been before. By mid-2007, I was practically living on a diet of coke, booze, and nitrous. The voices in my head that I'd begun hearing months before were now near-constant companions. They came in two basic varieties: demons and angels. The demons encouraged me to do more drugs—especially nitrous. They'd call me a pussy if I stopped huffing or even thought about stopping. They'd tell me I was worthless, I was nothing, and that I should keep huffing and holding my breath until I suffocated. The angels tried to convince me I was out of control and needed to stop. I often reacted to those voices the same way I did to anyone else who suggested I had a drug problem: I'd have a tantrum. It was a regular occurrence for me to be yelling "Shut up! Shut up! I'm fine! Leave me alone!" while I sat by the computer in my empty apartment.

One night, after sending a particularly cruel message to Kat, I was screaming at the voices, telling them that I hadn't been wrong to send the text, though I clearly knew I had been. In response, the voice of an angel in my right ear told me, "You're going to have to answer for that." The message was clear, and it came up again and again during my subsequent Internet research on the spirit world: We have free will to make any choice we desire in this life, but our choices have consequences that we can't escape. *Karma*—it is a bitch.

The voices shared space in my head with increasingly frequent hallucinations. Again, these phantasms often seemed to have my best interests in mind. At one point, I saw Jen's head pop out of a case of beer and patrol the apartment with a video camera to make sure I didn't do more drugs. I watched that eighteen-pack of beer move around the apartment as Jen's head monitored me with a camera. Another time, I remember watching a wall of my shoes, sitting on shelves, tapping their toes impatiently, telling me they were waiting for me to throw away my drugs.

I even hallucinated three well-organized interventions. Friends would materialize in my apartment, sit down, and express their concern for me. I considered these "divine interventions," and despite being completely fictional, they were not totally ineffective. After each of these divine interventions, I'd go tell Ryan or J.P. what had happened, and swear off nitrous or coke or both.

SIMONETTI: He'd come down to my apartment and be like, "Dude, I found God. I'm done with all this." I'd be like, "Okay, that's good. You need to settle down, bro." But the next night he was just right back to it.

None of these hallucinations really scared me much. It's not just that they seemed benevolent; I was convinced that I'd crossed over to the spirit world and reached a higher plane of enlightenment than most people ever achieve. Those hallucinations felt so real, so tangible, that to this day I have a hard time dismissing them as simply drug-induced lunacy. I felt like they were revealing profound truths to me, some that still feel valid now.

But as 2007 wound down, it was becoming painfully obvious—even to me—that I couldn't keep this up. My thoughts were jumbled and my breathing was frequently labored. I was huffing so much nitrous at this point it was like I was trying to cut air out of my life. I remember sitting in my swiveling office chair, facing my computer, alone in my apartment with my drugs, and having the crystal-clear realization that I was killing myself. If I didn't stop this, *I was going to die.* Then I remember looking at my cocaine and looking at my whippet container and thinking, *I don't care if I die.* I really didn't.

A moment after that thought crossed through my brain, I felt the chair I was in spin around so powerfully that I was nearly thrown out of it. A doctor would've probably called that a tactile hallucination. To me it was a message from the spirit world: Some powerful entity or god was trying to tell me I wasn't supposed to die yet. That's not just how I felt about that then, either. I still believe that today.

DESPITE MY raging drug problem, I had a pretty strong hand in the creative side of *Dr. Steve-O*. It was the first time I'd been asked to carry a show all by myself and as fucked up as I was, I recognized that if I had any hope of staying in the public spotlight, I needed the show to succeed. It took only about two and a half weeks to film the whole season, and I managed to pull it together enough to get through the shoots.

Well, mostly. One day, I had a few drinks with lunch and completely lost my shit. We had planned to shoot something with Kat, but in between the planning and the execution, she'd decided she wanted nothing more to do with me. But the other shooting location that day was right next door to her tattoo shop. When I realized that we were parking behind her studio, I threw a vicious tantrum. *How could the producers do this to me? How could they be so thoughtless and uncaring?* The rejection by Kat still stung, but the other real lesson from that outburst was that my tolerance for alcohol had dwindled so much that it took only two or three drinks to turn me into a monster.

Because I didn't have a license, we needed someone to drive the ambulance for *Dr. Steve-O*. Initially, the idea was for Trishelle Cannatella, a former *Real World* star I'd known for a few years, to be the driver, but the producers decided they didn't want to hide her behind a steering wheel. So they found Big Regg.

Reggie Pace was a six-nine 375-pound ex-college football star–turned–rapper–turned–bodyguard from South Central Los Angeles. He'd been working security for Paris Hilton when he met one of the

Dr. Steve-O producers. Having Regg driving allowed Trishelle to interact more with "the wussies" the show was aimed at helping.

I loved Big Regg right away. He was an easygoing, intensely amiable guy who was down for anything. He loved smoking pot and encouraged my rap career. Just after we met, we went into the studio and recorded the theme song for *Dr. Steve-O*. After that, we began hanging out on and off the set, and soon, he became more or less a full-time chaperone/bodyguard.

REGGIE "BIG REGG" PACE (*Dr. Steve-O* co-star/ friend): I was always honest with Steve. That's why I think we became close. On *Dr. Steve-O* we did a thing called Fart Art where each of the "wussies" got an enema with this nontoxic paint and then they'd have to fart on this piece of paper. Well, this one kid was from South Central L.A., right in the hood. The kid didn't want to do it and walked off the show. Steve got really upset. I had to pull Steve aside and explain to him, "Brothers don't necessarily play like that. If that kid did that on national TV, he might have a lot of problems when he went home to the hood." Steve thought about it and got what I meant. That was the beginning of our relationship.

Dr. Steve-O wasn't a bad show but I was in no condition to be carrying any sort of project on my shoulders. I was so involved in being a drug addict that nobody could ever get in touch with me. I rarely answered my phone or returned messages and when I did, I acted like a dick. I went on *Howard Stern* and insulted the WWE, the USA Network's cash cow, as a bunch of "fake-ass bullshit" that I'd never watch. And whenever I was confronted with a problem on the show itself, I became an unreasonable, arrogant, grandstanding jerk-off.

PONTIUS: When he was doing *Dr. Steve-O*, a lot of the dialogue was stuff he learned from me. That was annoying but he was so unaware of when he was taking other people's stuff because he was a sponge. The thing was though, he wasn't saying the lines right. A lot of what's in jokes is how you say it. So it pissed me off.

For one of the episodes, one of our "wussies" was a twenty-six-year-old guy who'd never had any sort of romantic encounter with a girl. We brought this guy over to a sperm bank at UCLA and had this porn star put a rubber on his dick and blow him. The whole thing was filmed and as far as I was concerned this was the greatest thing I'd ever done. This was the crown jewel in the *Dr. Steve-O* franchise.

The USA Network did not see it the same way. For reasons that probably don't need explaining, the executives there wouldn't allow any of the footage anywhere near the air. We couldn't even insinuate that this was going on. I wasn't so dumb as to think we could show an actual blowjob on basic cable, but I thought maybe we could show the footage of the girl going down and then the dude's face while it was happening. USA was having none of it. In fact, the network was so worried about their liability, they ordered all the tapes of that scene sequestered, and every person present for it had to photocopy their driver's license and promise not to leak any footage. The network was terrified of the repercussions if people found out what had happened on the set of the show.

I was furious at this injustice. My greatest accomplishment would languish forever on a cutting room floor. So I wrote an e-mail that not only expressed my disappointment but also did exactly what the network feared by describing in lurid detail exactly what had happened and then distributing it to the most powerful people in the entertainment industry whose e-mail addresses I could come up with—celebrities, journalists, producers, network executives, agents, lawyers, and anyone else (family, friends, associates) who I really wanted to impress. This was the first of what I called my "Rad E-mails." The network was livid.

Dr. Steve-O didn't exactly fail on its own merits. It was the highest-rated show in its time slot on basic cable and retained something like

72 percent of the audience from the WWE broadcast that preceded it. But despite these undeniable positives, the show was canceled after one season. As these Rad E-mails became my typical way of communicating with people regardless of the subject matter, the network decided I was more trouble than I was worth.

For me, I just thought the whole Rad E-mail List was great. I don't know that I believed all these people really cared about the ins and outs of my life, but I figured stirring up controversy with these e-mails was another good way of keeping myself relevant. There was no information too personal, no problem too trivial, no business negotiation too important, no thought too fleeting, that it couldn't be shared with those hundred or so incredibly influential people who were cc-ed on each message. In reality, I would've been hard pressed to put together a mass e-mail list of people who it would've been less appropriate to send all that stuff to.

So I used the Rad E-mail List as a megaphone. I amplified personal spats. I aired dirty laundry. I philosophized. I threatened people. I rambled on and on about shit I knew nothing about. In retrospect, I don't think anything in my life has made me more embarrassed, or more ashamed, than that Rad E-mail List. And knowing the kind of shit I've done in my life to be embarrassed and ashamed about, that's *saying* something. I wrote some vicious shit about my family on the Rad E-mail List and really laid into Pontius over some ridiculously minor dispute. It was all so erratic: I'd often get angry about the craziest things, then quickly come to my senses and apologize, but nearly always do so in a fashion that made me sound like even more of an asshole.

Eventually, my ranting and raving on the Rad E-mail List caused friends to write me off and probably ruined more career opportunities than I'm even aware of. At one point, I got convinced that Jon Murray of Bunim/Murray Productions had done me wrong, so I sent out multiple Rad E-mails detailing what I saw as his transgressions. I made all sorts of threats—mainly to sue him—if he didn't make it right. To quote from one choice e-mail: "Jon Murray is a greedy, immoral man. I am not, which makes me a lot richer than him in the courts. I will not bend or budge with this Bunim/Murray situation—I call that 'principle.'"

Friends, family, lawyers, and agents all tried to talk me off the ledge, pointing out both that Jon hadn't actually done anything wrong and that making these public threats to one of the most powerful people in the television business was the equivalent of career suicide, but I wouldn't listen.

Far from being an exceptional example, this was the norm for what went on with the Rad E-mail List. Reading back through some of those e-mails and responses now, the overall vibe is of one crazy asshole spouting off complete nonsense (me) while a bunch of totally reasonable people around him try to coax him back toward sanity (Dad, Cindy, my agent, my lawyers, my friends).

TED: Up until the Rad E-mails, the stuff that he was doing was enhancing his career. We didn't like it, we didn't agree with it, but you could see the rationale that it was helping him be more successful. He reached a point though where he was sending all these crazy e-mails and that was clearly destructive to his career. That was the point of no return.

CINDY: E-mails to Steve became e-mails to Steve and the whole audience. Part of my contributions to the whole e-mail craziness was to try to be the voice of reason. So I would put tons of thought into every paragraph. There came a point in time when I didn't want to respond at all because it would just fan the flames. Or if I was going to respond, I was going to have such unassailable logic that even if Steve completely missed the point, people around him would understand my concerns and maybe act on them. There was this fine line with the entourage between them being our connection to him—if you couldn't reach Steve, maybe you could reach Ryan or Jen—and them being enablers. But everything got taken the wrong way. He couldn't hear me.

It's pretty hard to describe how out of control my life had gotten by this point, but luckily there is plenty of video evidence to help. By late 2007, I had cameras running near-constantly, creating my own little personal *Truman Show*. Simonetti had basically become my full-time videographer. I'd often make him post video to my Web site, my Myspace page, and YouTube several times a day. It was as if I was afraid that if some part of my life went undocumented—either by my own cameras, the paparazzi, or at the very least described in detail to the Rad E-mail List—then I might cease to exist at all.

Most of that video footage was pretty worthless. Occasionally, I'd be doing a stunt—like having Pontius tattoo my ass using air rifles—but mostly it'd be the most inane shit you could imagine.

> **PONTIUS:** We went over there to film this BB gun thing and he was all swollen up. He was doing so much nitrous, his neck was wider than his head and his stomach looked like when you put a pillow under your shirt. When we were setting up, Dimitry was laughing, but he wasn't laughing at the skit. He was laughing at how engorged Steve's belly was. It was really sad. There's a point when if you're filming every single action you do, are you just living for the camera? He was so concerned about how he would be remembered. It was like, "Why don't you live for yourself?" It's great to film everything, but at a point you kind of lose yourself.

One popular subject of the footage for a while was the guy who'd moved into the apartment next door to me. He was a lawyer and would frequently complain about the noise from my apartment. I used to blast music, yell, and scream (often at the voices in my own head), break things, whatever. He'd either call down to the leasing office or call the cops. It galled me that he couldn't walk six feet to knock on my door and ask me himself—though, in retrospect, it makes complete sense that he wouldn't want to involve himself in the affairs of a person who was so clearly unstable—so I declared war on him. I'd turn my speakers toward his wall and crank my music up at 3 a.m. I'd pound on the walls and yell at him. At one point, I even punched holes through the wall separating our apartments. All this was documented on video and posted on the Internet.

> **SIMONETTI:** The first time he really started messing with the neighbor, I filmed it. Then the second time he went back in there, I was like, "No Steve. The cops were already here." He's like, "Dude, you gotta film this." I'm like, "No, I'm going home." Working for him, it wasn't like I could ever say "no" but there were several occasions when I just walked away. We did have one pretty major falling out when he was off the deep end, probably drugged out. He would get so excited talking that spit would fly out of his mouth. One night, he was being too obnoxious and spit right into my face. I intentionally spit right back on his face and told him to settle the fuck down. Then I told him I was out of there and it's over. That was the worst of it.

> **BIG REGG:** I would go to Steve's apartment every day or every other day to make sure he was all right. He was crazy, just doing this footage, putting it online, and e-mailing it out. He had a sixty-inch monitor for his computer and he just stood in front of it. He had really just turned into this evil, demented dictator on his computer.

Both Dad and Cindy were convinced by this time that I was suffering from some drug-induced bipolar disorder, and I'm sure they were right. I was having wild manic episodes during which I'd be up for days filming whacked-out footage and sending e-mails full of grandiose proclamations about how my latest stunt/rap song/idea was going to save the world. Often this would be followed by dark, disturbed notes about my mom or angry accusations toward family and friends for various imagined slights.

I'd made Jen, Ryan, and J.P. employees of Ballbag Inc., and along with Regg (who worked for me in a more unofficial capacity), they were frequently tasked with getting me to where I was supposed to be and keeping me out of as much trouble as they could. It was a thankless job.

By the end of 2007, every public appearance was a potential disaster waiting to happen. I got kicked out of the A&E roast of Gene Simmons for pissing on the stage. Regg and I got arrested on misdemeanor assault charges after Regg pushed our way into the opening of Paris Hilton's clothing line at some posh store in Beverly Hills. I threatened to kill George W. Bush, then passed weed out to the paparazzi (and smoked some), while standing in front of the notorious celeb hangout spot the Ivy in the middle of the day.

JEN MOORE (personal assistant): It became very difficult. Because on one hand you had Steve, who we were calling the CEO of the company, telling me "Do this. Do that." Then his dad would get upset because I'd make decisions but I was making them based on what Steve told me. So I was in many, many a compromised position where the decisions came from Steve but they came out of my mouth. It was so nuts—oh Lord, it was like a tornado for a while in my apartment.

BIG REGG: It was awkward, especially when we'd go on the road. I was worried that I'd go to his room one morning and his heart would be stopped. It was scary. But I used to be a dope

dealer way back in the day, so I know how people in those
situations react if they feel they're being judged or preached to.
So I wouldn't come at Steve like that. I'd come at Steve like,
"You're going to get me in trouble." Because I knew Steve loved
me to death. I'd be like, "Steve, if you fucking die on my watch,
you're going to get me in trouble." I'd try to make him feel
guilty, like he's doing something to hurt me. That's how I would
try to get him to tone it down.

SIMONETTI: There were a few times when it got so bad
that I told him, "You need to settle down." As far as people
maybe thinking that I didn't care, there were many nights when
he was crying on my shoulder. There was an occasion I can
specifically remember when he was literally crying and I'm
hugging him, telling him, "It's okay, bro. We'll get through
this. You'll get through this." But you can give your friend
advice—you can't tell him what to do.

I'm squeamish about needles, so I've never shot up anything, but a
drug dealer who lived around the corner from me used to shoot up all
the time and had squirted blood all over his place. If he wouldn't answer
my calls, I'd just show up at his place. Once, I walked in to find him
passed out with a needle hanging from his neck. Another time, I found
him jerking off with a needle sticking out from in between his toes. On
a third occasion, I found him sleeping near a table that was covered in
cocaine residue and dried specks of his own blood. I tried waking him
up but he was sleeping so heavily he couldn't be roused, which presented
me with a problem: How am I going to get *my* coke? I looked down at
the table and didn't even hesitate before I started scraping the blood-
tainted cocaine residue on the table into lines and snorting it. Sure,
shooting up made me squeamish, but I was *fine* with snorting a drug
addict's dried blood up my nose. It really gave me something to think

about later, when I got tested for HIV/AIDS and hepatitis C in rehab. Thankfully, those viruses can't survive for more than a few minutes when exposed to the air, which may be the only reason I didn't test positive for any of that shit.

It's pretty comic that amid all this craziness, I decided to become a vegetarian. During my obsessive Internet research on the spirit world, I came across a YouTube clip of a Hare Krishna dude from India talking about how difficult it is for Westerners to be "saved" because of our lack of respect for life and the planet. At one point, he bluntly asked, "How can you expect to be saved if you eat meat?" This reminded me of what I'd heard that angelic voice tell me about having to "answer" for my actions later on. I became terrified of having to pay for the suffering of every animal I'd eaten or worn, so I immediately gave up eating meat and wearing leather. Never mind that my apartment was strewn with pill bottles and platters of coke and ketamine. Never mind that my fridge had nothing in it besides vodka and beer. Never mind that I was a raging asshole to everyone around me. I was going to achieve salvation because I stopped eating burgers. (I justified continuing to eat fish because "Jesus fed people with fish.")

Not only did I become a vegetarian, I became the worst kind of vegetarian. I was a self-righteous, holier-than-thou judgmental jerk about it. I had a shoe sponsor at the time, but since they made leather shoes, I felt it was my duty to slam them publicly for killing cows. I'd tout my vegetarianism as a badge of honor and wield it as a hammer to bludgeon others for not living up to my lofty moral standards. It was really pretty impressive: even when I was doing something that could reasonably be considered noble, I found a way to be a dickhead about it.

WHERE KAT recoiled from me at my worst, that's all Brittany ever really saw. She endured me at my absolute lowest and rarely, if ever, said anything about it. It wasn't like she was my drug buddy—she was just a sweet twenty-one-year-old girl. Whether she was traveling with me on the road or visiting me in California, she'd typically keep normal hours while I binged on coke and whatever else for three or four days then crashed for fourteen to twenty hours straight.

I'm not really sure what Brittany got out of this relationship, but it couldn't have been much. She genuinely cared about me, but I think she was probably also a little enamored by the trappings of show business and fame.

BRITTANY (ex-girlfriend): I really loved him but I felt like I was babysitting. I was scared to leave him alone. I'm not Little Miss Innocent. I've done my share of partying, but I had never even dreamed of doing some of the things he's done. I mean, I can hang out and party, but I want to go to bed at three o'clock. I don't want to stay up until three o'clock the next day. So I'd be like, "Come to bed," and he wouldn't. He'd just sit there on his computer for hours and hours. I'd go to bed and then wake up at ten o'clock in the morning and he'd still be sitting at the computer. It would piss me off because he'd be up for three days, and then I'd wake up the next morning and he'd want to go to bed. Then he'd sleep all day and I'd be sitting around his apartment going, "Okay, now what do I do?" I was just kind of there.

In February 2008, I went with Brittany to visit her grandmother in Georgia. It was at her grandma's house that I got down on both knees and asked Brittany to marry me, right in front of Grandma. There wasn't a lot of forethought involved in this proposal. It was just one of dozens of horrible ideas that came to me during a fit of drugged-up mania that I thought was totally genius. I didn't even have a ring. I told Brittany to get online and pick one out. She ordered herself a Hello Kitty ring.

Not content with the exciting prospect of my impending marriage, I also decided I was ready to have a baby. To be fair, that wasn't entirely my idea. That one was first suggested to me by one of my drug-induced hallucinations. I remember closing my eyes and seeing pictures of babies projected on the insides of my eyelids. I was certain this meant my spirit friends were waiting for me to reproduce. I even recall voices confirming this and telling me they were urgently awaiting my offspring.

Brittany's grandmother told us that she recognized that we lived in a different time than she had grown up in, and offered to let us both sleep in her bed while she slept on the sofa in her living room. The morning after my ridiculous proposal I sat down with Grandma in the living room and announced to her that we had tried to make a baby in her bed. I'll never forget the horrified expression on Brittany's face when she heard me say those words to her grandmother. Thinking of that, and all the times I repeated it (including this one), makes me feel horrible.

CINDY: When I got an e-mail saying that they were trying to have a baby, I called Brittany on the QT and said basically, "This is a really terrible idea. Steve's in no shape to be a daddy." And Dad called Brittany's grandma several times. Because at that time, Steve was crapping all over us. He didn't want to hear anything Dad or I had to say, but he was smitten with Brittany's grandma.

I was scheduled to fly directly from Georgia to New York City in order to be part of *Jackass*'s "24 Hour Takeover" of MTV. The idea behind the "Takeover" was that the *Jackass* cast would have "control" of MTV for a full day—we'd play videos we liked, do some stunts, just generally screw around. It was all part of promoting the launch of the Jackassworld.com Web site.

Brittany was supposed to meet me back in California after the

"Takeover"—she was going to move in with me out there—but first had to go back to Florida to take care of some things. Before heading to the airport in Atlanta, I met some random guy in a bar who went by the name G-Music. I got a bunch of drugs and went with him on an all-night psychotic tour of Atlanta during which I recorded four more songs in two different studios for my then still-impending rap album.

I'd perfected a method of flying with cocaine on airplanes—I'd fold it up with the cash in my wallet and the TSA people would never want to touch the money—so I arrived in New York City with coke still on me, but hardly enough to make it through another day. There were two nights before the "Takeover" began, and I slept through the first, then scored a whole bunch more coke before the second. Things didn't go well.

PONTIUS: Steve-O, Wee-Man, and I all got taken to do interviews with a bunch of radio stations. We divided up the stations between us but about twenty minutes into it, the producer comes in and is like, "Hey, can you guys finish up for Steve-O? He's just too fucked up. He's on the phone with his dad while he's on the phone with the radio stations. He's speaking into his headphones instead of the microphone."

At one point, while I was in Central Park with a bunch of the *Jack-ass* guys filming a stunt where we sledded down some park steps, I gave an inadvertently hilarious interview to a reporter from the Associated Press. I was supposed to be promoting the "Takeover" but instead told this straight-laced news reporter, "I'm really more caught up in my own little world of narcotics and alcohol. I just sit in my house, piling all the narcotics into my body that I possibly can, namely ketamine, nitrous oxide, PCP, and cocaine, and I just get all kinds of results." The clip is still pretty easy to find on YouTube should you want a quick laugh.

I'd already been awake for at least twenty-four hours when the "Takeover" began but was so out of control that I didn't last through the night before my friends kicked me out. I'd brought tons of coke with me to the MTV studios and was sharing almost as much as I was doing. I did a quick rap thing with Big Regg, announced on live TV that Brittany and I had sex in her grandma's bed and were trying to have a baby, but was mostly just incoherent and intolerable.

KNOXVILLE: It was at its darkest. Just a complete fucking shit show. Normally with Steve, if he was out of control, you could talk to him and at the very least, he'd hear you in the moment. But at the "Takeover," you couldn't even talk to him. I was contemplating just knocking him out because he just wouldn't shut up.

TREMAINE: I had a show called *Rob and Big* on the air at the time and Steve was offended that I would be doing that and not something with him and Big Regg. But mostly, he was loud and incoherent. He was completely blown out, just a shell of himself. It was really troubling to all of us. We were like, "What the fuck do we do?" We were stuck live on the air with this really loose cannon. We didn't want to kick him out because he was one of us, but at the same time, he was really a mess. He was practically speaking in tongues. We couldn't really show him on TV because his pupils were so dilated, his eyes were completely black. He just looked like a demon. We really kept him around a lot longer than we should have.

After I got booted, you'd think I'd just go crash, but instead I went back to the hotel and stayed up until the next afternoon doing more coke. Eventually, I did finally sleep for a good fourteen hours or so, then woke up, smoked a joint, ate some breakfast, and went over to Howard Stern's studio to appear on his show.

I got on the air, rapped, hurled random insults at Martha Stewart, Eminem, K-Fed, Britney Spears, Bam, Universal Records, Hillary Clinton, George W. Bush, and a few others, and again talked up my plan to impregnate Brittany. Howard told me that Knoxville had been in the studio a few days earlier saying that everything had turned bad for me and that they were all really worried. Bam had been there recently, too, saying I was at the end of the line. I insisted I was fine, but my labored breathing and haggard appearance told a different story. I asked Howard, "Who do you think is going to live longer, me or Artie Lange?" Artie had his own well-publicized drug problems and was also significantly overweight. Howard didn't even hesitate: "Steve-O, you don't have a chance of living as long as Artie." He wasn't joking.

WHEN I got back to California after the "Takeover," Brittany was still in Florida. Immediately after arriving home, I snorted massive amounts of coke and ketamine. I wasn't hallucinating, but by this point, my hallucinations had become such a regular part of my life that I got really disappointed when they weren't happening. So I did more and more drugs in an effort to spur them on. In the midst of this binge, I sat down at the computer and began "researching" the fourth dimension. This "research" led to what I considered an astounding breakthrough: *the fourth dimension is time.* I realize this sounds like nothing but idiotic blather, but back then I was sure I'd stumbled on an invaluable nugget of wisdom.

I had a paid appearance to make in Vegas the day after I got back to California. Big Regg and I flew from the Burbank airport, and I can remember sitting on that plane, closing my eyes, and seeing a cartoon projection of two hands with handcuffs closing on them. The vision was clear as day. What I took that to mean was that since I'd cracked some code with my fourth dimension research, the spirit people had got me and now they weren't going to let me go. I'd soon find out that it meant something else entirely.

Vegas was a disaster. I got on the microphone at this club where I was being hired to show up and began rapping, much to the displeasure of everyone there. The whole place started booing me.

"Oh yeah?" I responded. "Well, whatever. I have more money than any of you."

It would've almost been funny in an Andy Kaufman sort of way if I'd been joking. But I wasn't. I was just the ultimate douchebag. I was regularly referring to fans who came up to me asking for photos or autographs as "pigeons." I'd complain to Regg about how sick I was of all the pigeons pecking at me. In retrospect, I guess I thought so little of myself that anyone who looked up to me seemed lower than dirt.

That night, I was in a hotel elevator with Regg when a fan approached me.

"Man, Steve-O, you look like shit," the guy said. He wasn't trying to be a dick—he seemed genuinely concerned—but I just went crazy and attacked the guy. I got in his face and started shoving and hitting him. It was such a cowardly move. Even in my fucked-up state, I never would've done that if Big Regg wasn't there. By no fault of his own, Regg—like the security detail in New Orleans, which only seemed to encourage me to shove the dude who was harassing Knoxville—gave me license to be an even bigger asshole than I'd normally be. Regg pulled me off this poor dude and somehow got me back to California in one piece.

I RETURNED home desperate to see Brittany. I'd made a big deal about us opening the FedEx package with her ring in it together, and in my mind, I expected her to be waiting at my apartment for me, anxious to share in this magical moment. Instead, she was at a friend's house and didn't seem to be in an incredible hurry to come see me.

While I waited for her, I remember writing this preachy, pompous, hypocritical essay that I sent out to my Rad E-mail List and posted on my blog. (Sample lines: "My name is Steve-O, my nation is 'The World,' and my religion is 'To Do Good.' We are accountable for everything that we do, say, or even think, and all the activity we are responsible for is eternal, and waiting for us to answer to it—In the Fourth Dimension. Time.")

When Brittany finally arrived at my place a couple hours later, she didn't have the FedEx package with the ring in it. She told me she'd forgotten it. I was outraged. If that wasn't enough, she then told me she didn't want to get married anyway. To me, that was the ultimate betrayal. She was a liar and I couldn't ever trust her again.

BRITTANY: The engagement wasn't something that I took seriously. I mean, I was only twenty-one years old. He was obsessive with everything in his life, not just drugs. It was like, "I want to get married!" "Okay." "I want to get married next Wednesday, because it's national nonsmoking day and I'm going to quit smoking!" And I'm like, "That's on Wednesday. You can't just plan a wedding like that." And he was already telling his assistant, Jen, to book it. It was just crazy. So I was like, "No!" I just didn't know how to handle it. I mean, I wanted to be there to support him, but I didn't want to get married. I was confused. I had all these emotions. I had just left my family and my parents. They were crying at the airport because their little girl was going to live in Hollywood. He didn't even ask me how I was doing. It was just all about him. He was self-centered and selfish and didn't even realize it.

I was devastated that Brittany didn't want to get married. I grabbed my skateboard and left the apartment, barefoot. I made it about a block before I jumped in a cab and went to the Rainbow. It took only two or three drinks there before I was basically in a blackout. While I was there, I bought five baggiess of cocaine from this gangster dude and called up another drug dealer who brought me a few vials of ketamine. At some point, I snorted lines off some girl's thigh, which I know about only because a photo of it surfaced in the *National Enquirer* a few weeks later.

I eventually had this random dude drive me and the gangster back to my place. They came in with me and filmed as I cooked up a vial of ketamine in the microwave, snorted a ridiculous amount of it, and began antagonizing the neighbor. I pounded on his door, banged on the wall, and told him I was going to kick his ass. I dared him to call the cops, which he did. When the cops showed up, I tried to hide all my drugs around the apartment—no easy task considering the sheer amount of illegal narcotics I had in that place. I left the video camera running on a stool aimed at the door when I opened it for the police, and thus managed to film my arrest on vandalism charges.

I was barefoot and shirtless, and the cops offered to let me go back inside to get dressed before they took me to jail. I brazenly declined, then spent the whole ride to the police station telling the officers they were doing me a huge favor because the publicity from this arrest was going to get me more media attention than a Super Bowl commercial. At the station, they found one of the baggies of coke—ironically folded into the cash in my wallet in the way I used to fool the TSA—and rebooked me on felony cocaine possession charges. It occurs to me that had I taken the cops up on their offer to go get some clothes on, I could've easily ditched my wallet in the apartment. But I was way too messed up to remember the coke was there. By that point, I was too far gone to understand much of anything.

21

I THINK THIS IS WHAT THEY CALL "CIRCLING THE DRAIN"

I got bailed out on Wednesday, March 5, after a day and a half in jail in West Hollywood. When I walked out of the place, TMZ.com cameras were waiting for me and I didn't disappoint: I'd smuggled my jail linens out in my pants, which I proudly displayed for the cameras and then hung out the window as my bail bondsman drove me home.

Any way you slice it, my life was pretty fucked at that point. Brittany had broken off the engagement, my friends were rapidly distancing themselves from me, *Dr. Steve-O* was dead, the rap album was a disaster, and I'd burned bridges with my shoe sponsor and pretty much anyone else in a position to offer me gainful employment. The most promising thing on the horizon for my career was a potential offer from ExtenZe—a penis-enlarging soft drink—to become their national spokesman. On top of all that, now I was facing felony coke charges.

In the weeks before my arrest, unbeknownst to me, Dad and Cindy had been talking to Dr. Drew about trying to get me into rehab. At Dr. Drew's recommendation, Dad recruited a lawyer, Barry Sands, who specializes in cases arising from alcohol and drug addiction. Barry met me at the jail the day I got out, along with the bail bondsman and Big Regg. Dad had made them promise to get me to an appointment he'd set up for that day with a psychiatrist at the chemical dependency clinic at Las Encinas Hospital, where Dr. Drew was the medical director. So after driving me to my apartment, the bondsman made me swear I'd get to this shrink appointment. Then he and Barry took off. Brittany was at a modeling gig in Orlando, so that left just Regg and me at the apartment.

Immediately, I began scouring the place for all the drugs I'd hidden when I'd been arrested. I found two vials of ketamine in the bathroom and three of the one-gram bags of coke that I'd bought at the Rainbow. Regg rolled a few joints and I pounded a few beers. Then I cooked up one of the ketamine vials into a powder in the microwave, snorted a frightening amount of it, and scraped the rest into the cellophane wrapper from my cigarette pack. I stocked my pockets with the coke, some joints, a handful of Xanax, and the ketamine, then grabbed two beers and told Regg I was ready to go see the shrink.

I drank, smoked, and snorted the whole ride there. When we arrived, I walked into the reception area, scribbled something barely resembling my name on a clipboard, walked back out, and cracked open another beer.

BIG REGG: He was like, "Okay, I was here. Let's go." I'm like, "Steve, you gotta stay." I could tell things were getting bad because he got furious with me, like, "Fuckin' Regg, don't tell me what to do!"

We drove from there over to Regg's house and I had what I thought was a fantastic idea to film myself teaching Regg to juggle. The resulting five-and-a-half-minute clip is pretty shocking: I'm shirtless, with a clump of white powder caked to the underside of my left nostril. After a few halfhearted attempts at juggling three lemons in Regg's backyard, I just start spitting, mumbling, and babbling incoherently. Then I walk close to the camera lens, cradle my hands in front of my face as if I'm holding a tiny, imaginary Earth, and quote a rap song that I'd recorded just days earlier in Atlanta: "God is one / God is two / God is me plus all of you / Think about everything you do / Be real careful of every move / Because it's trapped—like us, to time we're glued / We're glued to time, dude / It's the fourth dimension." The song, by the way, was titled "Spit on My Dick." Really.

Regg needed to pick up his girlfriend at work, so we drove over there and kept the camera running. Waiting in the parking lot for her, I climbed on top of Regg's car, raised my fist in the air, and shouted, "God is the sun! God is one!" Some security guards saw me and called the police. The cops questioned me (Q: "Where are you living now?" A: "Well, I just got out from behind bars for making a ruckus!"), but chose not to search me. That surely saved me from being hauled back to jail mere hours after being released, though clearly that was not really something I was all too worried about at the time.

I thought all this footage was genius, so we went back to Regg's house and posted it online immediately. Then we went over to a friend's home studio and recorded a song about crack that Regg had written. I'd run out of ketamine at that point, so I started working on the coke, which perversely enough, straightened me out a bit.

Eventually Regg dropped me off at my apartment. I cooked up some more ketamine and binged on it for hours. Whatever manic high I'd been on since getting out of jail was dissipating, and I was crashing hard. Just after midnight, I sent an e-mail to a buddy of mine from high school, Abdalla Zarroug, which, of course, I also copied the entire Rad E-mail List on.

From: stephenglover420@yahoo.com

Subject: a bullet in the head
To: [redacted]
Abdalla,
I am in the worst pain I have ever felt. I can hear my Mother crying. This
is so bad. Please squash this in 4d. Love...

Steve

My brain was so scrambled that I was convinced that Abdalla was this angel who had special powers and operated in other dimensions. I was coming apart at the seams. A little before 9 a.m. on Thursday morning, I sent out a Rad E-mail with the subject line "making babeeeeeeeeeeeeeeees" and a body that read simply, "Essssssssssppppppp pppeeeeeeeeeeeeeeeeeeeeessssssssssssn,,,,,wssssppppppppppppppppppppppppp kkkkkkkkkkkkkkkkkkkkkkkkkkkkkkkkkkkkkkkkkkkkkkkkkjjjjjjjjjjjjjjjya knnooooooooo."

The drug binge continued all day Thursday, until I finally crashed for at least twenty-four hours. I must have woken up sometime in the wee hours of Saturday morning because at 4:20 a.m., I fired off a Rad E-mail that opens, "I've never really given very serious thought to the idea of committing suicide, but . . . I did some major spiritual digging over the last couple days. Everything I've been studying had led me to believe that death was merely a 'wardrobe change,' and that being the case, what would be the difference?" I attached five YouTube clips to the e-mail that I described as "the fruits of my spiritual digging," and in a separate note to Dad and Cindy at the bottom of the same e-mail, I wrote:

If viewing the following clips doesn't ease the discomfort your pointless worrying about me causes, then, let me know and I will absolutely quit letting it bother me. I am not what is 'broken'—YOU ARE. I have the serenity to accept that which I cannot change, and, just like I did when I left Mom's house after her annyeurism—to set out to make Her proud of me—I will walk the fuck away from you and you're ability to see nothing good about shit and waste your life to worry and fear. I don't live in fear and I mean that very, very sincerely . . . I gave up eating/wearing any meat other than fish (so did Brittany), I've been working with Brittany at having a healthy relationship with her and her family, I've been the utmost professional in my career, and, if you guys can't see anything good in that, THEN I WILL OFFICIALLY FUCKING GIVE UP ON TRYING TO MAKE YOU PROUD. Please give these following video clips from YouTube a GREAT DEAL of attention. Completely undivided attention . . . and give some serious thought to this idea: you could've very, very easily lost a son/brother yesterday.

The clips I'd sent were some pretty whacked-out shit, but looking back at them now, there are moments that really scratch at the core issues that were tearing me apart.

"You will die. No one will remember you," is the way this Polish philosopher and sociologist named Zygmunt Bauman put it in a clip titled "How to Survive Death." Later in the same clip, he puts into words a profound riddle I'd been struggling with since I was a teenager and which had only grown more troubling as I watched Mom die: "How can we put some meaning in our earthly lives if you know in the end it is all in vain?" I'd thought all my video footage would be my immortal legacy, I'd thought fame could ensure I survived death, I'd thought obliterating myself with drugs could keep me from thinking about it, but now I was running out of ideas. The closest thing I found to an answer to this riddle was in one of the other clips I sent with that e-mail. It's a seven-minute video of Hare Krishna founder Prabhupada explaining reincarnation, or death as a "wardrobe change."

AS THE sun came up on Saturday morning, I was confronted with a new, more earthly concern. There was an eviction notice tacked to my door. Among the offenses listed were kicking in my neighbor's door while yelling, "I hate my neighbor—get out of this building!", spitting on my neighbor while brandishing a BB gun, busting a mop pole through the wall between our apartments, and calling my neighbor a "fucking faggot." All of this stuff had happened in the past thirty days. The property management company had no trouble documenting it in detail since I'd posted video of it all on my Web site, my Myspace page, and YouTube. I was given three days to move out.

My reaction was to send out a Rad E-mail alerting everyone that I was throwing an "eviction party." I was going to leave the apartment with a bang by performing two stunts: jumping a motorbike out of the sliding glass door that led to my balcony onto the roof of the building next door, and leaping from my bedroom window into a hot tub on the sidewalk three stories below. In the e-mail, I asked the *Jackass* guys for help setting up and filming the stunts, and stated that everyone "should be very aware that I am a man on a ruthless spiritual mission."

Then I kicked off my eviction party by trashing the apartment. With Simonetti filming, I destroyed a light fixture, ripped down a curtain rod and plunged it through the sliding glass door, and busted nearly every mirror or piece of glass in the place.

I didn't get many responses to the mass e-mail—most people ignored it, Tremaine said no one from his production company, Dickhouse, could come—which pissed me off. I sent a few more e-mails dialing up the pressure and letting everyone know I wasn't kidding. Still, very little reaction. Finally, just before 11 p.m. that night, I sent out the following Rad E-mail:

From: stephenglover420@yahoo.com

Subject: I promise...
To: [Redacted]
THAT I WILL KNOW HOW MANY BONES GET BROKEN IN A 25 FOOT
FALL ONTO FUCKING CONCRETE IF SOMEONE DOESN'T AT LEAST

BRING CARD BOARD BOXES OR FUCKING TRASH CANS...I'M READY TO FUCKING DIE...

I was definitely threatening to splatter myself on the sidewalk if people didn't pay attention to me, but I don't think I was that serious about committing suicide. I think I was simply acting like a douchebag in one way to try to distract attention from other ways in which I'd acted like a douchebag. It's really a pretty funny concept: I was simultaneously desperate for attention and embarrassed about the attention I'd been demanding. But I couldn't help myself. Throughout the day, I was also sending a constant stream of text messages to Brittany in Orlando.

BRITTANY: He was texting me and texting me, saying he was going to commit suicide, that I was driving him crazy, and that I was cheating on him. And I was like, "I'm working. I can't be on my phone." He was just freaking out. I was three thousand miles away, so I just started forwarding the texts to Jen Moore and everybody else.

KNOXVILLE: It's funny because his veiled suicide threat essentially wasn't that dangerous. He was going to jump this mini-motorcycle to the apartment next door. There was a twenty-five-foot fall, which sounds like, "Fuck, that could be heavy," but it was literally about four feet between his apartment and the apartment next door. He had that. But he was in such a state that something could've happened accidentally. It was just the thought of him saying, "I don't care if I die or not." And "Oh yeah, can you bring some boxes in case I do fall?" So even in his suicidal threats, there were safety precautions. That's what led me to think, "Boy, maybe this is more of a cry for help."

TREMAINE: We had been thinking about trying to do something already. A few months earlier, when he was really doing a lot of whippets, one of the sound guys we always work with, Cordell Mansfield, and I talked to him about it. It was sort of a half-assed attempt at a semi-intervention. Then when he was in jail on the coke charges, I got Jen, Brittany, Knoxville, and [*Jackass* associate producer] Shanna [Zablow] to come into the office to talk about it. We actually called and talked to an interventionist at that point because none of us knew what the fuck we were doing. He was like, "Are you all ready to commit?" and I needed to do some more diligence on getting Steve's dad involved first.

JEN: We all met at the Dickhouse offices and were talking about how we needed to do an intervention. We got Ted on the phone and worked out the bail and everything. At that point we knew that something was going to have to be done.

KNOXVILLE: Everyone was deciding what to do about him but the last straw was those suicidal e-mails. I called Jeff and was like, "We've got to go get him." Then we put out calls to about six or seven friends and they said, "We're there." And I contacted Dr. Drew to see the best way to go about this because all we had was an urge but no plan. Dr. Drew just ran me through everything.

DR. DREW: I told Johnny, "He's going to die. You need to go in there, tie him up, throw him in the car, and take him to the hospital." He was way too psychiatrically impaired to do a traditional intervention. He was really manic, talking about the world coming to an end. He would engage in these crazy spiritual conversations. I said, "Do not have a conversation with him. Put him in the car, call the cops if you have to, and take him to the psychiatric ward. Otherwise, he's dead."

TREMAINE: Dr. Drew told us we could do what's called a 5150, where you can hold someone for seventy-two hours on a psychiatric evaluation. So we decided, "All right, let's just go there. We'll tell him we're coming to film but we're really just gonna take him to the hospital." I called Steve's dad and let him know what we'd found out. I wanted him to come out right away, be a part of it and take the lead.

TED: It was one of the most difficult decisions of my life, but I decided not to go. As much influence as I had with Steve in other areas, I had absolutely none in the area of lifestyle. I couldn't even start a discussion about his addiction problems without him blowing up and slamming the door in my face. I believed strongly that his friends would have far more influence than I ever would, but that if I were there, they'd defer to me and drop into the background. So rather than an intervention with his friends and peers, it would quickly deteriorate into a vicious battle of words—or worse—between Steve and me. I explained this to Jeff, and told him that I wouldn't come out for the intervention, but would be on a plane as soon as Steve had had a few days to detox.

CINDY: In the weeks before the intervention, Dad and I were the ones sorting out Steve's insurance, trying to identify an ideal place and have it all set up ahead of time, so there would be no, "Sorry, we won't have a bed for three weeks." We were also trying to figure out all the legal options. If you do a 5150, that's for seventy-two hours, but how do you do it right so seventy-two hours later you haven't burned the family ties forever? Dad and I were already so deep in the crapper as far as Steve was concerned, so we weren't the right messengers. We didn't speak the right language. Johnny and Jeff and the other guys did.

Knoxville and Tremaine both e-mailed me late on Saturday to say they would in fact be coming the next day for the stunts. I was stoked. As far as I knew they'd be filming. I was convinced these stunts would build momentum for a third *Jackass* film, which, in turn, would bring me at least a few more years in the spotlight. But the good news didn't exactly settle me down. I stayed up most of the night firing off crazed Rad E-mails, breaking shit all over my apartment, and putting guns to my head, while Ryan filmed all the madness, compressed the video, and posted it online virtually in real time. The last video before I finally passed out had me lighting my pubic hair on fire and threatening to kill the president.

22

5150

Regg was the first person to arrive at my apartment on Sunday morning. I'd been asleep for only a few hours when he and his brother, Swizz, showed up around 10 a.m.

BIG REGG: Steve was in some drawers and a bathrobe, and the apartment was fucked up. There was shit everywhere. He was getting pissed because the guys weren't there yet. I was nervous because I'd never lied to him. I felt like I was betraying his trust.

Regg and Swizz actually left for a little while and then came back around noon with a big *Jackass* contingent—Johnny Knoxville, Jeff Tremaine, producer Trip Taylor, soundman Cordell Mansfield, and cameramen Dimitry Elyashkevich and Rick Kosick. They all walked in and began blocking the doorways and windows. Knoxville came running through to seal off the window I'd been talking about jumping out of. He posted up right next to it.

I knew something was wrong when I saw that they didn't have any camera equipment. Then they told me they weren't there to film, they were going to take me to the hospital for a seventy-two-hour psychiatric hold.

I didn't really take them all that seriously at first. I turned on my own video camera and tried to film the whole thing. Knoxville knocked it out of my hands. I don't know if I've ever seen a more serious look on that guy's face. The whole thing got very real at that point.

RICK KOSICK (cameraman, *Jackass*, *Wildboyz*): The plan was Knoxville and Jeff were going to do most of the talking. Me and Regg would stand in the back so he couldn't make a run for it. We'd block the door and grab him.

KNOXVILLE: I'm not that tough, but I took some tough guys with me that day. We knew he was going to be defensive and wouldn't want to go, but I kind of told everyone that if he says he doesn't want to go, just knock him out and then we'll take him anyway. Steve-O is not violent at all, so I pretty much knew that if there were a bunch of big dudes in the room, he wouldn't resist.

TREMAINE: It was always hard for us to intervene because we all partied pretty hard. We all go to bars, live it up, and act a little crazy. So for us to even contemplate intervening, it had to be horrible. It'd be a little hypocritical for a lot of us to be involved otherwise.

My first reaction to realizing that this was really happening was to get defiant. I started yelling, "I'm not going! I'm not going! I'm fine!" They tried to explain what was going to happen at the hospital but I wouldn't listen. I started blasting one of my rap songs and then lit up a joint.

I walked around trying to ignore the intervention going on in my apartment as if it had nothing to do with me. The guys wouldn't let me go into my bedroom without following me in there and kept insisting that this was going to happen whether I agreed to it or not. I kept telling them I was fine.

BIG REGG: It really got to the point with Tremaine and Knoxville where they were going to have to take him forcibly. I remember Steve gave me this look like, "Regg, stop 'em! Make 'em stop!" I'll never forget that look. He looked like a five-year-old kid. I felt so bad. Even though I knew it was the right thing, that really fucked me up.

It became clear I wasn't going to win this battle. They'd let me carry on like an asshole for a while, but eventually I was going to the hospital even if they had to kick my ass in the process. So I started trying to bargain with them. I said I'd go for twenty-four hours but not seventy-two. I also wanted to bring my video camera so I could film it all.

CORDELL MANSFIELD (soundman, *Jackass*, *Wildboyz*): It was really Dimitry who negotiated the whole thing. Steve was like, "Fuck that, I'm not going for seventy-two hours. I'll go for twenty-four hours." Knoxville and some of the rest of us were like, "No, man. You've got to go for seventy-two." And Dimitry was like, "Twenty-four is good. Let's try twenty-four!" He was lighthearted about it. Steve was like, "I want to bring the camera," and we were like, "No fucking cameras!" And Dimitry was like, "Let him bring the camera!"

DIMITRY ELYASHKEVICH (cameraman, *Jackass*, *Wildboyz*): Whatever it took to get him in the car and to the hospital, that's what we did. If he agrees to go for one day, just take him and leave him there for three days. "You want to bring your camera? Bring your camera." I knew they wouldn't let him bring it in the hospital.

I gave in and said I'd go. At the time I had hundreds of one-dollar bills stapled to the walls of my apartment and strewn all over the floor. (This was my idea of home décor.) I walked around scooping up fistfuls of cash and stuffing it into a plastic folder, which also held a bunch of release forms that I planned on getting people at the hospital to sign after I filmed them. I figured I'd film myself calmly convincing the hospital staff I was just fine, then, after they released me, I'd use the cash to take a cab somewhere to buy more drugs. It'd be a great stunt for my next DVD.

The drive to Cedars-Sinai Hospital was awkward, though a lot less heavy than the intervention. I spent most of the ride, sandwiched between Regg and Kosick, making fun of Tremaine while Knoxville drove. When we pulled up to the hospital and got out, some dude tried to get me to sit in a wheelchair. I said something like, "Get this asshole out of my face before I snap!" Then I think I spit on him, or at least threatened to if he wouldn't leave me alone. This was the kind of guy I'd become.

We walked into the ER through a side door, past the waiting room, and into a little room with a shower curtain instead of a door. My video camera never even made it as far as that little room. Tremaine was with me in there, partially to show his support and partially to ensure I didn't try to make a break for the exit. When a nurse came in and asked me why I was there, I told her there had been a big misunderstanding. I was fine.

TREMAINE: Steve is really smart. Even in his most blown-out phase, he could all of a sudden turn it off and talk to cops. And he was doing that. He just all of a sudden turned into "normal dude Steve-O" and was talking to doctors. But I had collected all the e-mails I could, brought them to the doctor, and said, "Just know that he's a really good talker and he's going to convince you everything is fine. But here's why we did this."

The guys had provided the hospital with printouts of all my suicidal e-mails, which easily qualified me for 5150 status as "a threat to myself or others." There was really no opportunity to talk my way out of this one. Soon, I said good-bye to Tremaine and was led to a part of the hospital that was completely locked down, where the doors don't open when they're pushed.

I figured I was going to be stuck in that hospital for a while, so I quit trying to be "normal dude Steve-O," and reverted to just being a pissy asshole. My highest priority became smoking a cigarette. A nurse told me I'd be able to smoke one soon. "Soon" was not soon enough, so I threw a massive tantrum—I screamed, I made threats, I flipped over a chair. A staff member told me that such behavior wouldn't be re-warded. He was so calm when he said it that it actually made me more pissed off. As soon as I picked up another chair and began to throw it, a pack of security guards appeared seemingly out of nowhere. This was my first experience with the concept of "surrender."

I was carried into a room and slammed down on some sort of table, equipped with heavy straps. I began panicking and getting claustro-phobic just looking at those straps. I quickly promised to be on my best behavior, so they skipped the straps, but still rammed a needle into my butt cheek. I have no idea what flowed through it but it was some po-tent shit that rendered me powerless to break my promise.

AFTER NAPPING for who knows how long, I awoke and got my first real look at what the Cedars-Sinai psychiatric ward was all about. There were two wings: one for the run-of-the-mill crazies, the other for the more drastic cases. When I got assigned to a room, it was on the more disturbed wing, and my roommate was a good indication of exactly what that meant.

As soon as I walked into this nondescript little room—I'd sort of expected it would be a padded cell and was half-disappointed to be wrong—I knew this guy was seriously messed up. Voices in his head were telling him that everything was horribly wrong and that he was going to be punished for it. He was panicking about his clothes—he needed different ones but was frightened to change them. Everything seemed to terrify him, but the idea of anything changing scared him even more. He wouldn't stop crying, screaming about horrible things that were going to happen to him, and pleading with the voices in his head for mercy. I, of course, had my own voices and hallucinations to contend with, but mine were like a friendly sewing circle compared to the demons haunting this poor fucker.

I felt really bad for the guy—at least for the first hour or so. After that, I just couldn't stand it. Unfortunately, my roommate was about par for the course on this wing of the ward. Another guy blatantly shit himself and was rolling around in it in the hallway, making as much of a mess as he could. It was all very *One Flew Over the Cuckoo's Nest*.

While I was certainly no less nuts than I'd been when I'd walked into the loony bin a few hours before, I was sane enough to know that I needed to get the fuck out of this place in the worst kind of way. I went to the nurses' station and told them I needed to leave. They seemed pretty used to hearing people say that and calmly gave me a handbook titled *Rights for Individuals in Mental Health Facilities*. I didn't have to read much to realize it wouldn't help me get out of there.

Back at the nurses' station, I demanded to use a phone. They told me I was welcome to use a pay phone in the hall, but only to dial 1-800 numbers and collect calls. The only person I managed to reach was my lawyer, Barry Sands. He told me it would look much better to the judge if I stayed where I was. I didn't give a shit what the judge thought and said as much, but Barry seemed totally unruffled. As I hung up with him, I began to sense that the conspiracy to keep me locked up—at least that's the way I saw it then—ran deeper than I'd been aware of. Thanks to Knoxville and the rest of the gang, there wasn't a single person in the world I could've reached by phone who either could or would have gotten me out of there.

So there wasn't much more to do than sit around and wait for my chance to have a cigarette. Just about everyone in there was jonesing to smoke, and most patients had cigarettes, but we weren't allowed lighters. There was this cigarette lighter contraption on the wall in the patio area, but it was activated only three times a day. That was worse than fucking jail. You can't smoke at all in jail and quickly come to terms with that fact. Waiting around six hours for each cigarette though was pure torture.

On my second day in there, I got a visit from a large group of people, including Knoxville, Tremaine, Brittany, and a doctor whose job it was to determine my fate. It did not go well.

> **TREMAINE:** Once Steve came in, the doctor was real confrontational with him. I was like, "Oh, god. This isn't going to work." The doctor was telling him the cold, hard truth, but he was being so aggressive with Steve that they butted heads right away. That meeting turned ugly real fast.

> **BRITTANY:** He was like, "I'll get better if Brittany will help me and stay with me." And Knoxville was like, "No. Don't put this on Brittany. This is you." But Steve was freaking out and blaming everything on me. I didn't know how to handle it. I was absolutely devastated.

I ended up storming out of that meeting and promising everyone I'd see them in twenty-four hours, once my seventy-two-hour psychiatric hold had expired. It wasn't too long after that that I was informed that my three-day 5150 hold had been officially changed to a 5250 hold, which meant I could be kept against my will for up to two weeks. At that point I began to try really hard to start telling the staff what I thought they wanted to hear.

I was gradually detoxing but hadn't exactly given myself over to getting well. Jen would visit me just about every day, and every day I'd hand her folded-up pages with messages I'd written on them. It was her job to type them up, post them on my blog, and blast them out to the Rad E-mail List. I'm probably the only person who has ever kept an online journal while locked down in the nut house.

The first entry from the psych ward, titled, "You Should All Know I'm In The Looney Bin," was surprisingly thoughtful considering I was in such sorry mental shape. It begins, "They call it 'code 5150,' that means 'psycho,' legally, fuckin bat-shit, certifiably. I'm outta my mind, believe-you-me. How'd I get this way? How can this be? It's gotten so bad there's nothing left of me."

The post goes on to describe how I had previously thought of bipolar disorder as a good thing—a way to ensure I made the most of my short life by limiting my experiences to intense highs and lows, "ANYTHING but to crash on the rocks of mediocrity," I wrote. But now, I was beginning to realize that much of what I churned out during these chemically enhanced "highs" was just "a bunch of manic bullshit that made little-to-no sense and, furthermore was devastating to those who loved me."

I'll pretty much stand behind those sentiments today, but after handing that first note to Jen, my writing grew increasingly unhinged. Here's a choice quote from my second entry: "Before being committed to the 'funny farm' I only contemplated the 4th and 5th dimensions . . . There are, actually, no less than nine dimensions . . . For those of you that are interested in hearing from entities that exist in other dimensions, I present you with the word: Pleiadians."

That was a reference to a book by Barbara Marciniak called *Bringers of the Dawn: Teachings from the Pleiadians*, which another patient had given to me. For those who dig intergalactic, apocalyptic conspiracy theories, this book is a real gem. As Marciniak's Web site explains, the Pleiadians are "a collective of multidimensional spirit beings from the Pleiades star system, and have been speaking through Barbara Marciniak since May of 1988. The Pleiadians are here to assist humanity with the process of spiritual transformation in the years leading up to December 2012." I thought all that shit was pure genius.

On my fourth day in the psych ward, I was moved over to the tamer wing, where the other patients were much friendlier, or at least less stark-raving mad. There was a group of three older ladies who stuck together the whole time. They all appeared quite wealthy, and none of them seemed like they belonged there. They carried on as though they were enjoying a cocktail party, joking and laughing the whole time. They almost made that place fun. I also met an oddly cheerful and mild-mannered lawyer. He'd hacked his wrists and arms so severely with a razor blade that hundreds of sutures and staples had been required to close the wounds. We got along great.

Each night before bedtime and the final opportunity to smoke a cigarette, there was a mandatory meeting during which each patient talked about his or her day, and how it had made them healthier. Nobody wanted to stay there, so it was basically an exercise in everyone begging the staff to be released. One lady broke my heart: She'd been in there for more than a month and had been declared incompetent to control her own money. The state had seized control of everything she had and didn't seem prepared to give it back or let her out any time soon. I never figured out how the whole mental health system worked, but from what I could gather, psychiatric patients have almost no rights at all. That being the case, I was going to need to convince everyone that I was ready to clean up my act if I was ever going to get out of there.

My problem wasn't denial. I knew I was an alcoholic drug addict, but thought of myself as hopeless, a lost cause. I'd been an alcoholic from before I even had my first drink. As a kid, I ate candy alcoholically—no amount was ever enough. And I came from a long line of alcoholics, few of whom met with a particularly happy ending. I figured that was my destiny too.

Fortunately, one of the first guys I met in that friendlier wing was a heroin addict who gave me a book about recovery from alcoholism. Although I started reading it only to kill time, the message I got from it was clear: The most seemingly hopeless alcoholics and addicts are the ones who have the greatest chance of getting sober, staying sober, and being happy about it. In fact, in some ways, hopelessness is an addict's only hope, because until you surrender to the idea that you have no power over alcohol and/or drugs, you're going to keep finding excuses, justifications, and reasons to get loaded again. That book felt like a lifeline—albeit, a very fucking thin one—like someone was saying that there was a chance for me. But I didn't feel ready to do anything about it. At least not yet.

The next day, three guys came in to talk about their problems with drugs and alcohol, how they got sober, and what life was like for them in sobriety. Those guys weren't being paid to be there, hadn't been sentenced to it, and were there only because they wanted to help people who needed it. Had I been anywhere else, I can't imagine I would've listened to a single word they had to say, but the alternative was sheer boredom, so I heard them out. Something about those guys cracked through at least the outer layer of my defenses. Whereas the staff at Cedars-Sinai seemed like an opposing team whose job it was to be against me, these three guys had no such agenda. They didn't care why I was in the psych ward and just wanted to talk about their problems on the off-chance that one of the patients could relate. Seeing these three guys for myself, and hearing them tell their stories, made me believe that sobriety actually worked for them. It wasn't some lame copout because they weren't rad enough to handle living life at its most extreme.

At the end of their talk, these guys handed out a list of twenty questions that help people determine if they have a problem with drugs and alcohol. My answer was "yes" to almost every question. After taking that quiz, I felt like I was backed into a corner. My life was a motherfucking wreck. If I wanted to get out of this place, I had to try to get sober. And I clearly wouldn't last very long once I got out if I didn't stay sober. Something had to change. So I walked back down the hall, and by the time I got to my room I had decided that I wasn't just going to go to rehab because it was the only way out of the psych ward. I was genuinely going to learn how to live clean and sober.

As soon as I made that decision, I got very excited about the potential I had to do a lot of good in the world by getting sober. I somehow got the idea in my head that I would be doing the world this big favor if I cleaned up my act, and that the world was going to owe me for it. I was going to be the guy who made sobriety cool! It makes me laugh when I think about it now: There I was, locked up on suicide watch, career in the toilet, an embarrassment to my family and friends, but totally convinced that the world needed *me* to lead by example. Once again, even when I tried to do the right thing, I ended up doing it like a douchebag.

23

THIS DOESN'T GET FIXED

I spent a week in the psych ward at Cedars-Sinai before I entered rehab at the chemical dependency clinic at Las Encinas Hospital. Dad had come out to lend his support and actually sat in on my admittance interview over at Las Encinas. I think it was a real eye-opener for him. I was asked to list every drug I could recall doing with details about the history, duration, frequency, and quantity of my use, and as I went down a list that included not just the main culprits, like booze, coke, weed, ketamine, PCP, and nitrous, but also things like video head cleaner (inhaled it) and aluminum cleaner (drank it), I'm sure he was learning about things he'd never heard of before. Hell, even I was shocked by the truthful answers that were coming out of my mouth. Dad, to his credit, remained stoic and calm throughout the interview.

He was obviously happy that I was going into rehab but still didn't really understand what addiction was all about. At one point, he said something like, "Once you put this behind you, once we get this fixed, everything will be terrific." I snapped at him and yelled, "Dad! This doesn't get *fixed*! We don't put this behind us! Dad, I'm a drug addict! I'm going to be a drug addict for the rest of my life! The fact that you were married to Mom for twenty-five years and never figured out what addiction is is disgusting!" I really went off on him.

> **TED:** I'll never forget that. It required considerable thought
> and discussion just to understand what was going on. In my
> life, you identify a problem, you determine its causes, you define
> the solution, and you implement the solution. Then it's done
> and on you go. I now understand that addiction problems don't
> work that way.

Because I never really fucked with opiates, I was lucky enough not to experience much in the way of the harsh physical withdrawal symptoms that everyone associates with detoxing (vomiting, fever, diarrhea, and so on). But I'm convinced it took several months for the drugs to get completely out of my system, and my behavior during that time was its own kind of withdrawal. After I stopped drinking and doing drugs, I continued acting like just as big an asshole as I'd been when I was loaded. Maybe worse.

Just after I got to Las Encinas I remember talking to Big Regg on the phone and hearing him tell me that he'd seen on the Yahoo homepage that I was the second most popular Internet search at that moment. To me, this was great news. This rehab thing was better publicity than all my previous arrests combined.

I convinced myself that my road to sobriety needed to be a lesson for the world, so I was intent on documenting every step of it. When during my first week in rehab I was required to complete a writing assignment describing my addiction, its origins, and its consequences, and then pen a good-bye letter to my drugs of choice, I made sure to give a copy to Jen so she could post it online and share it with the Rad E-mail List. That was wildly inappropriate and resulted in multiple tabloid stories highlighting the most controversial parts. At the time I claimed that I was "holding nothing back," being completely honest so as to be a better role model to all the people who could benefit from my experience. This was a crock of shit. The bottom line was I only wrote those things for attention. I was as desperate for fame as I'd ever been, if not more so. Sobriety was just going to be my newest stunt to ensure the spotlight was pointed my way.

AFTER A week or two, Knoxville and Bam came to visit me in rehab and I couldn't resist busting out a new trick. I threaded a shoe-lace up one nostril through the hole I'd just discovered in my septum (the result of all the coke and ketamine I'd snorted), and then out the other nostril. It was a nifty little clip for the Jackassworld.com site and, as far as I was concerned, a reminder to the world that just because I was going to be sober didn't mean I couldn't be rad.

I had a pretty steady stream of visitors in rehab. The *Jackass* guys would come by sometimes, and Regg and Jen were almost daily presences there. One person who never visited was Brittany. I was such a dick to her at that first meeting over at Cedars-Sinai, she had every reason in the world not to come back again. But because she didn't come, I continued to blame all my problems on her.

BRITTANY: After that first visit, he wrote me this long note saying he was sorry and asking if I'd come see him during his visiting hours. I didn't know what to do. I didn't know how to react if he said anything to me. I didn't want to say the wrong thing. So I called [*Jackass* associate producer] Shanna [Zablow] and Jen and was like, "Should I go see him?" They were both like, "No, no, no, no. Don't go." So then I didn't. He freaked out and said he never wanted to see me again. Either way, I would've lost. If I would've gone, something would've happened and then they would've been pissed off at me for going. So either way I was the bad guy. It just sucked. I was very confused. Then his dad and everyone just stopped talking to me. They started pushing me away. What I understand now is people were telling Steve that because he was obsessed with us, he had to completely cut ties with me. But I didn't know that. When you break up with someone you go through that whole thing— you fight, you yell, you scream, you say everything, you vent. You get everything out you need to get out. I never had the opportunity to do that. He changed his phone number, changed his e-mail. I was just completely cut off.

Even after I broke up with Brittany, I continued to find ways to be an asshole to her. I'd feel bad about the way I'd treated her and then reach out to her to try to be nice. But once we got back in contact, I'd end up being a dick again. It was an abusive cycle. Eventually, the relationship ended completely. She wanted to be friends and I couldn't. I cut it off but did it so badly. It wasn't fair to her at all.

FROM THE minute I got to rehab, I was treating it as a career opportunity, which I suppose makes some sense considering I had pretty much nothing else on the horizon, work-wise. I was still droning on about the rap album to anyone who'd listen, working under the assumption that Universal for some reason would actually put that mess out. But while the idea of my rapping about doing tons of drugs and acting like a crazy person once had been mildly amusing, it was no longer remotely so in light of my institutionalization for doing tons of drugs and acting like a crazy person. So I got dropped from the label.

My delusions of grandeur would've been obnoxious on their own, but just as I'd wielded my vegetarianism as a moral battering ram, now my sobriety gave me one more thing to make me feel like I was better than everybody else. In retrospect it was all so ridiculous considering how fucking nuts I still was. Although the voices in my head had died down, I continued to hear murmurs and to see occasional visions when I closed my eyes. When people in rehab started talking about surrendering to a Higher Power, I had no problem with that. As far as I was concerned I already had an intimate relationship with all kinds of Higher Powers.

What's more, the "spiritual digging" I'd been doing before I was thrown in the loony bin only accelerated. In fact, I more or less disappeared down that particular rabbit hole. I was writing bat-shit insane messages about religion and spirituality on an almost daily basis and making sure Jen distributed them as widely as possible online. But it was worse than just being crazy—I generally managed to turn whatever nonsense I was spewing into a pompous, moralizing lecture.

"It's Time To Stop Lying And Cheating," I wrote on March 21. "It's time to stop doing anything that you don't want everyone, and I mean, literally, everyone, to know that you have done. Call it a hunch, but I believe that the time for us humans to be seeing through only two eyes and thinking with individual minds is EXTREMELY limited (i.e. only until 2011, when the Age of Aquarius Begins)." This was mild compared to some of the stuff I'd start spouting off about later regarding the Pleiadians, the Fifth Sun, the Fourth World, Planet X, and Keylontic Science (look it up . . . actually, on second thought, don't). I think most of my friends and family recognized that I was in a really vulnerable state at that time, so the general reaction to all that ranting and raving was sympathy rather than criticism. That said, FunnyOrDie.com featured a cartoon that made fun of me and my whacked-out, apocalyptic proclamations, which was both right on point and incredibly funny.

I stayed at Las Encinas for thirty days and then moved into sober living apartments at the Gooden Center, which were a sort of secondary level of rehab. Basically, I'd have group sessions and rehab-related activities from 8 a.m. to 3 p.m. every weekday and had to be home every night by 11 p.m. (midnight on the weekends). Beyond that though, I was more or less free to come and go as I pleased.

EVEN THOUGH I was getting sober for all the wrong reasons, I was fully committed to it and very serious about it. I was always present in my groups and very involved. In fact, I wouldn't fucking shut up. I really gave it a genuine effort and in doing so began to take an honest, no-bullshit look at myself and my actions. As the last remnants of narcotics finally left my system and the fog around me lifted, I finally could see the guy I had become. And I didn't like what I saw.

It became clear to me what a fucking asshole I had turned into. And not just since I stopped getting loaded—since I *started* getting loaded when I was a teenager. It had been a gradual descent but over the past twenty years I'd become a nasty, arrogant, mean-spirited douchebag. I felt like I didn't deserve forgiveness for all the shit I had done. I didn't deserve forgiveness for the way I had treated people. I didn't deserve forgiveness for what I had put my family and friends through. I couldn't forgive myself for the humiliation my behavior brought about. I looked in the mirror and I fucking hated myself.

When people talk about addiction, they tend to ask, "How bad did it get?" "What made you hit bottom?" For me, I didn't bottom out when I was getting drunk and doing drugs. Right up until the time of my intervention, I was pretty sure I was still having a blast. I hit bottom when I'd been clean for a hundred days and finally saw what I'd become.

For all my previous suicidal thoughts, I don't think I ever came as close to really considering it as I did at that moment. I can remember scoping out places where I might be able to hang myself. Those thoughts scared me enough that I spoke up about it to sober friends whom I trusted, and agreed to check myself back into a psychiatric ward, this time over at Las Encinas, where I'd been in rehab.

The psych ward at Cedars-Sinai had been kind of a cross between a hospital and a jail, but Las Encinas was more like a cross between a hospital and a country club. Not that I was enjoying it. When I got there, I was so depressed I couldn't even get out of bed. My only recreation, the only thing I got any enjoyment out of, was eating. So I'd sleep all day, wake up for breakfast and lunch, which I would eat while still lying in bed, and then go right back to sleep. After a while of living this regimen, I got straight-up fat.

My doctor prescribed me a shitload of psych meds. The staff called me "medicine boy" because I was downing this ridiculous pile of pills every morning. I know that some of these medications really improve people's lives, but I didn't see any positive results. They turned me into a zombie. I'd sleep all the time and routinely pass out in the middle of group sessions.

After two days in that second psych ward, I wrote in my journal:

Depression. Suicidal thoughts. Spending a whole week thinking about killing myself is exactly where I'm supposed to be? Maybe the psychiatric ward is exactly where I'm supposed to be, that's where the fuck I am, anyway . . . I feel like a big fat pussy for checking into a psych ward with 101 days clean. It's on the same grounds as the rehab I came to get clean at. I'm embarassed to go outside to smoke. I'm embarassed to say I've got 103 days clean with the last two spent in bed. Let me say it again, I feel like a fucking pussy. A real badass would kill himself is what my dumbass is thinking. I know lots of people who love me, but I'm not one of them. I did shit that's too fucked up to forgive myself for and, even worse, using drugs and alcohol isn't an option— and I'm always going to be that fucked up little kid. This is what we call self-pity, fuck.

That journal entry was unbelievably significant. As soon as I recognized that I was wallowing in self-pity, something happened. It finally occurred to me that the rest of the world didn't need me to do it a favor by getting sober. I needed to do that favor for myself. That hadn't ever really sunk in before I checked into that second psych ward. I didn't need to kill myself—I just needed to stop being the asshole I couldn't forgive.

After three weeks in the psych ward at Las Encinas (I would've left earlier but the psychiatrist in charge of my care wouldn't release me), I had come to terms with the fact that my motivation for getting sober had been misplaced and decided to start the entire process over, despite having been clean for a full four months already. I moved into the main rehab house of the Gooden Center. I stayed in this primary level of treatment, with around-the-clock supervision, for another sixty days. Then I moved into a sober living house in Pasadena. For a while, I didn't do much besides concentrate on staying sober. The rules and regulations of the facility really helped give some structure to my life. I shared a bedroom with another dude and had to be up, with my bed made, every day by 9 a.m. and home by curfew, which was again 11 p.m. on the weekdays and an hour later on the weekends. There were chores to do—scrubbing toilets, cleaning the common area—and randomly administered urine tests twice a week. It was all a far cry from the entitled celebrity life I'd been leading. I never really got any special treatment in any of these rehab and sober living situations. After some initial nods of recognition or mentions of *Jackass*, almost everyone just got used to my being around.

I quit taking the psych meds pretty quickly after leaving the main rehab house at the Gooden Center. I just felt like I didn't need them. For all the talk of my being bipolar, I think if anyone piled as many drugs into his body as I did into mine, he'd be bipolar too. Once those drugs got out of my system, the worst of my mania and depression mostly left with them. I don't have advice for anyone about psych meds and certainly don't recommend quitting them cold turkey the way I did, because it can be extremely dangerous, but I was fortunate. Once I stopped taking all those pills, I immediately started feeling better.

As most people know, one of the keys to staying sober is getting yourself out of the environment where you used to get loaded and away from the people you got loaded with. In that sense, a lot of the shitty things that had happened in my life before going into rehab turned out to be lucky breaks. Because I'd been evicted, I had no apartment to go back to, so I had no choice but to get out of that environment. Additionally, when I was evicted, I once again had relied on Simonetti to put all of the stuff from that apartment into storage. In that process, my cell phone went missing and with it, the numbers of all the drug dealers and drug buddies I'd relied on for years. (When I finally went and emptied out that storage unit in 2010, I found the phone in the pocket of the sweatshirt I'd been wearing the day I was arrested on coke charges. I destroyed it immediately.)

In another accidentally lucky move, I'd burned nearly every bridge I had in my career, so there were no nagging phone calls from agents or producers with job offers and thus no work at all to distract me from sobriety. Finally, since I'd severed ties with Brittany, there was no drama from a relationship adding any stress to my life. I was alone and my life was being drastically simplified whether I liked it or not.

In some ways the rest of 2008 was a period of hibernation for me. I read a bit, watched some TV, and later spent a lot of time with a girl I began dating named Beth and her dog Boogie. But I didn't work, I didn't film, I didn't post anything on my blog, and I killed the Rad E-mail List dead. I started realizing that my addiction to fame, to being the center of attention, was nearly as crippling as my substance abuse. I needed to put some real distance between myself and that world.

In show business, the question everyone always wants to know is "What comes next?" You just finished a successful movie—okay, what comes next? You're in the middle of a sold out tour—what's next? It had been the dread of not knowing the answer to that question that sent me off the cliff after *Jackass: Number Two*. The last two years of my life had been a constant, desperate scramble to maintain my fame, and it literally drove me crazy.

It occurred to me that maybe I needed to get out of the entertainment business entirely. So many of my problems stemmed from being massively self-involved and obsessed with being the center of attention. I mean, is it even possible to break those habits while working in an industry built on them? I wasn't sure.

One day, with this on my mind, I started thinking about other things to do with my life and decided I might want to join the Peace Corps. So I looked them up on the Internet and clicked the box that said "Contact Us." I wrote a little message saying I was throwing in the towel on my entertainment career and wanted to become a Peace Corps worker in some foreign country. I filled out a short questionnaire and heard back from them quickly: I was ineligible because I didn't have a bachelor's degree from a four-year college.

It was just as well. Although I was serious at the time, it's likely I would've changed my mind. The people who run the Peace Corps are smart enough to protect themselves from people like me by making the whole process of getting in pretty tough. They don't want to deploy a bunch of flaky dudes who want to go home after six weeks.

Another requirement of the sober living house was that I work, or do some sort of community service, for a certain number of hours a week. I chose to volunteer at a nursing home. If you remember, when I was in high school, I completely abandoned the Maje, the elderly British man who relied on me to take him everywhere. The last I'd heard from him, he was leaving me message after message on my answering machine and was desperate to get to his cataract surgery, but I was too involved with drinking and smoking weed to give a shit. Although I didn't quite make this connection at the time, I guess in some karmic way, I hoped working in that nursing home would help make amends for the Maje.

The first time I walked in there though was tough. I was immediately confronted with all my issues about my mom's suffering. I remember seeing an old woman there who was in bad shape—she was all contorted, in pain and afraid. It ricocheted me back to seeing Mom at her worst. I asked a nurse who worked there how she could be okay with seeing this woman like that. This nurse looked at me and said, "She just wants what everybody wants—to be loved."

That really hit me hard. Here was this poor woman who clearly needed love, probably more than any other person in that place, yet because she was suffering, because it made me uncomfortable to look at her, I wanted nothing to do with her. I believe this attitude is deeply ingrained in our society as a whole. We hide away our elderly and our infirm because they're an inconvenient reminder of where we're all going to end up. We believe ignorance really is bliss and then wonder why we're lonely and terrified when the end finally comes. It's really tragic. As I write this, it dawns on me how wrong I was not to join my sister in comforting my mom as she died.

It took quite a while before I got comfortable with being at the nursing home. Eventually, though, it became like a sanctuary for me. Whenever I felt like I was too wrapped up in my own little problems, talking with these old people, playing Bingo with them, would usually make me feel better. I continue volunteering there to this day, long after my sober living community service requirements expired, because—to lean on a cliché—I've always gotten more from that place than it has ever gotten from me.

24

DO I DARE TRY THIS AGAIN?

Eventually I had to come out of hibernation. In late 2008, I got a call from my agent. When I picked up the phone, he said, "I've got an idea to run by you and you're either going to want to punch me in the face or you're going to love it." He had an offer for me to appear on *Dancing with the Stars*. The first thing I told him was, "You couldn't find a worse dancer than me." He assured me that would only work in my favor.

I'm not exactly sure why I said yes, but I guess after sitting around doing nothing for so long, just doing something felt like a positive move. I was still pretty iffy on the whole idea of even having a career in show business, but I figured this would at least open the door to that possibility should I decide I wanted it and could handle it. The fact that it was family entertainment, on ABC, and wouldn't really require me to play the part of the reckless, insane maniac Steve-O that

I'd been since *Jackass* started also made it feel like a healthy move. And, in retrospect, I guess it was, but at the time, being back in the spotlight on live national TV doing something I was horrible at and doing it *sober* was terrifying.

Part of me really wanted the world to see that there was more to me than a guy willing to hurt himself for the amusement of others. But part of me was afraid that once the world saw that they wouldn't be too interested. And another part of me knew it was important for me not to care either way.

I was really careful about the way I talked about sobriety while I was on *Dancing with the Stars*. Blabbing at every turn about how I'd gotten sober would not only set me up to fall even harder should I end up getting loaded again, it also would draw me back to the flawed motivations I went to rehab with in the first place. I couldn't be doing it to be a role model for everyone else. I had to do it for myself.

The whole experience was nerve-racking. I can remember lying in bed the night before the season premiere and freaking myself out so much that I seriously considered backing out on day one. Once the series started, I was incredibly uncomfortable the whole time, but I think a lot of people watching the show sensed that and found it somewhat endearing. I was just in such a fragile, vulnerable state that the littlest things seemed to have the potential to make me crumble. One day, the producers asked if I could get some of my *Jackass* buddies to be filmed at my rehearsal. That was a real blow to my ego. *What, I'm not enough on my own?* With elimination from the show obviously drawing near, a depression was beginning to consume me. I felt the whole *Jackass: Number Two* syndrome cranking up again. It was almost as if I could hear the *click-click-click-click* of my psychic roller coaster as it was climbing a hill toward a steep, swift, inevitable fall. I started thinking, *Oh man, what's the difference if I stay sober for a year and then get loaded, or stay sober two years and then get loaded? I'm going to just wind up getting loaded anyway. So I might as well just go get loaded.*

Fortunately, I had a whole support system of sober people who I lived with in Pasadena at the sober living house and was in contact with every day. I remember a good friend named L.W. said something at that point that really stuck with me. "There's no rule that says you always have to feel good in sobriety," he said. "You're allowed to feel bad and you're going to feel bad sometimes. It's okay. But when you feel bad, the one foolproof thing you can do that will always help is to act like a gentleman. If you do, you'll have something to feel good about." Hanging on to those words and that idea really helped me through that dark time. I know if I had tried to get through all that on my own, I never would have made it.

In the end, I'm not sure what was more amazing—that I survived the six weeks I was on the show before being eliminated without falling off the wagon or that I survived six weeks on the show before being eliminated. My dancing was atrocious, but all the people who called in and voted for me kept me alive from week to week, perhaps in more ways than one. Knowing that after all the horrible shit I'd done I still had people pulling for me was definitely gratifying.

MY FIRST inclination after surviving *Dancing with the Stars* was to return to my hibernation, but a year earlier, when I was still very new to sobriety, I'd started a project that now seemed to be coming back to haunt me. My original concept was a DVD that would pair footage of me at my drug-fueled worst with new footage of me sober. The point was to show that I was just as much of a badass sober as I'd been loaded. The footage would be augmented with interviews of me and my friends telling my story. It was all part of that whole ill-conceived idea about sobriety turning me into a hero.

After a few months of working on the project, my confidence was wavering, so I turned it over to Tremaine and Dickhouse. They transformed it into a more straightforward documentary about my journey to drug hell and back that would eventually be called *Steve-O: Demise and Rise*. My feelings about it fluctuated wildly. At first, I thought all the footage of me incredibly fucked up was awesome; later on, I was appropriately horrified by it. I'd regularly phone the Dickhouse offices and tell them I wanted to call the whole thing off, but they'd always calm me down and turn me around on it—by the end of the phone calls, I was usually scheduling more interview times. But I had second thoughts about that project right up to the day it aired on MTV.

I tried to console myself with the idea that it could be helpful for some people to see what I'd gone through, but it definitely didn't do me any good. Watching the rough cut and seeing myself huffing, snorting, smoking, and drinking myself into such a tragic state didn't serve as a reminder of why I needed to stay sober. It actually made me want to go huff, snort, smoke, and drink. I can't really explain it logically, but I guess that's why I'm an addict. When I saw the footage of myself doing drugs, it felt like I could smell them, feel them, and taste them, and it made me want to go do them again. The humiliating footage of me also failed to serve as a deterrent. Rather, being humiliated by the footage just felt like another reason to get loaded. In the end, I got through it (with a lot of help), but I never actually watched *Demise and Rise* in its full, finished form.

There was talk for a while about the documentary serving as a pilot for a new reality show for me on MTV. There were several ideas thrown around, including one in which I'd travel around making amends for all the wrongs I'd done—kind of a reality version of *My Name Is Earl*. I'm incredibly grateful nothing came of that. That would've almost certainly been a disaster for my sobriety.

FIRST WITH *Dancing* and then with *Demise and Rise*, it seemed like I was heading back toward a life in front of the camera. I spent a lot of time thinking about whether or not this was a good idea. It seemed to me that if I was going to do it and make it work, it would have to be a very different trip than the first time around. For starters, work would always have to take a backseat to sobriety. If some opportunity was going to put my sobriety at risk, I'd have to have the discipline to walk away from it, no matter how great an opportunity it was. Second, I had to find a way to draw a sharp distinction between who I was and what I did.

From even before I had the barest whiff of fame, I had created a character named Steve-O who had almost immediately taken over my whole life. Steve Glover never stood a chance. I'm not saying that I'd been putting on an act as Steve-O—that was completely me. But it wasn't *the complete me*. Steve-O is a part of me with the volume turned all the way up all the time. It never occurred to me during the time that I was running around like an out-of-control maniac that I had a choice not to be that guy *all the time*. That I could go home and turn down the volume. If I was going to survive in the entertainment world I needed to be able to keep some safe distance between my work as Steve-O, professional idiot, and my life as Steve Glover, amateur idiot working to stay sober. If happiness for me is contingent on having a thriving showbiz career as Steve-O, I have no doubt that I'll be miserable for the remainder of my years.

This contrast became sharpened in the summer of 2009, when talk first got serious about making a third *Jackass* film. I knew it would be a different experience for me from what I'd been used to. I also knew I was potentially throwing myself back into an environment full of temptation and bad influences. Sobriety issues aside, we'd set the bar so high with *Jackass: Number Two* that I genuinely worried that any attempt to outdo it would be either fruitless or extremely dangerous. Maybe it was time for me to quit while I was ahead.

On the other hand, I genuinely love doing the crazy shit we do for *Jackass*. This has nothing to do with being wasted—it's just my sense of humor. It was important for me to prove to myself—and to others, I guess—that I could still do it, still be a lunatic stuntman, without drugs and booze. I was more eager than ever before.

FILMING BEGAN in early 2010. I made a decision before we even started that I wouldn't be willing to do any stunt that had major potential to put me in a wheelchair or a coffin. If I'm being totally truthful, even when I was loaded, I always took more care with my stunts than I made it seem. But never had I been so explicit about it. After everything I'd managed to live through, and all the work I'd done to become healthy, it would be a real waste to get paralyzed or killed doing a stunt.

One myth I would dispel is that being loaded helped numb the pain of my earlier stunts. That shit hurt whether I was sober or on day three of a coke and nitrous binge. Maybe if I'd been a heroin addict, the drugs would've been a nice anesthetic, but the only thing being wasted ever did for me was to help me not consider the consequences of whatever I was about to do. Let's face it, when you're fucked up, you do more stupid shit without thinking about it. Being fully present and clearheaded really isn't a bonus when you're about to have a baseball hit into your nuts. You can see the dread on my face in almost every one of my scenes in *Jackass 3D*. Fortunately that only makes for better footage. If we were all gung-ho all the time, it would be boring as hell.

A good illustration of the differences between working sober versus working wasted was the opening sequence of *Jackass 3D*. In it, I'm launched headfirst into a ceiling fan. I'd done almost that exact same stunt eight years earlier when I was jacked up on coke and booze in my apartment. I remember staring at that fan in my apartment and getting all psyched up, thinking, *Fuck you, fan! You're going down!* And when the camera rolled, I went after that fan. This time, sober, I sat there staring at the fan, paranoid about the fact that something might go wrong and I'd land on my head and break my neck. In the end, I counted, "One . . .

two . . . three," and went for it just as hard as I had the first time. I wasn't any more careful or reckless. I just fretted about it more.

Despite my clear-headedness and the precautions against death and maiming—or perhaps because of them—I ended up getting injured more during the filming of *Jackass 3D* than I had on any of the previous movies or TV shows. During a fire gauntlet skit that didn't make the final film I had to walk across a balance beam while kerosene-fueled fireballs swung back and forth trying to knock me off onto a bed of hot coals. We filmed it in a warehouse, but the guy in charge of the place didn't want the coals on the floor for fear they would damage the cement. The crew came up with the idea of putting the coals on these gigantic steel sheets, which was great except that with the hot coals on them, these steel sheets turned into a fucking frying pan. So when I inevitably got knocked off the balance beam, I fell into this frying pan and seriously burned my right butt cheek, hip, arm, and leg. As much as that fall from that tiny red wagon in Orlando during the second season of the show had been excruciating, this was considerably worse and warranted a trip to the hospital.

I also went to the hospital for two other injuries from stunts that didn't make the film. (Much to my dismay, they didn't even get included in *Jackass 3.5*, which, like its predecessor *Jackass 2.5*, collected the "best of the rest" of the bits that we'd filmed for the movie in a separate DVD release.) For one of them, I tried to pierce my nipple using a high-powered BB gun. There were fears it would shoot my nipple right off, and Tremaine even told me he wasn't sure if it would make the film because it seemed so dark. Still, I wanted to do it. The first shot barely nicked my nipple. The second went straight in and didn't come out. Blood poured down my chest. It hurt badly but I probably wouldn't have even gone to the hospital except for what happened next.

As I was standing there giving the "postgame wrap up" to the camera, Bam snuck up behind me and punched me in the nose with a boxing glove on. This was a recurring gag in the third film—"The Rocky"—and whenever Bam was planning on doing that to someone, they used this "phantom" camera that shot one thousand frames per second so the punch could be captured in extra-high definition. At this point, though, the phantom camera had been shut down and Bam had been told not to bother with "The Rocky." But he was drunk and did it anyway. In doing so, he broke my nose. I was fucking pissed.

The doctors didn't really do much for me at the hospital. They said that I should wait for my nose to heal a bit if I wanted it straightened out and reset, and I told them that I needed to keep the BB in my nipple for work. It goes nicely with the copper BB in my left butt cheek and the lead pellet in my right one. Amazingly, for all the minor battle scars I've incurred over the years—burns, scrapes, stitches, broken bones, a shark bite—my body is still in remarkably good shape. I did get most of my teeth reconstructed with caps and veneers—vomiting, cocaine, chewing glass, and various accidents had pretty much destroyed them, and as a result, I've spent more time in a dentist chair than anyone I know. But I've done no real permanent damage to the rest of my body, and I don't think my daily aches and pains are any worse than your average thirty-six-year-old's.

Because of my self-imposed prohibition on any potentially lethal stunts, it seemed like I ended up doing a lot more really gross shit for *Jackass 3D*. Like the "Poo Cocktail Supreme." The original idea was for me to be strapped into a very full Porta-Potty, which would be attached to a bridge with a bungee cord, then pushed off it.

I actually hate bungee jumping and am deathly afraid of it. I know logically that it's perfectly safe, but I think because I've spent so much time jumping off bridges and buildings without a bungee, my brain has been reprogrammed. I can look at a fifty-foot drop off a bridge into a river and say, "That's doable." But I can't look at a three-hundred-foot drop and convince myself everything will be fine just because I'm attached to a glorified rubber band.

My fear of the bungee made me the perfect candidate for this stunt. The more terrified and reluctant I looked, the better it'd be. After some consideration, this potty drop was reconfigured into a potty launch, in which I'd be propelled skyward while sitting on the toilet. It all worked great—I was miserable beforehand and covered in shit afterward.

Sometimes, all the gross-out stuff really bothered me. The "Sweatsuit Cocktail," in which I drank Preston's sweat after he ran on the elliptical machine wrapped in Saran Wrap, is a good example. Essentially, the whole point of the skit is for me to vomit, which I did so quickly that I actually thought I'd be in trouble for ruining the shot: after all of the work it took to get that little cup of sweat, I puked before I even managed to drink a drop of it. But the studio decided that because we were doing the film in 3D, they needed a shot where the audience would get puked on, so we re-created the scene to film a pickup shot of me puking onto the phantom camera.

Back when I was boozing, smoking, and eating meat, vomiting came much more easily to me. It's not that I could do it whenever I wanted, but rather that I couldn't seem to help from doing it. I've always had a really active imagination and just the thought of something disgusting would have me retching. (I think that imagination is the same reason I've always been a two-pump chump in bed, but that's another story.)

Ever since getting sober and healthy though, my puke reflex isn't what it used to be. From a health standpoint, this is actually a good thing. I've vomited so much and so often in my life that my esophagus is in really bad condition. I have what's called Stage 3 esophagitis, and every time I throw up it gets worse. (I guess I forgot to mention that when I claimed my body is still in tip-top shape.) But to get this "Sweatsuit Cocktail" shot, I needed to puke on demand all over this ultra-expensive 3D camera, and it was crucial that the first bit of puke to leave my mouth land precisely on the lens. Preston's sweat wasn't making it happen, so I had Dimitry run his fingers through his ass crack and then rub them on my upper lip. Having to puke on target like that really gave me "puker's block"—I was just dry heaving and it hurt. When I finally vomited, it wasn't in the right spot. So then I had Preston sticking his fingers up his ass and putting them in my nostrils.

That didn't get us the shot either. I felt like I was just annihilating my throat. Finally, Ehren pissed in a cup and I drank it. That did the trick.

Afterward, I felt spiritually drained. It was not just the damage that I willingly did to my already fucked-up esophagus, it was also the battering my dignity took through the whole ordeal. I left the set late that night and wanted to do nothing more than crash into a parked car, then drive straight to a bar. I didn't.

In the end, they didn't even use that pickup shot in the film. It sucks ass to go through hell in vain, but it happens quite a lot in *Jackass*. Some stunts and some shots just work better than others. Ideas that look good on paper sometimes look like crap on the screen. Other times, Tremaine and Knoxville just feel like the tone is wrong. The BB gun nipple piercing was probably my favorite footage of everything I did for *Jackass 3D*, but in the end, it was deemed too "dark." There were also related concerns that some kid would try to do the same thing, shoot himself in the heart, and die. I suppose that's a legitimate point, but it doesn't make the disappointment that much easier to take. It's always a pisser when your best material gets cut. Then again, these films have done well because Tremaine, Knoxville, and Spike know what they're doing. Their track record speaks for itself.

A BIG part of *Jackass* has always been the camaraderie between the cast and crew. During the TV show and the first two films, after a day of shooting—and sometimes during it—we'd typically spend most of the time drinking. Early in the filming of the third movie, we did all of our shooting locally around Los Angeles, and Knoxville complained that after work everyone was going their separate ways instead of hanging out together like we used to do on the road. For me, the fact that everyone was going home instead of getting drunk at the end of the day was only a good thing—one less temptation.

Soon enough though, we were on the road again and the rest of the cast and crew were all regularly in the same bar after shooting. That became a challenge for me. I'd avoid the whole bar scene entirely and then start feeling sorry for myself for all I was missing out on. I felt like I wasn't a part of the gang anymore. The reality is, though, that if I go and pick up a drink after a day's work then there won't be any more day's work. My sobriety was the reason I was able to be a part of the film at all. I was showing up on time, eager to work and contributing a lot creatively in ways that simply hadn't been happening in the latter days of *Jackass*. I don't think a single idea I submitted for *Number Two* was even filmed. What's more, now I was easy to get along with. For maybe the first time in my life, I was not an overwhelming, annoying son of a bitch. Some people might have even described me as downright likable. Sure, I was giving up something by not hanging out with the guys in a bar, but it was completely insignificant compared to what I was getting in return.

KNOXVILLE: Steve had never really written a lot of stuff for the past *Jackass* movies—maybe something here and there—but when we were writing stuff for *Jackass 3D*, he came in with some really good ideas. It was a whole new Steve-O. He and I would sit in the same room and have conversations, instead of in the past, when we were both fucked up, just kind of talking at each other. We were actually enjoying each other.

All the guys in the cast and crew were supportive of my sobriety if for no other reason than they'd seen the alternative. Knoxville told a few interviewers that they'd banned alcohol from the set for my benefit, but as I had always understood it, booze had been banned from the set ever since the first film. Back then, we'd been doing an onstage Q&A hosted by Kurt Loder in front of a very conservative-looking studio audience. It was all for some MTV special. We'd spent the whole day drinking beers supplied by the film's beer sponsor, Miller High Life, and were not sober. I seemed the most likely candidate to fall apart at any moment—I'd been bingeing on ketamine right up until the taping—but, in fact, it was Dave England who went off the rails. While a woman in the audience was standing at a podium asking a question, Dave dove off the stage and knocked over both the podium and the woman. Pandemonium broke out and the woman ended up suing. She was eventually awarded more money than we'd spent making the whole film. (Really.) I had long thought that the no-alcohol rule dated to that debacle and was just something that everyone always ignored.

> **KNOXVILLE:** Alcohol wasn't banned because of the Dave England incident from the first movie. We had booze all over the set in *Jackass: Number Two*. We had coolers of it, and had Steve not been sober we probably would've had coolers of it on the third movie. But because he was and we loved him and wanted him to stay sober, we banned it from the set of *Jackass 3D*. I'm not saying that people didn't break the rule, but we tried our best to monitor it. In the end, there was 98% less booze than before, and the 2% that got snuck in, we tried to deal with and dispose of the best way we knew how.

During most of the filming, I was still in sober living, sharing a room with another dude, scrubbing toilets, and peeing in plastic cups a couple times a week. This was my choice. Those same long odds that had helped me justify staying loaded for years convinced me to stay in sober living until I had two years of sobriety under my belt. If only 5 percent of addicts get sober and stay sober, I needed to give myself every advantage I could in order to be part of that 5 percent. Nobody can ever tell you they're going to stay sober forever, especially not me, but I can say with absolute certainty that if I get loaded again, I am absolutely fucked.

I HAD my worries that *Jackass 3D* wouldn't do as well as the first two movies. It had been four years since the last film, and I still felt like it was going to be impossible to top *Number Two*. As it turned out, it was our biggest success yet. It made more than $50 million in the opening weekend alone, setting all kinds of box office records, and went on to gross more than $115 million in the U.S. and $160 million worldwide. It was fucking huge.

Looking back on it now, I still like *Number Two* better, but *Jackass 3D* has a wider, more mainstream appeal. I think the fact that we'd been around so long also helped us. It wasn't just the brand name and that people were happy to see it back—although that may have been some of it—but it was also the case that nobody was really shocked or appalled (and therefore turned off) by what we were doing anymore. Not only did people know what to expect from us, I think mainstream culture has moved our way in the last decade too. Thanks to YouTube and all the other Internet bullshit going on, there are shocking videos being e-mailed around on a daily basis. Shows like *Fear Factor* brought gross-out stunts to prime-time network TV. While on the surface that all may seem to be competition for us, the bottom line is I think we do this stuff better and funnier than almost anyone else, and that is why people came out to see the film in droves.

It was also interesting to see that a lot of the same people who probably once held their noses and dismissed *Jackass* as the triumph of lowbrow humor came around to it with *3D*. *The New York Times* ran multiple, reasonably complimentary stories about the film, the *Atlantic Monthly* had a column showing their appreciation, and the Museum of Modern Art staged an advance screening in New York City. Personally, I've never really thought of *Jackass* as art—I just thought it was dangerous and silly—but I think in general, the question of how to interpret what we do is always up to the audience, not the creators. I can pretty much guarantee you, though, that if we'd set out to make it "art," rather than to just make each other laugh, it would've sucked.

EPILOGUE
WHAT COMES NEXT

Having a number one movie is a great rush and, for me, after all I'd been through, it felt like a personal triumph, even if it was hardly my triumph alone. But there was also something bittersweet about it: in a sense you're at the top of a mountain and the feeling is, there's nowhere to go from there but down.

After *Number Two*, it was that feeling—amplified by a whole lot of narcotics—that sent me off the deep end. Even clean and sober though, that anxious voice in the back of my head kept prodding me: *What the hell are you going to do now?*

By the time of the film's release, my life—from the outside looking in, anyway—appeared pretty unremarkable. I lived with lots of plants and my two dogs, Walter and Bernie, in a small, unglamorous two-bedroom apartment in a quiet neighborhood in Glendale populated largely by Armenian immigrants. The dogs are both rescue dogs and they're crazy: they bite, they growl, they bark, they piss all over the apartment, and I love them for it. The dogs ended up with me essentially because other people couldn't deal with them. Maybe it just took someone with a healthy dose of their own insanity to relate to them. It occurred to me only recently that these beasts were the first pets I'd had since my teenage years when I'd let that poor hamster, Doyle, die of thirst because I was too busy getting wasted to fill his water bottle. It seems as if Walter and Bernie are my chance to make amends with the animal world.

On a related note, I've been a vegan for almost two years now. Back when I was still getting loaded, vegetarianism was something I turned to out of fear—fear of not being "saved," fear that I was going to take on the suffering of every animal that I caused by eating meat. Over the course of the first year and a half in sobriety, I learned that it's highly problematic to be motivated by fear. I became conscious about trying to replace fear with love or faith. I realize now that I'm a happier person if I lead a more compassionate lifestyle and that's what being vegan is all about to me. A lot of people in recovery talk about building self-esteem through "esteemable" acts. There's really no way around the fact that I was such an asshole for such a long time, that I've got a lot of catching up to do in this department. The more stuff I can do that I feel good about, the better.

Veganism has never been a particularly difficult thing for me to adopt and stick to because it feels so rewarding. When I cut eggs out of my diet, I immediately felt better about myself. The same thing happened when I stopped eating fish. At that point, I remember thinking, *I can do more! I can do more!* Then I went to the grocery store and bought a carton of soy milk. Once I tasted that, I felt like "I can really do this." There are vegan alternatives to all kinds of animal-based products in most supermarkets too, which makes it incredibly easy to be vegan without feeling like you're making any sacrifices. Veganism has benefited every aspect of my life. I'm healthier, I feel good about myself, and I'm really doing something I believe in, all of which, in turn, only helps my sobriety.

As of this writing, it's been nearly three years since I've had a drink or any drug stronger than Advil (legal or otherwise), with the exception of the anesthesia required for the endoscopy procedures to monitor my esophagus once in a while. I quit smoking and now have been a vegan for almost two years. I was on probation for a while from the felony coke charge, but that got cleared from my record and now, apart from a lingering 2003 assault charge (stemming from an incident during one of the Dunlap tours) that I was completely unaware of until I was arrested for it in Calgary this March, I have no legal issues to speak of. If I could only stop jerking off to Internet porn, I think I could be a candidate for sainthood.

In all seriousness, I'm striving for normalcy these days. But for a guy who has spent pretty much his whole life dedicated to extremes, it's a daily challenge not to mistake serenity for boredom. I still have nothing resembling a handle on moderation, and I don't know that I ever will. But at the very least I'm learning to channel my obsessive behavior toward things that won't hurt me or anyone else: sobriety, veganism, my dogs, my family, being of service to others, and, of course, Internet porn.

For me, part of being of service to others involves helping other people who are in recovery or in the grips of addiction. At one point, I actually ran into one of the three guys who had come into the psych ward at Cedars-Sinai when I was there and finally gotten through to me. I told him how much his words had helped me, and he arranged for me to go back to the Cedars-Sinai psych ward to talk to patients there in the same way (and the same room) as he'd spoken to me. That was a really big deal to me. I'm not sure if I got through to anyone there that day but it didn't matter. As I've come to learn, one of the main points of trying to help people like that is to help yourself. That's why those guys had come to the psych ward in the first place: because it helped them stay sober another day.

Besides helping others in order to help myself, I often find inspiration in the unlikeliest of places. Nikki Sixx is still a hero of mine today, but for very different reasons. He has more than ten years of sobriety under his belt, is still a badass, and is still on the road with Mötley Crüe. After inspiring me to be a degenerate for years, the fact that he's now a mentor in sobriety just rules.

I've got a lot of friends but also spend a lot of time by myself these days. I've had only one real girlfriend since getting sober, Beth, but after about ten months together we decided we work a lot better as friends. I was only seven months sober when we first got together, so maybe it was a little early for me, but she's awesome and now one of my closest friends. I suppose I want to get married one day and have (or adopt) kids, but at the moment I'm working on being responsible for myself, my plants, and my dogs. If I can manage that, it might be time to move on to bigger challenges. For now, I quite enjoy being single and am not in a rush to change that status.

The success of *Jackass 3D* created a lot of opportunities for me, including the chance to start getting booked again for paid appearances in nightclubs. I decided against doing them though. I could probably hang out in nightclubs for a while without getting loaded, but as they say, "If you spend enough time in a barber shop, you're going to wind up getting a haircut." I don't need to be in places where everyone's number one goal is to get loaded, and I don't care how much money I have to pass up to avoid them.

A few months before the film came out, I started doing standup comedy at some comedy clubs around L.A. I'd done it quite a few times back around 2006 when I was completely loaded, but this was the first time I'd tried it sober. It was terrifying at first but also exhilarating. My entire act began essentially as one long riff on how terrible I am in bed. It's probably not the kind of thing I'd want to be doing if I was looking for a serious girlfriend, or even just a one-night stand. Really, any chick who sees my act and then still wants to come home with me must either really love me or really hate herself. Either way works out okay for me. (Just kidding.)

My routine was really, really rough around the edges at the beginning, but with each performance, it's gotten better and my confidence has grown. For better or for worse, I feel completely at home onstage, and at the moment, I'm working hard at it and really having fun. I've spent a lot of time writing the material and working with more established comedians to hone the jokes. I recognize how lucky I was from the start to have the audience already on my side, rooting for me. Once *Jackass 3D* premiered, I went almost immediately from doing twenty-minute sets for free on a Friday or Saturday night to headlining famous comedy clubs. That went well enough that I got an entire tour booked, which I dubbed the "Entirely Too Much Information Tour."

I don't know if standup is what my future is all about or not but it seems pretty safe to say that I won't be joining the Peace Corps or completely disappearing from the public eye anytime soon. Having just finished the last *Jackass* film, we haven't yet started thinking seriously about a fourth one, but before too long, it's certainly a possibility. I've done a lot of agonizing since getting sober about how long it's really going to be productive for me—or for any of us—to keep putting our bodies at risk for laughs. I no longer believe that we'll run into a creative wall. If the third movie taught me anything, it's that there's really no limit to how many new ridiculous ideas we can come up with. But there is a worry that we're pushing our luck. We can take safety precautions, we can get smarter and smarter about our stunts, but in some sense I worry if it's just a matter of time before something goes horribly wrong.

THERE IS no getting around the fact that even as I close in on three years sober, show business remains a perilous proposition for me. With each new project, be it *Dancing with the Stars* or *Jackass 3D*, I recognized the pitfalls as if they were signposts on the road back to oblivion. Of course, it's not the ones I recognize that worry me, it's the ones I don't see.

For the longest time when I was growing up, I had a two-pronged motto: "The meaning of life is to get off your ass and pick one" and "It doesn't matter what you want, only how badly you want it." I thought those adages were serving me well for a long time. I wanted to get famous by doing the craziest shit I could think of, and I applied myself to that task with a dedication that was, quite literally, insane. Now I realize that it wasn't my philosophy that let me down. It was my goal.

I've learned that fame can be an addiction no different from alcohol and drug addiction. At first, it's all so much fun. Then you get to a point where rather than want it, you need it. Finally, you lose control. You want to stop but can't, and it starts to destroy you.

I feel like I'm at a crossroads in my life. The path forward is clearer than it once was but still filled with thorns, potholes, and potential dead-ends. I've got standup dates booked and there's talk about maybe doing a new TV show. Opportunities are all over the horizon, so for the moment, that dreaded question of "What comes next?" is answered. But if I'm going to stay sober and stay sane, I need to accept that there will come a day when nothing comes next. No gigs, no shows, no movies, no footage, no stunts, no books, no nothing. Eventually it all ends. I'd be lying if I said I was okay with that right now. Hell, I may never be. But I'm trying.

PHOTO CREDITS

INSERT A

Page 1: Stephen Glover *(all)*; *page 2:* Ted Glover *(top)*, Stephen Glover *(bottom)*; *page 3:* Ted Glover *(top)*, Stephen Glover *(bottom)*; *page 4:* Ted Glover *(top and middle)*, Stephen Glover *(bottom)*; *page 5:* Stephen Glover *(top)*, Tracie Smith *(middle and bottom)*; *page 6:* Donna G. Glover *(top)*, Stephen Glover *(middle and bottom)*; *page 7:* Cindy Glover *(top)*, Stephen Glover *(middle)*, Photo courtesy of Dennis McGrath. MTV Networks *(bottom)*; *page 8:* Stephen Glover.

INSERT B

Page 1: Photos courtesy of Rick Kosick. MTV Networks. All Rights Reserved. *(all)*; *page 2:* Photo courtesy of Dimitry Elyashkevich. MTV Networks. All Rights Reserved. *(top)*, Photos from *Jackass: The Movie* and *Jackass Number Two* courtesy of Paramount Pictures *(bottom)*; *page 3:* Photos from *Jackass: The Movie* and *Jackass Number Two* courtesy of Paramount Pictures *(top)*, Candy *(middle and bottom)*; *page 4:* Cordell Mansfield *(top)*, Photo courtesy of Dimitry Elyashkevich. MTV Networks. All Rights Reserved. *(bottom)*; *page 5:* Photos from *Jackass: The Movie* and *Jackass Number Two* courtesy of Paramount Pictures *(all)*; *page 6:* Terry Richardson *(top)*, Stephen Glover *(bottom)*; *page 7:* Cordell Mansfield *(top)*, Stephen Glover *(middle)*, Cordell Mansfield *(bottom)*; *page 8:* Cordell Mansfield *(top)*, Mike Carano *(bottom)*.